A Life Stolen

Sarah Sak

with Jacquie Buttriss

SEVEN DIALS

First published in Great Britain in 2022 by Seven Dials,
this paperback edition published in 2023 by Seven Dials,
an imprint of The Orion Publishing Group Ltd
Carmelite House, 50 Victoria Embankment
London EC4Y 0DZ

An Hachette UK Company

1 3 5 7 9 10 8 6 4 2

A CIP catalogue record for this book is
available from the British Library.

ISBN (Mass Market Paperback) 978 1 8418 8400 4
ISBN (eBook) 978 1 8418 8401 1
ISBN (Audio) 978 1 8418 8402 8

Typeset by Born Group
Printed and bound in Great Britain by Clays Ltd, Elcograf S.p.A.

www.orionbooks.co.uk

In loving memory of my son, Anthony Walgate.
Loved and missed every day.
May you now rest in peace xx

Contents

CHAPTER 1	The Nightmare Begins	1
CHAPTER 2	Disbelief	12
CHAPTER 3	Nothing Suspicious?	24
CHAPTER 4	The Wrong Charge	40
CHAPTER 5	A Cry for Help	55
CHAPTER 6	Wading through Fog	66
CHAPTER 7	Shouting Out Loudest	80
CHAPTER 8	Yelling in the Dark	91
CHAPTER 9	Anthony's Funeral	99
CHAPTER 10	An Empty Victory	114
CHAPTER 11	The Fourth Body	131
CHAPTER 12	All Change	140
CHAPTER 13	Looking Both Ways	151
CHAPTER 14	The Wrong Sort of Fame	167
CHAPTER 15	Gross Misconduct?	176
CHAPTER 16	The Day Before	185
CHAPTER 17	The Trial Begins	193
CHAPTER 18	Shock Revelations	205
CHAPTER 19	Too Much to Bear	221

CHAPTER 20   Away Days with a Film Crew   235

CHAPTER 21   The Jury's Out   244

CHAPTER 22   The Final Verdicts   258

CHAPTER 23   The Aftermath   270

CHAPTER 24   Anthony's Legacy   278

Epilogue   288

Acknowledgements   311

CHAPTER I

The Nightmare Begins

Sunday, 22 June 2014

The day my world came crashing down. That afternoon, that moment, changed everything. The shockwaves still resound inside me, every day and every night.

The day started off with a beautiful view out of the bedroom window of our Turkish holiday hotel – a perfect blue sky over a shimmering sea. We had a leisurely breakfast before stepping outside and straight onto the golden sands of the beach at Gümbet. We had enjoyed meeting new guests in the bar the evening before and well into the early hours, so hadn't had much sleep. This was the penultimate day of our week-long holiday. We spent it sunbathing, resting and chatting with the bar staff and other holidaymakers.

At four o'clock in the afternoon, after a swim, I felt tired so we went in, back to our room to have a nap before our last night out with friends. We were both still in our swim-things and Sami, my Turkish husband, went to have a shower first, while I pottered about, still in my wet swimsuit.

I suddenly realised I hadn't turned my phone on once since our arrival six days before. It was my work phone as well and I hadn't wanted work to intrude on our holiday, especially because Sami lives down south and we normally spend only two weekends a month together, so that week of our holiday was our time, just for the two of us.

If I had left the phone untouched until we returned to the UK, I would have been in blissful ignorance for at least another 36 hours. But while Sami was in the shower, I decided to have a quick look.

Feeling relaxed, I switched it on . . . and that's when the nightmare began. I expected to find two or three messages from work and maybe one or two from my younger son, Anthony, a university student in London, who was always sending me funny texts. But not this time.

Beep-beep-beep-beep it went . . . and kept going.

Something must be wrong. I held my breath . . . When the screen lit up and I saw the long list of more than a hundred missed calls and texts, I knew for certain. A shiver ran through my whole body. Something was terribly wrong.

I quickly glanced down the list of names and almost every other one was from Paul, my older son, and most of the rest from my ex-husband Tom with several from my sister Kate, plus some from my mum . . . but nothing from Anthony.

It was Tom's name that stood out. Tom was Anthony's father and we only ever communicated when it was about Anthony, so as soon as I saw his name, I knew. I didn't even look at any of the messages. I knew something had happened to Anthony. His was the only name missing. It had to be Anthony. I turned ice-cold and trembled beyond control. Yet still I hoped I was wrong – was this really happening?

I didn't want to know . . . yet I knew.

I felt an almighty punch in the chest, so hard that it took my breath away. He could have had an accident; he could be ill or in trouble, but it had to be something worse than I dared think. I just knew it . . . My whole body shook and white noise filled my ears, deafening me to the world. At that moment, I could hear nothing but my worst fears resounding round my head.

I held the phone at arm's length, not wanting to look at it, let alone use it. But I knew I had to. I just had to ring Paul, desperately hoping he would answer, that it was nothing bad after all – maybe my house had been burgled, or burnt down. Please, anything but . . . The seconds seemed endless but he answered quickly.

'Paul, it's me,' I said, my voice wavering.

Straight away I heard him burst into tears. 'Mam, I'm really, really sorry,' he blurted out, 'but Ant is dead.'

'No!' I shrieked and threw the phone away from me, onto the bed. I didn't hear what else he said. I couldn't listen. I wasn't ready to hear what came next. But it was too late. I knew . . . and I could never un-know those three words: 'Ant is dead.'

I wasn't aware of it at the time but I started to scream. Paul must have heard me – he was still on the phone when I threw it on the bed.

Sami heard it too and came running out of the shower.

'What's the matter?' he asked, putting his wet arms around me, his face lined with worry. 'What's the matter? What's going on?'

'Anthony is dead!' I said in a little voice as I shrank into myself. I was going to repeat it, but nothing came out, so I just pointed at the bed with a wavering finger.

Sami saw the phone and picked it up. Paul was still there. 'What's happened?' demanded Sami.

That was it. As he listened, I ran out of the room. I could hear nothing now but a distant scream and I had to get away from it. I didn't know where I was going. I ran down the corridor past some people, all of them staring at me with grotesque faces, though now I realise they must have become distorted in my brain.

There was a cleaner we had chatted with the day before and she came towards me but I just ran blindly past her, down the stairs, trying to get away from the long scream . . . yet I couldn't. That's when I realised it must be me screaming. It was weird, like an out-of-body experience. I just ran on, still screaming, lower this time, like a wail, a howling wail. I had no idea where I was going, no plan or intention, other than to get away from the phone that had brought me the terrible news.

People must have been looking at me, thinking I was a crazy lunatic. And in a way, perhaps I was at that moment. My hair was soaking wet and I was still wearing my swimsuit, as if straight off the beach.

'I have to go home now,' I screeched as I ran past them, out of the building. 'I have to go home.'

As I ran on, alongside the pool, towards the beach, still wailing, a middle-aged woman in shorts and a T-shirt came out from one of the poolside apartments. She turned towards me and stepped in my way so I had to stop. I think I must have needed to stop by then. My lungs were bursting and I gasped to catch my breath.

'What's the matter?' she asked in a soothing voice.

'My son's dead!' I shrieked, shaking all over.

She put her arm around me and led me to a low stone wall. 'Let's sit down here,' she said, 'and you can tell me all about it.'

'I don't know,' I howled, in a high-pitched voice that I didn't recognise.

She sat me down on the wall, just as her husband came out to see what the noise was.

'This poor lady's son has died,' she explained. 'Go and fetch the holiday rep from the hotel next door.' She pointed in the general direction. He nodded and off he went. She turned to me. 'Now, you stay here,' she insisted, taking charge in a quiet manner that cemented me to the spot, 'while I go off and make you some good English tea.'

I obeyed her. I didn't know what else to do.

She quickly returned with a steaming mug of tea and put it down next to me. 'It's got lots of sugar in,' she explained. 'It's good for shock.'

She was a lovely lady – very calm, which was just what I needed. I don't know who she was or where she came from. I don't even know her name. But she put her hand on mine with gentle reassurance, soothing my hysteria.

'I have to go home,' I said, again and again. 'My son is dead. I have to go home straight away. He needs me.' It was all a muddle in my head.

'I know,' she said. 'And you need to be there for him and for the rest of your family.'

'Yes.'

'Do you know how he died?' she asked, with concern in her eyes.

'No. I threw the phone away . . . I didn't want to hear it.'

'I don't blame you,' she empathised. 'I'm sure I would have been the same.'

Just then, only minutes after we'd sat down together, her husband returned with the young travel rep, who ran towards me, swinging her blonde ponytail. She sat down next to me and took her laptop out of her bag.

'When are you due to go home?' she asked in a sensitive voice.

I wanted to reply but I couldn't get my thoughts straight at first. I was just trying to order them enough to answer her when Sami ran down the path to join us.

'Thank God I've found you!' he exclaimed, looking dishevelled, still holding a towel round his waist with one hand and my phone in the other.

'When are you due to go home?' repeated the rep to both of us.

'Tomorrow night,' Sami replied, giving her the full details.

'Do you want to get a flight today instead?'

'Yeah, yeah, yeah.' Sami nodded, looking at me.

'Yes, straight away,' I agreed.

'I'll go back to the room to get my credit card,' he said, passing the phone to me before he ran off towards the building.

As the rep searched for any available flights, I looked at my phone. My first instinct was to throw it into the water but I knew we might need it later. Almost immediately, my mothering instinct kicked back in and my thoughts went to Paul. I had left the poor boy hanging on after he'd told me the terrible news. I felt really bad about that now, so I called him back and apologised.

'It's all right, Mam,' he said, sounding close to tears again.

'Do you know what happened?'

'No. I don't know anything about it,' he replied. 'Nobody does.'

'Not even Tom?' I asked. Tom was my first husband, Paul's stepdad, but they had a good relationship and I was sure they must have talked to each other.

'No, they wouldn't tell him anything.'

'So you don't know how he died?'

'No. All we know is that the police had a post-mortem done on Friday but they told Tom they couldn't find anything, so they're going to do another one.'

'Right.' I paused. 'Where are you now?'

'At home.'

'In your flat?' Paul lived alone and I was worried about him being on his own so much over the weekend, getting more and more depressed. Anthony was his only sibling but we have a very close extended family with my sister Kate and her children living nearby. They had all grown up together.

'I'm all right,' he said, his voice sounding hesitant.

'Well, I don't want you to be on your own. Go round to your Auntie Kate's.' I knew he would be better off with people who loved him. 'Just go round to your Auntie Kate's now. Do it for me, so I don't need to worry about you.'

'OK Mam, I will.'

'And we're hoping to fly back tonight. I'll be home as soon as I possibly can.'

Just as I finished talking to Paul, Sami got back with his card and the rep finished her trawl for flights back to England. She was very efficient and reassuring – quick too.

'I can get you back to the UK, but I'm afraid I can't get you a flight back to Leeds Bradford Airport,' she said, looking up from her screen.

'But that's where we left our car,' I blurted. 'Never mind,' added Sami. 'Just back to somewhere in the north of England if you can. Anywhere, as soon as possible.'

'Well, there is only the one flight,' she continued. 'It's to Manchester. Would that be OK?'

'Yes,' said Sami. 'We'll take it.'

'There is just one problem,' she added, looking from one of us to the other. 'You may not make it in time. It goes from a different airport that's further away. The flight leaves in three hours' time and it usually takes three and a half to get there. But it's the only flight I can get you on.'

Sami thrust his card at her. 'Book it, please.'

'OK,' she said, filling in his card details and handing it back. 'You'll have to pack very quickly and I'll find the fastest way for you to get there.'

Just as we were about to rush off, the manager of the hotel came up to us. Somebody must have told him about us. 'My car is out at the front of the hotel and I will drive you to the airport as soon as you are ready.'

We were so grateful for his offer, and didn't have time to argue, so we agreed.

Back in our room, we quickly threw everything from around the bedroom into the cases any old how, wet and dry, all in a jumble together. I later discovered we'd left behind everything in the bathroom, but never mind. Sami phoned the friends we were due to meet for dinner and explained we had to go, while I closed the cases and locked up the room. We dashed down to reception and straight out to the car, which accelerated off like a Ferrari.

The roads to that airport were all motorways, so the manager put his foot down and drove at 100 miles per hour all the way. We seriously broke the speed limit! As we went, Sami spoke with the manager in Turkish. They were talking so fast that I couldn't keep up with it and all I could think about was Anthony, my baby. He was 23, but to me he was and always would be my baby. He was always so alive, so full of fun and energy. How could he be dead? Might he have had a heart attack or a stroke? No, surely not – he had a strong heart. Someone must have killed him then. Had he been shot, stabbed, beaten . . .? I don't remember much after that, as the miles flew by, until my phone rang. I answered an unknown number, holding my breath . . . then let it out when I heard the young rep's voice.

'I've just rung to give you an update,' she explained. 'I've called the airport and told them the situation. I asked them to let you straight through all the security and hold the flight as long as they possibly can. They said they would try so I hope you get on the plane OK and home to your family as soon as possible. Our thoughts go with you.'

'Thanks for everything you've done,' I said. 'We're very grateful for your help.'

I relayed the information to Sami. Now we just had to hope there weren't any hitches, though with us being different nationalities that could be tricky. It usually caused us quite a hold-up, so I desperately hoped it would be different today.

With my phone in my hand and miles to go, I couldn't resist scrolling back several days to Anthony's last text.

'What's the goss, Sezzer?'

I froze in a silent howl. I keyed to 'reply' but his phone was 'not available'. That soulless phrase punched me, resounding in my head: not available . . . not available . . .

I kept looking at the time, anxious that we'd be too late, but finally we reached the police checkpoint at the entrance to the airport. It usually takes us ages to get in as they check the car thoroughly and look at all our papers. But this time the hotel manager said something to the policemen. I've no idea what, but it worked and they just waived us through.

We had only minutes to go when he dropped us off and we rushed inside the terminal building.

The check-in had stayed open for us and there was a lady behind the desk, ready to rush us through. The plane should have been leaving at that moment but she let them know we were on the way and we ran through the airport, all the way to the boarding gate, where they took us straight onto the plane. We were the last people to board and they were ready to go. It was all so brilliant. It helped us enormously to know that so many people were rooting for us and making the impossible happen.

A member of the cabin crew showed us to our seats at the front and the plane started taxiing almost immediately towards the runway. It had been a hot drive to the airport. But now, sitting down in the plane, I suddenly felt freezing cold. It must have been the shock, as well as the cooler air in the cabin. I started to shiver violently. All I had on was my swimsuit, now dry, and a pair of shorts. I didn't even have a T-shirt with me.

'Have you got any blankets?' I asked a steward. 'I'm so cold.'

'I don't know,' she replied. 'But I'll go and see what I can find.' She went off, then returned a few minutes later, empty-handed. 'No, I'm afraid I can't find one but I'll give you my jacket.' She took it off and helped me put it on without undoing my seatbelt.

I think she must have known. She was so kind to us. They all were.

We couldn't use our phones on the plane, so we just sat back in our seats and tried to relax. Neither of us said a word. What was there to say? We didn't know anything. And neither of us felt like making small talk.

All I could think about as the plane took off was Anthony. Had he been in a road accident, or died from a sudden illness, or what . . .? Why had they had a post-mortem? As I later wrote in my diary notes:

> I went over and over all the scenarios of how my baby could have died. Even though he was 23, he was and always will be my baby. My heart pounded so hard I thought I would pass out.

We didn't speak the whole flight. We had both been tired out before all this. Now I tilted my seat back but I know I didn't sleep. I couldn't. Though I don't remember anything else about that flight. Not a thing. I just went blank, detached from my surroundings. I didn't even think, my God what's happening? I didn't think at all. It was as if my brain had shut down, perhaps to block out all the questions and the unknown answers. The nightmare had begun . . . but it was an empty abyss.

CHAPTER 2

Disbelief

23 June 2014

We went through the motions, disembarking from the plane, walking the long walk to the passports area. Here in the queue my agitation increased. Soon it would all be real. Although it seemed like an age, I quickly reached the front. As I handed over my passport, I wondered whether all the emotions of the past few hours had changed my face. Was I still me? I must have been as the girl behind the desk handed my passport back with a sympathetic smile – could she know?

I came straight through but had to wait for Sami, still way back in the foreigners' queue. Finally he joined me and we went to claim our cases, then on through the arrivals gate. As we emerged to the sea of expectant faces, we caught sight of our good friends waving at us. That was a great relief – to see them and to be back in England. Sami had phoned Ahmet to come and meet us at Manchester Airport, which he and his wife kindly did, in the middle of the night, in order to drive us across to Leeds Bradford Airport where my car was parked. Now at last we really did feel we were on our way home.

As we left the airport, Sami told them what we knew – hardly anything. The three of them spoke in Turkish some of the way, while I sat gazing out of the window as the dawn broke, knowing that each mile took us closer to Paul and our wider family. I was desperate to find out what had really happened to Anthony, yet still reluctant to hear it. That was the war that was going on in my head as we crossed the Pennines to Yorkshire.

I don't know how or when it happened but as we were getting out of Ahmet's car and into mine, there was a change of plan.

'Kate rang my phone,' Sami explained.

'When? I didn't hear it.'

'No, Ahmet had the radio on, so you probably couldn't hear in the back.' He paused. 'Kate said that she's sent Sophie to drive Phil and Paul to meet us at Ferrybridge Service Station so that Phil can drive your car the rest of the way home and Sophie will drive us back in hers.'

'Why are they doing that?' I asked.

'First of all, she wanted to know if we had arrived back in the UK yet, and I told her we had but we are very tired.' Sami yawned, as if on cue. 'Kate knows that I'm not allowed to drive over here, so that's when she suggested sending them to meet us so you wouldn't have to drive all the way.'

'Oh, I see.'

Phil is my sister Kate's husband and Sophie's their daughter. I was glad they were bringing Paul. I had been so worried about him – the way I had left him hanging on the phone. And I expect he was worried about me too, so I couldn't wait to see him and give him a hug.

It's true. I was shattered. We hadn't slept more than three or four hours in the past forty-eight, so, what with fatigue and the shock as well, I felt quite weird as I sat and programmed the satnav for Ferrybridge . . . At least, I thought I did, but it went wrong on the way and we got completely lost in the middle of Leeds, which made me so cross. I could have cried but Sami calmed me down and kept me going. I was so exhausted that I nearly crashed the car a few miles further on but the near-miss shook me up and I knew I had to get us to Ferrybridge somehow. Then I could finally give in.

When we reached the service station, we drove round and round, trying to find Sophie's car. I was just about to give up when I saw Paul walking towards us, waving his arms wildly in the air.

He was quite emotional when he saw me, so we just hugged and cried together in the middle of Ferrybridge car park in the early morning light. We didn't care who saw us. Paul came and sat in the back with me while Phil drove my car and Sami went to keep Sophie company in hers, as we all made our way back to Hull. On the way, Paul told me about the day he found out.

'I was at work when the policewoman phoned the office and asked to speak to me,' he said.

'What did she say?'

'She asked me if I had a brother called Anthony, so I said yes. Then she asked me where you were. So I told her you were in Turkey and why did she want to know? She told me they needed to talk to you. I asked her what had happened but she said the police couldn't tell me, as they had to tell you first. I asked her if they'd talked to Tom. "Somebody went round to see him earlier," she said. He must have told her where I work. That's when I knew it had to be something serious. She asked me where you were staying in Turkey and when would you would be back. I didn't know where but I told her what day you would get home. Then I suggested the police ring Auntie Kate. She might know.'

'So they didn't really tell you anything?'

'No, but the manager saw my face when I came off the phone and asked me what the matter was, so I told him what the policewoman had said. Then I rang Tom. He told me it was a policewoman who came to see him too, and what she had told him, that Anthony was dead.' He paused. 'I was stunned.'

'Did the manager let you go early?'

'Yes, I told him my brother had died. Then he said I should go home but I didn't want to go back to my flat on my own and worry all evening, and they were short-staffed that day, so I finished my shift. I kept thinking about Ant and about telling you but working helped me cope. Then I went round to Tom's and stayed with him that night.'

'I'm glad.'

'Yes, Tom suggested it. We spent the evening together, talking about Ant, trying to puzzle out what had happened and why the police wouldn't tell us anything.'

When we finally arrived at my sister Kate's house in Hull, not far from home, we all piled inside. She was still up, waiting for us to get there, and her other daughter Lottie had been sleeping on the sofa, so she got up as well. We all hugged and had mugs of tea together in her lounge.

'How much do you know?' Kate asked me.

'Nothing, except that he's dead,' I said, the tears welling up again. 'What do you know about it?' I asked her. 'Do you know what happened?'

There was a hush in the room as we all listened.

'All I know is that last Thursday, which was 19 June, a police constable turned up here at around 6 o'clock in the evening. When I opened the door, she said she was looking for Kate Whelan. "That's me," I said. "What's it about?" She asked to come in so I showed her in here. She sat on that chair and told me they were looking for you. "Why?" I asked her. She explained they had to find you to tell you about Ant. Then she went on to say that he'd been found dead in a street in Barking, London.'

I gasped. 'Found dead in a street?' I repeated, my thoughts racing, so that I hardly heard what else Kate said.

'Yes. But that's all I know. She seemed very vague and wouldn't tell me anything else, not till she'd spoken to you. She kept asking what flight you'd be on and which airport, so they could come and meet you off the plane. I told her: "Not bloody likely!" We didn't want her breaking the awful news to you badly, like she did to us and Tom. Anyway we only knew you were in Turkey. You hadn't said where, or who you were flying with, or anything like that.'

'So that was Thursday evening?' I asked, trying to work it out

'Yes.'

'Was that before they went round to see Tom?'

'No. I asked her if anyone had told him and she said she'd been to see him herself earlier and had also spoken to Paul.'

I looked at him and he nodded. 'Yes, she must have been the one who rang me in the afternoon,' he said. 'After she'd been to Tom's.'

Kate handed me a list of names and numbers. 'These are the people you need to ring when you've had some sleep,' she said. 'They're all Metropolitan police officers, down in London. Call this one first,' she said, underlining the name O'Donnell at the top of the list.

I was shattered and badly shocked by this new piece of information: 'found dead in a street'. Those five words echoed round my brain but, as Sami and I finally arrived home, I still couldn't think how or why Anthony had come to be found dead in a London street. It was all too much to process. I needed some sleep first to clear my head.

It was about half past nine in the morning when we got home so we went straight upstairs and fell into bed, exhausted. My last memory before sleep was the horrifying image of Anthony's dead body, his eyes still open and looking straight at me, pleading for help. I remember reaching out into the darkness, but nothing more.

When I woke I was completely disoriented. Only three or four hours of sleep and it took me several minutes to process my thoughts. The shock hit me all over again as I remembered Paul's first words: 'Ant is dead.'

Sami made us some brunch, though I didn't have much appetite.

'I'd better phone the police,' I said with a heavy heart, part of me not wanting to know . . . and yet also desperately needing to know. I had to know everything. So I took out the list Kate had given me in the early hours of that morning. With my hands shaking, I called the number at the top that Kate had told me to ring first.

'Can you please put me through to Detective Sergeant O'Donnell.' There was a short pause.

'O'Donnell,' snapped a gruff voice.

'I'm Sarah Sak, the mother of Anthony Walgate.'

'Oh yes,' he replied.

'Can you please tell me the details of how my son Anthony died and any other information you have.'

'He was found on Thursday morning in Barking,' said O'Donnell. 'That's all I can tell you.'

'But I need to know what exactly happened!'

'Detective Constable Slaymaker has been appointed your family liaison officer. Now we know you're back, he will ring you later today.'

'Can't you tell me anything?'

'No.' There was no empathy or compassion in his voice. In fact, he sounded rather bored. 'DC Slaymaker will call you later and you can ask him. He will be able to update you with whatever information we can pass on to you.'

So that was that. I was fuming. How could he be so terse and uncommunicative? Not to mention the pain it caused me to have to wait yet longer to find out the simplest facts. Hopefully our family liaison officer would be more humane.

Next I decided to call my ex-husband Tom. It had been too late to call him the night before but he might have more information about the circumstances of Anthony's death.

'Sarah,' he said. 'Thank God you're back. I've been trying to get hold of you ever since . . .' I could hear the relief in his voice. 'Have you spoken to the police yet?'

'Yes, Kate told me to call this guy O'Donnell, but he was no help at all. He wouldn't tell me anything or answer my questions. He didn't even sound as if he cared. He said I'd have to wait till his colleague, Slaymaker, rings me later today. I'm furious with them already! Kate said that a policewoman came round to your place and told you on Thursday night?'

'Yes. I just can't believe it. It's . . .' He swallowed hard, suppressing his emotions. 'It was such a terrible shock. It still is.'

'I know what you mean. I feel the same.'

'It's stunned me. I can't think about anything else. I can't work for thinking about him. I don't even know what happened. Nobody has told me anything.'

'I'll make sure the police tell me how he died, or, more likely I think, how he was killed,' I assured Tom. I could tell he was very relieved because he was always the calm, steady one who didn't like to make trouble, whereas I was the doer, the one who organised things, the one who stirred things up, who dared to say the things that needed saying.

'What makes you think he was killed?' he asked.

'Well, why else would his body have been found on a street in Barking – a place I don't think he'd ever been to?'

'I didn't know that!' His voice rose in shock.

'That's what the policewoman said to Kate,' I explained. 'When she was looking for me, Kate asked why she wanted me and the policewoman told her that Anthony had been found dead on a street in Barking.'

There was a stunned silence at the other end of the phone, as Tom processed that information.

'What did the police tell you?' I asked.

'Well, it was a young policewoman who came round and asked if I was Thomas Walgate. I told her I was and she blurted straight out that my brother Anthony had died.'

'What?'

'Yes, that's what she said. So I said, "I don't have a brother called Anthony. My brothers' names are Paul and Graham. But I have a son called Anthony." "Well, it must be him then," she said. I was shocked. "So which is it?" I asked her, as she turned to go out of the front door. "Is it my brother or is it my son?" She just shrugged and said, "If your son's the one called Anthony, then it must be him," and off she went.'

'That's terrible, didn't she even apologise, or make you a cup of tea or show any sympathy?'

'No, nothing at all.'

'That's appalling, the offhand way she broke the news to you that your only son, your only child, has died. On top of that, to get it wrong as well – that's inexcusable.'

'Yes, I have to admit, it did make me angry.' Tom is not easily riled but this was too much even for him.

'I'm not surprised when it was such a disastrous way to inform you.' I was fuming on his behalf.

'Well, it's all right. No need to make a fuss,' he said. 'She was only doing her job. It probably wasn't her fault. Complaining about it won't bring Ant back.'

'I know that in her mind she was doing a job,' I said. 'But where was the f***ing human kindness and compassion that anyone should show towards a man when she's breaking the awful news to him that his only son has died? I think the police have handled all this atrociously. I shall tell them exactly what I think about it!'

'After she'd gone,' added Tom, 'I tried Ant's phone, to see if it could all have been a mistake. Maybe it wasn't him at all. There was no answer so I kept trying his number, on and off all evening, for about six hours I think. But it always went to voicemail. I left several messages, asking him to ring me. He didn't. He couldn't. So, in the end, I knew.'

We commiserated a bit with each other and ended up wondering what Anthony would be making of all this if he could only see it all.

As I put the phone down I turned to tell Sami what Tom had told me. He was as shocked as I was.

'But you always told me how wonderful the Great British police are,' he said. 'Not like Turkish police.'

'Well, I grew up being told that I could always trust a policeman or woman,' I explained. I had always told Sami: 'If there's an emergency, dial 999 and the police will turn up like superheroes, to help and reassure you and solve your problems. If you ever have any troubles, just speak to the police and they will always help you.' I explained, 'And I always thought that was true . . . till now.'

Sami and I had been in love since the moment we met, at the party of one of his friends in Turkey. Somebody introduced us and, with me being English, we shook hands, smiling at each other. It was a very strange feeling. The time really did seem to stand still as our eyes locked for several seconds before we let go. Everyone there noticed and later teased us about it. The next day, he told me that when he'd seen me arrive, he knew he wanted to marry me.

'But you didn't know anything about me,' I protested.

'I see you – I know you a lovely girl and I want we marry.' His English wasn't so good then but he spoke from the heart and I knew I loved him too.

We only spent a few days together and then it was the end of my holiday. I had to go home with my friend. But not long after, I went out there again, we married and he came to England.

I don't know what his family thought would happen to him but they all clubbed together and bought him the most expensive gold watch they could afford. They gave it to him when he left for this strange country of England and told him that if it all went wrong, or I was horrible to him, he could sell it and pay for his journey back home to Turkey. The funny thing is that he never wears a watch, so he just put it in a drawer and there it stayed . . . just in case!

As always, Sami was my rock, from the moment I first heard Anthony had died, but I didn't want to take all my pain and frustration out on him as I knew I had to focus on finding the truth, somehow. I had to make some other phone calls and I needed some time on my own as well so I asked Sami if he was going to go back and check up on the guys at his restaurant in Essex, to make sure it was all OK since his holiday.

'There's nothing you can do here,' I said. 'I have so much to do but you can't do any of it for me. I'll be all right.'

He reluctantly agreed. He wanted to stay with me and look after me but he also knew he needed to get back to his business.

It was a relief, to be honest, as I'm probably better on my own when I'm in a state. I needed to focus fully on finding out what happened to Anthony, to make sure the police investigate it and get justice for him. So I really wouldn't have the energy to have Sami to worry about, as well as everything else.

But I did miss him . . . and oh, how I missed those funny phone calls from Anthony.

CHAPTER 3

Nothing Suspicious?

24 June 2014

After our holiday, we had planned that I would come back up to Hull and clear out my house, as I had already given my landlord notice that I would be moving down to live full-time with Sami in Essex. I even had another good job lined up down there and I was looking forward so much to seeing more of Anthony, who was a student at Middlesex University. I had made all the arrangements and was all set to go.

But now . . . Anthony had gone, and I couldn't go off and leave Paul, my only surviving son, at this difficult time. He wasn't Tom's son but he was so like him in the way he bottled things up and hoped they would go away. They got on very well but I knew he needed me, or if he didn't now, he would do when it really hit him that Anthony's death was forever. Despite the seven-year age gap, my two sons had always been close. When Anthony was little, he idolised Paul, his protective big brother, his hero whom he followed everywhere he could.

However, there was one time when that wasn't such a good thing. Anthony was two and just toilet-trained while

Paul was about nine. I woke up one morning to the house being very quiet. Tom was at work and there was no noise from the boys.

I went downstairs to find that Paul had found a DVD of the horror film *Candyman* and Anthony had sidled up onto the sofa to watch this 18-rated film with him. Paul looked guilty when he saw me and Anthony was white with fear. I grounded Paul for a week and cuddled Anthony but he refused point-blank to go to the toilet again, 'In case Candy Man gets me!' It took me weeks to convince him the toilet was safe.

A year or two later, I remember Anthony made a terrible scene because he wanted to go out and play with Paul's friends but I wouldn't let him. He was so angry that, when I went upstairs for something, he dialled 999 and reported me to the police for being cruel to him for not letting him play in the street. They told him to put the receiver down, then phoned me and asked me to make sure he couldn't do that again!

Paul would probably be remembering those bittersweet childhood memories too, so I just couldn't leave him behind. I think I also felt I needed my extended family right now. Kate in particular was an enormous help and support.

I called my landlord, who is also a friend. I told him that Anthony had died,

'God! That's awful!' he exclaimed, in shock.

'Can I stay on in the house?'

'Yes, of course you can. Stay as long as you like. I haven't advertised for a new tenant yet, so it's still yours for as long as you want it.'

'Thanks, that's a relief.'

'What happened? How did Anthony die?' he asked, then added, 'You don't have to tell me if it's too difficult for you to go over it again and again to people.'

'No, it's all right. I just don't know anything yet. Only that it was in a place called Barking.' I paused. 'I'm waiting for the police to call and give me more news.'

'I can't believe it,' he said, his voice a mixture of shock and sympathy. 'Would you like me to phone round and tell other friends?' He knew a lot of my workmates, so that seemed like a good idea. I couldn't face having to tell everyone myself.

'Yes, please.' I knew that within the day, every man and his dog would know! Within minutes, my boss, Angie, texted me: 'So sorry to hear about Anthony. Take off as much time as you want. Anything you need, just let me know.' People could be so kind. If only the police were more considerate.

I cancelled the van hire and the lads who were going to help me.

Next, I rang my work's head office and spoke to one of the senior managers, Gavin, who is also a good friend.

'Anthony's dead.'

'Oh no!' he said, shocked. I could hear the concern in his voice. 'How? What . . . ?'

'I don't know. He's dead and they won't tell me anything. I have to wait for a police officer to call me later.' In that moment, I realised just how impotent I felt, that I couldn't even tell Gavin how my son died.

'Don't worry about work, Sarah,' he reassured me, full of compassion. 'You don't have to do anything. I'll sort it all out for you.' Gavin hadn't even met Anthony but I was always talking about him and his funny stories, so everyone must have felt they knew him.

I didn't dare make any other calls until I'd heard from DC Slaymaker but just then Kate turned up. After a quick chat to update her on what I'd done so far, she suggested we went over to see our mother. I picked up my phone and my keys and she drove me over there. I hadn't managed to speak to Mam since I'd first heard the awful news, though she had left me some comforting text messages. We had a good hug in her hallway.

'I'm so glad you came,' she led me through to her lounge. 'I was terribly shocked to hear about poor Anthony,' she said in a soothing voice. 'I can't believe it.'

'None of us can,' agreed Kate.

'You sit yourselves down and I'll make us a nice cup of tea.'

'Thanks Mam,' I said. 'That's just what I need.'

At that moment, my phone went.

'Sarah Sak?'

'Yes.'

'I'm Detective Constable Paul Slaymaker. I believe my colleague DS O'Donnell had a brief conversation with you this morning?'

'Yes, far too brief.' I put the phone on speaker and beckoned Kate to listen in.

'Well, I've been appointed as your family liaison officer, or FLO. That means that I will be your first point of contact if you have any queries and I will be asked to update you with any information about this case.'

'This is not a case. This is my son you are talking about and your colleague wouldn't even tell me how he died.'

'He was busy on urgent matters this morning so I'm calling to fill you in on the details that I have to hand.'

'Are you telling me that my son's death isn't an "urgent matter"?' I was angry already.

'There was nothing suspicious about it, Mrs Sak. But I do realise that it's important to you.' He sounded so condescending that he nearly had me swearing at him before he'd even told me anything. But I knew I had to curb my temper.

'How did my son Anthony Walgate die?'

'Well, his body was found by a local resident, on the pavement, in a sitting position, propped up against a wall outside a small block of flats in Barking.'

'Where exactly is Barking?' I'd never heard of the place until Kate mentioned it.

'In east London,' he said, in a rather bored voice. 'It's part of London's Metropolitan police area.'

'You're talking about a body here but he was my son. You make it sound quite alarming, the way he was found. Was he still alive?' My tears welled up at the prospect of that appalling image but I tried to keep my voice steady.

'The resident who noticed him called an ambulance. They arrived but it was too late. He was pronounced dead at about twenty past four in the morning, last Thursday, 19 June.'

'But why? How?' I hardly paused for breath. 'Was he stabbed, shot, beaten up . . . ?'

'No, nothing like that.'

'Well, I'm telling you now – something's not right.'

'No, no, it's not suspicious, Mrs Sak.' He sighed loudly. 'He's not been killed or anything.'

'Was there any injury on his body?'

'No, not a mark on him. There's nothing to tell – nothing to investigate.'

'How did he die then? Was it his heart or his brain?'

'No, we had a post-mortem done, but it didn't show anything.'

'He must have died of something!'

I could almost hear him shrugging his shoulders. 'I can't say, Mrs Sak. But it wasn't anything suspicious. As I've already told you, nobody killed him. Now if you don't mind . . .'

'You are not ending this call till you tell me what the cause of Anthony's death was.'

'We don't know the cause of death. Maybe we'll never know.'

'So where's his phone?' I asked.

There was a definite silence at his end, as if I'd caught him by surprise. 'Oh, he didn't have it on him.'

'So he must have been attacked or mugged,' I said. 'He never went anywhere without his phone. He always had it on him and he never turned it off.'

'Well, he obviously didn't have it that day.'

'I'm telling you, if he didn't have his phone on him, something is badly wrong.'

'Nothing like that. I'm sorry to have to repeat it to you again but there was nothing suspicious. Nothing out of the ordinary.'

'That can't be right. There is something wrong – very wrong.' I had a sudden thought – a glint of hope. 'How did you know the body was Anthony?'

'We didn't at first. But your son's friend China Dunning reported him missing the next day. She gave his description and the postcode where he was going so we were able to identify him from that and confirmed it with the photo she brought us. Why don't you give her a ring? Here's her number.'

'I'll do that,' I said, scribbling down China's number. He then terminated the conversation as quickly as he could.

I was shocked by Slaymaker's condescending manner and was relieved to end the call. I was fuming.

'He's treating you like a f***ing druggy's mam!' said Kate, who had heard it all. 'As if you're some druggy's mother, whose son has no value, no worth. He as near as told you that Ant had killed himself! Who does he think he is? It wasn't enough for him to give you only the basic facts; he was completely heartless, as if he was bored. He'd seen it all before and he didn't care. He just wanted to get rid of you.'

'Well, that's what I've got to deal with now,' I agreed. 'But I'm not going to let them get away with it! I always thought the police were supposed to protect and serve the public,' I said. 'But now I realise I've never been so wrong!'

'He sounded like he just wanted you to go away, didn't he?'

'Yes, but I won't stop until I find out who killed Anthony – until I get justice for my son.'

'Yes! You give them what for!' she said. 'I'll be with you all the way.'

*

Back home, it was evening and I was shattered but there was one more call I just had to make. DC Slaymaker had suggested I ring China Dunning. That was the only useful thing he said. Anthony had a strong group of very good friends at university – most of them girls! He trusted them and they trusted him. They would never have let each other down. In fact, Anthony relied on their friendship in many ways. China was one of his closest friends. I had met her a few times when I'd been down to visit him in London. I fished out the scrap of paper with her number on it and rang her.

'Hi China, it's Sarah, Anthony's mother.'

'Oh Sarah,' she said, with all the heartfelt empathy of a fellow victim and a long sigh of relief. 'I'm glad you've rung. I didn't want to disturb you on your first day home, I'm so sorry about Anthony.' I could almost hear her tears.

'Yes, I know,' my voice was cracking. I welled up too and I struggled to speak. 'I called the police this morning and again this afternoon but I hardly got any information from them. They told me you reported him as a missing person but I still don't know anything about how Anthony died or what they're doing to try to find out. Do you know?'

'No, I don't. They wouldn't tell me either.'

'When did you realise he was missing?'

'Well, we had this pact. Every time Neenee – that was my name for him . . .'

'Yes, I remember.'

'Every time he went anywhere unfamiliar or to meet a new contact, he would always tell me when and where he was going. So, this time, he told me he'd made contact with a man on Grindr and he was going over to Barking to see him. You know what Neenee was like – he was always very wary of new places and new people, ever since that time he was mugged, when he'd only been at uni for a week.'

'Yes, I remember.'

'So he gave me a piece of paper with the man's name on it, Joe Dean, and his postcode. He even showed me a photo of him on Grindr. He was smiling in the photo but I thought there was something quite spooky-looking about him. I even said that to Neenee.'

'And what did he say?'

'He said he'd be careful and wouldn't take any risks. He also said that he'd let me know when he was back and if I didn't hear from him by such a time I should tell the police, just in case he'd been killed or something. Those were the exact words he said: "In case I get killed or something." He laughed at the time . . . but it was the last thing he said to me.'

'NO!' I heard myself saying. I froze, unable to think of any other words for several seconds. Finally I responded. 'Did you tell all that to the police?'

'Yes. I told them everything I could but I got the impression they weren't listening very much.' She paused. 'Oh Sarah, I was so upset!' she blurted. 'They just didn't want to know.'

'It wasn't your fault,' I reassured her. 'They were like that with me too.' I paused for her to regain her composure. 'Was this all on the phone?' I continued.

'To begin with, yes. I rang to report him missing. They didn't seem to take it very seriously, but they asked me to come down to see them that afternoon, which I did. I gave them a statement but I'm not sure they wrote down everything I said. They did give it to me to read and it seemed to have all the main points.'

'What about the photo of that man?'

'I didn't have it. Neenee had just shown it to me on his phone. I did suggest they look at his phone and find it there. But they didn't seem interested. So I told them I thought he looked distinctive – in an odd sort of way. They wrote that down.'

'Who was it you spoke to?'

'I'm not sure who it was on the phone on Thursday morning but they asked me to come down to the station that afternoon and give them more details.' She paused, as if trying to remember. 'I think the officer who took my statement that afternoon was called O'Donnell – Detective Sergeant O'Donnell.'

'Oh him! He was the one I first spoke to and he wouldn't answer any of my questions.'

'Yes, it was the same with me,' she agreed. 'All he wanted to know was what drugs Ant took. I said nothing much. He took poppers, as you know, which aren't really drugs at all, and sometimes smoked cannabis, usually with us or occasionally on his own, but never anywhere else. I'm not sure O'Donnell believed me. He said he assumed Anthony was gay and I said, "Yes, but what does that matter?" When I asked him for more details about what had happened to Anthony, he wouldn't reply, other than to say: "There's nothing to tell." I couldn't believe it.'

'Did he not tell you anything at all?'

'No, he just broke the news to me that Anthony Walgate was found dead on a street in Barking. It was a terrible shock. I wanted to know more but he was being very cagey.'

'That's all he told me too.'

'So,' she continued, 'I asked him when, how and all that. But he just said: "It's no good asking questions that don't have any answers." So I said, "I won't stop asking questions until I get the answers because something is very wrong." Then he showed me out.'

'Well, at least Anthony confided in you . . .'

'And Kiera,' added China. 'She was there too when he told us where he was going. We were the last of his friends to see him alive.'

'If it hadn't been for Anthony telling you, we might never have known what happened to him. The family liaison officer they've given me said Anthony didn't have his phone on him or any identification.'

'I can't believe that!' she gasped. 'He always had his phone on him. It was like it was attached to him. He wouldn't go anywhere without it.'

'That's what I told them too.'

It was a great relief to speak to China and hear that Anthony had taken what precautions he could about meeting a new date. I'd always known he was gay, ever since he was about fourteen, or even earlier, so that was no surprise. I sat back and reflected on what China had told me and what a wonderful friend she had been to Anthony. In fact, thinking back, all his closest friends had been girls. At university it was China, Kiera and Ellie. At school and college there were others, but always girls.

I recalled a conversation with Colin, one of my work colleagues, some years back. He was gay and he told me most of his friends were women. For some reason, it made me think about Anthony.

'I sometimes wonder whether my ten-year-old son might be gay,' I said.

'What makes you think that?'

'A few things, I suppose. He mostly plays with the girls at school and he's always been a mummy's boy, preferring to stay in and play Ludo or watch telly with me than going outside to play ball or climb trees with the other boys down the road.' I paused. 'As soon as he could stand, he had a duster in his hand. He loves making things clean and he hates getting dirty or mucky. But he likes doing arty things, like cutting and sticking to make pictures. I know these things don't necessarily make him gay but it's just a case of is he or isn't he. It's a mother's instinct, I suppose.'

Colin nodded. 'Does it worry you?' he asked.

'No, not at all. He is what he is, whatever that might be. I just want to help him be happy. I don't worry about him being gay, if he is, but maybe later I might worry for him – only because of other people's prejudices. Teenagers can be cruel, and so can adults, come to that. But I just want him to be happy being himself.'

'Good answer,' said Colin with a grin. 'Why don't you bring him in to meet me? I can spot it a mile off!'

A few days later, that's what I did. Anthony thought we

were going shopping, so I made it seem like we had just bumped into Colin and we stood and chatted for a while. Colin asked him what he liked best at school and what games he liked to play.

'I don't like PE,' said Anthony. He was usually painfully shy with strangers but today he seemed quite relaxed. 'My favourite lesson is art,' he said. 'I like drawing and doing collages.'

As soon as I got to work the next morning, Colin came and found me. 'Your son is so gay!' he said.

'No, he's not!' I laughed, mainly at his certainty. 'How can you be so sure?'

'I'm telling you now. Your son is gay.'

It didn't make any difference to me or the way I thought of Anthony but it helped me to know it was likely he was gay. I didn't tell anyone else though – not at that point. It didn't make any difference.

Going into his teens, Anthony seemed to realise he was different and why that might be. I think he struggled with it when he was about thirteen and went through a quiet phase, perhaps still unsure. He was a bit depressed at times but at home he was always himself, spending a lot of his time with me, watching the telly.

Anthony, Paul and I used to watch *EastEnders* together, ever since Anthony was about six, even though he didn't really understand the storylines. He used to love watching *Friends* with me too. He especially loved the music and drummed it out on my legs every time.

While Paul still lived at home, he was always very good with Anthony, who loved watching his big brother play games on the computer. PlayStation 1 came out when

Anthony was about seven and he loved it. He always wanted to play on it, so when it was teatime I used to shout up to him that it was ready and he shouted back: 'I can't come now. It's got to an exciting bit!'

'Right,' I'd reply. 'You're banned!'

Eventually I let him go back to it but he became so obsessed that I had to limit him to just an hour a day after that – until he reached his teens, when he began to use the computer to design things, mainly clothes.

As he became more comfortable with being gay, at around fourteen, Anthony relaxed more and seemed happier again. His teeth were the only thing that bothered him now, so the dentist started him on a long course of monthly treatments at Leeds hospital. I used to drive him there and we always had a laugh.

One day, on the return journey, when he was about seventeen, it just seemed the right moment, so I said it.

'Are you gay?'

For a moment, he seemed shocked. Then he burst out laughing. 'You can't ask me that – you're my mam!'

'I don't mind if you are,' I said with a smile. 'So are you?'

'Well, I'm not a virgin,' he replied.

'Boy or girl?'

He laughed out loud again. 'Mind your own business!'

'So, boy then?' I asked.

'Yes.'

We were silent for a minute or two, listening to the car radio. Then he turned his head towards me. 'You don't mind then?'

'Not at all,' I smiled. 'I don't mind that you're gay, the only thing I mind is not having grandkids, but that's all. I just want you to have a happy life.'

That was the end of the conversation and we never mentioned it again. But it was as if I'd lifted a heavy weight off him and, as he grew up, I looked back on this as an important moment because we always used to talk naturally about his being gay as part of everything he was doing. Like me, our whole extended family loved him for who he was – gay or straight. It was never an issue.

Anthony had his first boyfriend when he went to art college in Hull. He was seventeen and Dave was about a year older. The first I knew was when Anthony told me he was going to move in with Dave.

'Dave's a college friend with his own flat and he said I can move in with him and sleep on his sofa.'

'Oh yeah?' I said. 'Right. That's fine.' I was happy with it. He was old enough to make up his own mind. They even got a puppy together, soon after Anthony moved in.

The first time I went to their flat was when I bought them some shopping and took it to them. I met Dave and he seemed quite pleasant.

'I'll show you round,' said Anthony. 'This is our bedroom.' He grinned.

I looked at him and burst out laughing. 'Yeah, OK,' I said. And he laughed too, so it all went well.

What I didn't realise was that this was not what it seemed. China told me when we spoke about it recently: 'Anthony always wanted the perfect relationship,' she explained. 'But Dave was the dominant one. He always told Neenee that if he didn't do what Dave wanted, he would chuck him out. Dave was matter-of-fact about it, but Neenee was struggling with himself over the situation. It might have seemed all right on the surface, but deep down he knew it wasn't a healthy relationship and he left after six months.'

His only other long-term boyfriend had been Mitch, a fellow student.

'But I don't think he quite got to grips with that relationship,' China told me. 'It broke up after a few months because Anthony reckoned that Mitch was leeching money out of him, so he stopped it.'

The trouble was, Anthony was just too kind. Although he absolutely loved his fashion studies at Middlesex University and really came out of his shell, with his fun escapades and flamboyant ways, the shy, sensitive, trusting boy was still there underneath right up until the night he died.

But now it was all over. I still couldn't believe it. Anthony's last words to China, 'in case I get killed or something', kept reverberating inside my head.

CHAPTER 4

The Wrong Charge

25 and 26 June 2014

The following morning, as soon as I woke up and felt again the shock that Anthony had gone, my head was full of questions. It was as if he was urging me to keep on digging, to find out more, to goad the police into action. *'Don't let them rest, Sezzer!'* That was his name for me. He never called me 'Mam' – only 'Sezzer'. So I knew it was him speaking to me.

I always used to call him 'Ant', always. But I'd just noticed I was only using his full name now. It wasn't deliberate, except with the police. I don't know why but I didn't feel able to use his shortened name. I couldn't bring myself to refer to him as 'Ant', not with all this going on. It was too personal . . . too painful.

I had got nowhere with DC Slaymaker so, after my conversation with China and knowing that she had given her statement to O'Donnell, I decided to call him direct. My call went straight through to him, but I could hear the disappointment in his voice when he knew it was me.

'It's no good calling and asking me endless questions. You have a family liaison officer now. Call him.'

OK, so that was the way it was? I took a deep breath and I called DC Slaymaker:

'Have you got any news? Any more information?'

'No. There's nothing new, nothing to investigate.'

'Why do you keep saying that? What do you mean nothing to investigate?'

'Well, he took the drugs and he died.'

'NO!' I gasped. 'That's just your assumption, but it's wrong. Trust me, that's not possible. Ask anybody—'

'Well, like it or not,' he interrupted, 'that's what did happen.'

'And I'm telling you it did not.' I felt my anger rising. 'Do you want me to come down there and f***ing investigate it for you? Because something is not right.'

'There is nothing to investigate,' he repeated in a mock patient voice.

I realised I was getting nowhere, so I enlisted China's evidence to support what I kept trying to tell him. 'When I called you yesterday, you told me to ring China Dunning, one of Anthony's friends. She's the one who reported him as missing and came to see DS O'Donnell on the Thursday afternoon to make a statement about it.'

'Yes?'

'She told him that Anthony had given her the name of the guy he was going to meet. Joe Dean, and his postcode.'

'Yes,' he said, followed by an awkward silence.

'Well, have you found this man, Joe Dean?'

'No.'

'Why not?'

'Because he's not on our records, not in this postcode, so he probably doesn't exist.'

'Have you spoken to anybody?'

'Only the people living in the block of flats where the body was found—'

'Not "the body",' I interrupted, outraged. 'It wasn't an object; he was a person – Anthony's body.'

'OK, I'm sorry.' At least he had the grace to apologise. 'But the residents said they didn't see or hear anything.'

'Are you sure? Did you speak to all of them? Were they all telling the truth?'

'Look, Mrs Sak, there's no need for all this. There's nothing suspicious about your son's death. He died on his own, during the night. There was no mark on him. He had a small bottle of something next to his body, so we're having that analysed and a second post-mortem done but we'll have to await the results. It may take some time, but I will update you when the results come in.'

'Who was the person who called the ambulance?'

'A resident of one of the ground-floor flats.'

'Have you spoken to him?'

'Yes.'

'How come he found him at that time of the morning?'

DC Slaymaker gave a heavy sigh. 'Because he's a chef, he was coming home from his late shift.'

'Did you question him?'

'Yes, one of my officers did speak to him but he couldn't tell us much. We might try him again.'

'Had Anthony been dead long when he was found?' I could hear papers rustling.

'It looks like it, yes. He was cold.'

'So he might have been dead a while?'

'I suppose so.'

'Then why didn't anyone else find him?'

'Look, Mrs Sak, there is no point in all this. It is not a crime. Your son had a drug next to him . . .'

'How do you know it was a drug?'

'We'll know soon . . . and Miss Dunning said he often took drugs.'

'No, never with strangers. He only ever smoked cannabis, occasionally, and only with his friends in his or their flats. But never any hard drugs. And I'm sure he would never have taken anything at all away from home.'

'Well, we found some drugs in his flat.'

Now I was really riled. 'No, not real drugs. Did you test them?'

'No need.'

'I know he had some poppers, which he kept by his bed. China told me that. But they're not drugs. They're certainly not illegal. They're just like gas to sniff. Anthony would never have taken anything like heroin or cocaine. He was very against those because he would never have done anything that might harm his health. He was a happy, successful university student, working hard and doing very well. He had a great future ahead of him.' I paused, but there was no response, so I carried on: 'Yes, with his close group of friends, he would party like there was no tomorrow but Anthony didn't trust anyone else. I'm certain he would never have drunk or taken any drugs with a stranger.'

'That's what—' he broke off. I felt sure he was going to tell me 'that's what they all say.'

43

'You think I'm just some druggy's mother who doesn't know her own son, don't you? Well, you couldn't be more wrong! I'm not in denial. This is not just a mother's instinct. It's me knowing Anthony as a man. Anyone who knew him would tell you. This death is no drugs overdose. There is something very wrong that happened to my son and I won't stop till I find out—'

'Well, Mrs Sak,' he interrupted wearily, 'we'll know more when the second post-mortem results come back but it will be quite a wait I'm afraid.'

'So can we at least have Anthony's body back, so that we can have a funeral for him? It's been a week now and I'm shocked that nobody's even mentioned getting his body back to us.'

'I'll make a note of your request but I'm afraid we can't release the body until the coroner's office has seen the post-mortem report and given us permission.'

'And what about all his possessions – all the things in his room?'

'All we have here is his laptop and that's locked away.'

'I assume somebody is going through his browsing history and messages for clues? There might be something there about Joe Dean, the name he gave to China, the man he had arranged to meet.'

'No, we don't have the personnel to go through that . . . all for a wild-goose chase.'

I ignored his insinuation. 'But surely you have to do that for any unsolved murder?'

'For the umpteenth time, Mrs Sak,' I heard his big sigh. 'Your son was not murdered. In any case, going through his laptop would be too expensive.'

I was appalled but also still worried about all his other things. 'So can you send me the rest of his belongings?'

'No, I'm afraid we've sealed up his room now, so it will not be possible to send you anything yet.'

'But what if his landlord wants to re-let his room?' I was horrified to think of it. 'He might just empty it and throw everything away.'

'No, he's not allowed to do that. It won't be for long.'

I felt completely drained when I put the phone down. I was hugely disappointed that we couldn't hold a funeral yet or have his personal items back, and alarmed that they weren't even looking at Anthony's laptop. But mostly I felt a mixture of fury and frustration that the police officer who was supposed to be supporting us was doing quite the opposite – blocking almost every question and pushing us away. How could he say it wasn't a crime, when he hadn't even investigated it?

I kept thinking of all the things they could do – try to track down his phone, check his laptop, take statements from everyone in the flats . . . They clearly just wanted me to crawl away and leave them alone. But they didn't know me. I was no detective but I couldn't just sit there and hope they would get round to it. It was obvious they had written off Anthony's death as just another gay druggy's overdose. I sat and fumed for about five minutes.

Then Kate rang and she could tell I was angry, so I gave her an update.

'Do you think they're being deliberately unhelpful?' she asked. 'Or just uncaring?'

'It's hard to say but it certainly feels like both of those

things, and worse!' I paused. 'I'm going to ring him right back and push him harder this time.'

'Good luck!'

So I called him again. 'You said you had interviewed the residents?'

'Yesss?' he said, in a slow, flat voice.

This time I stayed silent for several seconds . . . and it worked. I wanted him to give me at least some details, and he did.

'We are talking to them now and taking some statements but I can't tell you any more at the moment.'

'So it's ongoing?'

'Yes. But this is not really about Anthony's death.'

'What do you mean? It's six days now since Anthony's body was found. Why is all this taking so long? I'm sure you would have done things differently if it had been a young girl's body found in the street.'

'It wasn't, so let's keep things in proportion.'

'Are you saying his death doesn't matter because he was a gay young man with a small bottle beside him, that you assume is a drug and that anybody could have put there?'

'No, but it's not a crime.'

'How can you possibly know that if you won't even investigate it properly? I'm telling you, Anthony could not have done this to himself. He was killed – probably murdered. Why can't you at least look into that as a possibility?'

'I've already told you . . .'

'Do you know what?' I blasted at him. 'If Anthony's death had been in Hull, they would definitely investigate it. They'd be all over it.'

In a condescending tone, DC Slaymaker said to me: 'We get more murders in this area in a week than you get in Hull in a year.' He made it sound like this was just another one that wasn't worth looking into.

'Well, you've got a bigger f***ing police force than we have!'

He paused for a moment – I suppose to keep calm. 'I'll let you know as soon as we hear about the second post-mortem,' he said.

'OK,' I said abruptly. 'Goodbye,' and I slammed the phone down.

I needed a cigarette after that, and it was a warm day, so I went and sat in the garden. Our lawn backed onto a primary school's playground and I could hear the happy sounds of children playing. That had been Anthony, when he was small – always running around and laughing with his classmates.

I remember one time when he was about three and the house we lived in then was at the end of a cul de sac. All the children in that road used to play together. They'd play out all day when they could and the little ones used to play in each others' gardens. A couple of days before, Anthony's hamster had died. So we had a sort of funeral in the garden, as you do. On this particular day, all his little friends, about six of them, all three-year-olds, came round to play in our garden. They were outside, making lots of noise as usual. I was in the kitchen and, all of a sudden, it went deathly quiet.

I thought, 'Oh my God!' I leant over the sink and looked out of the kitchen window. They were all standing around something.

'What are you doing?' I asked.

'Nothing,' said Anthony. Then the others chimed in: 'Nothing, nothing, nothing!'

Well, that sounded rather suspicious, so I went outside to see what they were up to. I soon saw it. He'd only dug up his hamster to show them! They were all stood there. It was in the middle and they were all stood round it, prodding it and poking and feeling it. So I had to bring them all into the house and wash all their hands, one after the other, all six of them, all queued up at the sink. Finally they all had clean hands so I shooed them off to someone else's garden, then went outside to pick up the dead hamster and put it in the shed, to bury that night when he was in bed.

'What were you doing?' I asked Anthony later.

'Just checking it was dead.'

'I wouldn't have buried it if it wasn't dead!' I said.

Oh, bless him. He did remember that over the years. It was probably his first memory. I used to say to him: 'Do you remember when you dug your bloody hamster up?' And we'd have a good laugh!

I couldn't help but smile now as I thought of it and pictured them all . . . but in moments the smile dissolved as the tears flowed down my cheeks. I thought they'd never stop.

On the following day, the Thursday, exactly a week after Anthony's body was found, I woke up to bright sunshine pouring through the window. For a few short seconds, I actually smiled. But then I was suddenly hit all over again by the terrible truth. How could I smile when I would never see him again, never hear his voice or his laughter? I felt guilty that I was alive and he wasn't. A part of me didn't even want to be alive without him, but the other part was the battling me, the mother who demanded to know, who wouldn't give in. As I went through the motions of showering, dressing, making myself eat some breakfast, even though I didn't have any appetite, I recalled yesterday's conversations and made a decision. If the police wouldn't do anything, I'd damn well make sure somebody else did. But who?

Just then, our Kate arrived, so I put the kettle on.

'Have you got your laptop on?' she asked me.

'No,' I said. 'Why?'

'I'll do the coffees and you log on, then I'll show you.'

We sat in front of the screen and she put in a search. 'Here you are. It's the *Barking and Dagenham Post*.' She clicked and the image changed. 'Look. It's on the front page today.'

I read it in shocked silence. It was about the body that had been found in Cooke Street the previous Thursday morning. Anthony's body. 'Was it a murder?' the headline asked but it didn't mention Anthony's name.

'How did you know about this?' I asked Kate.

'I was up early, so I just looked it up on the off chance and there it was. And that's not all.' She scrolled down the page and got to the comments section. 'Read these. There are quite a few new messages now, just in the time it took me to drive over here.'

We started to read from the first onwards. They were all local people, in the Barking area. Some were saying it was a murder and one said 'No, it's another drugs death,' which sparked off a debate, going to and fro. Several people were obviously worried about their own and their families' safety.

'And look what it says on Facebook,' Kate said as she clicked onto the page. We read some of the comments together and then she pointed out one she'd seen earlier. 'Listen to this. It's from a young woman chatting with her friend, who lives in that block of flats. She read it aloud: '"What happened? Was it another murder?" And her friend replied: "No. I asked the police if it was murder and they said, "No, it was a drugs death." Look at the date on it,' Kate said. 'This was only a few hours after Ant was found.'

After Kate left, I had another read of the newspaper articles and messages, trying to find even the tiniest clue. The bit about a policeman talking to a resident just after Anthony's body had been found was what kept going round in my head, and the fact that he said it was a drugs death. Only a few hours ago, Slaymaker had said the same but he didn't know Anthony. How could he make such an assumption without at least listening to us?

I sat and breathed in the silence, while my brain was blank and buzzing by turns.

My ringtone went off, jolting me back to the moment. China's voice was a welcome interruption and I was glad to talk through what I'd read in the papers. She hadn't seen any of it, so she was as riveted as I was when I read some of them out to her.

Then she told me what she'd rung about: 'Have you heard about Ellie's phone message?'

'No,' I said. 'I had two useless conversations with the police yesterday and nothing today.' I knew Ellie was another of Anthony's close friends, so he probably used to message her quite often . . . before he died.

'Well, Ellie switched on her phone first thing this morning, as usual,' explained China. 'But this was different. Neenee's number came up.'

I froze.

'There was a text message from that number, so she clicked to open it.'

'What did it say?' I asked.

'Just four words,' replied China. "THIS IS THE END." She came straight round to show me, then down to tell the police, assuming they would follow it up, but she was upset that they didn't seem bothered.'

'Now, why doesn't that surprise me?' I said. 'They told me he didn't have his phone with him, either in his pockets or in his rucksack. I told them they should look for it, but they just said he must have left it behind that day.'

'Well, whoever has that phone now,' suggested China, 'is obviously using it to frighten us.'

'Yes,' I added. 'And whoever has that phone is probably the murderer.' I paused while we both took that in. 'But who? How? And why didn't the police call and tell me this morning?'

'Do you think we should follow it up?' asked China.

'Yes, I'll get onto it straight away. If they thought they'd got rid of me for a while, they have another think coming!'

I dialled Slaymaker's number again.

'Why didn't you call to tell me about Ellie Green's text message from Anthony's phone this morning?'

'Because it's not important.' He didn't even pause for me to butt in. 'He probably lost it or left it somewhere, so anybody could have it by now, and the message was very short, so it could even have been from a child, playing about.'

'I can tell you that this wasn't playing about. Whoever sent that message is the man who killed my son.'

'Well, we'll just have to agree to differ,' said my FLO. 'We'll never know, anyway.'

'Why not? You have put a trace on it, haven't you?'

'No, Sarah,' he said, unexpectedly using my first name for the first time as he tried to fob me off. But it didn't stop me now.

'This is a definite clue to the murder of my son,' I reiterated. 'And I insist that you investigate it. Surely you must at least put a trace on it?'

'No, we can't do that. It would be—'

I interrupted him. 'Let me guess,' I said, with as much sarcasm as I could muster. 'Too expensive?'

'Yes.' He ignored my dig. 'And in this case, it wouldn't do any good as Anthony's death was not suspicious.'

'Well that phone call certainly is suspicious, so I'm pleading with you. Please trace that phone. Track down where it is and who has it. Then you will have the killer . . . and save any other mother from losing her son.' This was followed by a short silence.

'Actually, I'm glad you rang,' he changed the subject, as if we'd been talking about the weather.

'Why, is there any news?'

'Yes. As you will remember, I told you we were interviewing the residents of the flats.'

'Yes, there's been something in your local paper about it. I saw it online.'

'Yes, that's right. But one of them, Stephen Port, whom we have interviewed on at least three separate occasions, has changed his story each time. So we have arrested and charged him.' My hopes soared . . . then crashed again. 'For perverting the course of justice.'

'What the hell does that mean?' I asked.

'It means he told lies and in the end he admitted it.'

'So are you going to charge him for murder as well?'

'No, we can't do that. Port didn't kill Anthony – nobody did, and we weren't investigating that anyway. This charge only came up because we wanted to try and clarify whether anyone had actually seen Anthony taking drugs.'

'Well, he didn't.'

'No, I have to tell you that he did.'

'What?' I was incredulous. 'Was it the liar who told you that?'

He didn't get the inference. 'Not at first. He made up some cock and bull story about finding him in the hallway of the flats and dragging him outside. But then he changed his story and told us something else and finally he told us the truth.'

'And what was that?'

'He told us that Anthony had come round to see him and that he had brought some drugs with him and took them in Port's flat. Port said he then had to go to work, so he left Anthony to sleep them off but when he returned, Anthony was dead in Port's bed, so he dragged him outside and rang the ambulance, then went to bed.'

'And you believe him?!' I almost screamed at him in horror.

'Yes, he stuck to his final story and it matches the facts.'

'So, when you say you've charged and arrested this animal . . .'

'He's been charged and will face a trial later in the year.'

'And that trial will be about . . .'

'Perversion of the course of justice,' repeated Slaymaker. 'We'll keep you informed if there's anything more to tell.'

'So at least he's off the streets then?'

'No, he's been bailed till the trial.'

'But it's the WRONG CHARGE!' I yelled at him in my frustration, unable to hold back the fury I felt. 'And he'll still be at large to lure in more victims. You mark my words – Anthony won't be the only one killed.'

CHAPTER 5

A Cry for Help

27–29 June 2014

I'd been trying to think what I could do to stir up the police
. . . There must be someone who could help me. Now, as I
sat, attempting to make sense of the snippets of new information, it suddenly occurred to me – if the police can't help,
then maybe I should phone our MP.

Karl Turner is what they call a man of the people. He's
very down to earth and I'd heard stories of the ways he
had sorted out problems for other constituents, so what did
I have to lose?

I went online and looked him up. I found a number and
rang it straight away. I expected to get his secretary and
have to book an appointment, but he picked up the phone
himself. That's what he's like.

'Karl Turner,' he said. 'Can I help you?'

'Yes, I hope you can. It's about my son, Anthony Walgate,
whose body was found in a London street last Thursday.'

'Was he the one I read about in the local paper?'

'Yes. They didn't give his name but it's an awful situation,'
I began. 'The Barking police are absolutely useless and they
refuse to investigate it. They refuse to follow up any leads

and they just keep saying it wasn't a crime. Well, I know it was. My son was a hard-working student at Middlesex University in London, doing very well and with a good career ahead of him. He loved his life and his loyal friends. Why would he jeopardise all that? They're saying he was a druggy but I know he didn't ever take any serious drugs. He would certainly not have taken any drugs or drunk with strangers.' I paused for breath. 'I've tried and tried, but the police just keep blocking me . . .'

'Are you free to come in to see me?'

'Yes,' I agreed, surprised and relieved that he was taking me seriously.

I remembered that Kate knew him and I thought I might want some moral support, so I rang her up and she came straight round to collect me.

He welcomed us in and sat us down with him. 'Right,' he said. 'What do you want me to do?'

I launched my tale of woe and told him about everything. He was wonderful, listening attentively and taking it all in, nodding and clicking his tongue in sympathy in all the right places.

I could see he was shocked by what I told him. But that day he wasn't just a listener – he was a doer. I'd heard he'd been brought up on a council estate and he'd been a barrister before becoming a Member of Parliament, so he knew about these things and had often had dealings with the police.

'OK,' he said. 'Let's sort this out. First things first: let's make sure they get Anthony home to you as soon as possible and safeguard his possessions until they can release them.' He took the details and made a couple of phone calls.

'Right, they're going to move all the things currently sealed in Anthony's room and put them into safe police storage until they can be sent on to you. I understand that they can't release your son's body until the coroner signs the release. I think that's what they told you, isn't it?'

'Yes. But we need to have a funeral for him as soon as possible, to help me and everyone else grieve and be able to visit his grave.'

'I do understand that, Sarah,' he said. 'I will keep on the case for you.'

'Thanks.'

'Now, what do you know about this man's charge for perverting the course of justice?'

'The only definite things we know are that he was the one who found Anthony's body and phoned for the ambulance and what the Barking police told me – that his name is Stephen Port and that he changed his story about what happened each time they interviewed him. One story was that he found Anthony unconscious outside, the second story was that he was in the hallway of the flats and the third was that he died in Port's flat.'

Karl Turner then explained what 'perverting the course of justice' really means and why the police would consider it so important to charge Port with that. He explained it all in the context of our scenario – what I'd told him about the residents of the flats being interviewed, what I'd been told Port had actually said each time and what his final version of events was.

'And they believed him that third time?' asked Karl in surprise.

'Yes, that's just what I asked them too. They said that, yes, they did believe his third statement, because he stuck to that story. Yet this, by his own admission, was the last man who saw my son alive.'

'Well,' said Karl, 'that is alarming. Do you know whether they probed him about the circumstances of Anthony's death, beyond what he said in his final statement?'

'Apparently not,' I replied. 'They always insist that his death was not suspicious and not to ask questions that will never have any answers.' I paused. 'I can tell you, I was fuming! I still am!'

'This all sounds horrendous for you. I'm going to get to work and speak to a few key people to help expedite things and ensure that you are kept more fully informed from now on. In fact, the first thing I'm going to do is to have a chat with my mate Paul, the chief inspector of Humberside Police. I'm sure he'll be able to set off a few rockets!'

We stood up to go and he handed me his card. 'That's my personal mobile number,' he said. 'I'm going to keep in touch with you to see how things are going but I want you to call or text me any time you need my help or advice. Is that a deal?'

'Yes, Karl. Thank you so much. You've been brilliant.'

'Yes,' added Kate, 'I'll stand you a drink next time you're over our way.'

'I'll keep you to that,' he laughed as we shook hands and left.

'Phew! What a difference,' I said as we walked back to the car.

'Yes, isn't that great? He's 100 per cent on your side. And it sounds like he's going to shake up that useless shower of so-called police and get things done.'

Later that afternoon, Paul Cunningham, the chief inspector of Humberside police, rang me himself to say how sorry he was that our experience of the police had been so poor and that he had rung my FLO, DC Slaymaker, and given him what for! I was stunned.

'I told him, "You need to sort yourself out," and I don't suppose he was very happy about that, Sarah. But it's no more than he deserves. I told him my friend, our Member of Parliament, rang me and told me that one of his constituents is really upset by all this. It isn't good enough. I think it will have the desired effect, and they will at least keep you in the loop from now on.'

'Thanks very much, Chief Inspector,' I said, genuinely relieved and grateful.

'Call me Paul,' he said. 'You've got my number now, Sarah. So let me know how it goes,' and he put his phone down.

'Wow!' I said out loud to myself as I saved his number in my contacts. Then I was straight on the phone to Kate to tell her about the call.

'How do you feel about things today?' she asked.

'Relieved to have some strong support . . . but I'm not holding my breath. I think the Barking lot are so entrenched that it might take a while for anything to change much at that end. But I do feel as if I got somewhere today.'

While I was genuinely pleased with these influential people's support and the knowledge that it might make a bit of difference in the short term, my main focus all the time was Anthony. Losing him was already a huge, gaping hole in my life and I didn't at that time realise the irony of the fact that I needed it to stay that way in order to keep me fighting.

I sat in my chair in the lounge – the 'Queen's chair', as the boys always called it, because it was my chair and no one else was allowed to sit in it. So, of course, cheeky Anthony, being the younger one, just waited till I left the room . . . 'Quick, let's go and sit on the Queen's chair,' he'd shout as he leapt on it! He would have a giggle with Paul until they heard me coming back and then immediately jump back to the sofa again. They thought I didn't know but of course I did, and I played the game sometimes, tip-toeing in, catching Anthony by surprise and giving him a mock telling off! We did have a laugh about that when he was older but he still used to do it to tease me.

I smiled briefly at the memory but soon my smile had gone and I sat there, staring into space for a while – I don't know for how long. Probably all evening, my mind full of cotton wool.

Promptly at half past eight the following morning, my phone went. I was so sluggish these days and I hadn't even had breakfast yet. Who could it be? Straight away, I recognised the number. I would have liked not to answer it but I knew I had to. It might be something important.

'Why have you landed me in the shit?' asked a very angry voice – my FLO. 'What did you do that for? Bloody hell, Sarah. You've really got me in trouble now.'

'What do you mean?' I asked, secretly pleased that he'd obviously got it in the neck.

'You know perfectly well. I had a call from the chief inspector of Humberside yesterday afternoon and he'd somehow got completely the wrong end of the stick. Apparently, he had rung you first and you'd told him I wasn't up to the job.'

'Well, you aren't are you? I went to see a friend of my sister's, who happens to be our MP. He explained exactly what Port's charge means, which is more than you ever did. He was very sympathetic to my situation and told Paul, the chief inspector, all about it. Paul then rang me, full of apologies about the Barking and Dagenham police not looking properly into Anthony's murder—'

'It wasn't murder.'

'That's just your opinion. You don't listen to anything China or I say, you give us the least amount of information you can and you expect me to just give up on my bright, intelligent, clean-living son. Well, Paul agrees with me that I should have far better support from you and be consulted much more to help you develop better-informed judgements.'

'I can only do what my superiors tell me,' he said. 'And I can only pass on information if we have any, but since there is nothing to investigate, there is usually nothing to tell you.'

'Well, Paul and I had a long and very helpful conversation.' I could tell that my deliberate use of the chief inspector's first name was irking him, so I kept doing it. 'Paul said he would ring you to ask you to be more sympathetic and helpful towards me, as a bereaved mother, who knew her son better than anyone and who has good reason to believe that your police force are not doing a good job.'

I paused but he said nothing, so I continued, on a roll now. 'You have to admit it: you're supposed to be my liaison officer and you don't liaise. You're rubbish. You don't support me at all. You haven't done, right from the start. To get any information out of you is worse than pulling teeth. You're useless!'

'Well, what do you want from me?' he asked in an anguished voice.

'Right. I want you to call me regularly and give me a full and honest report about what is happening. Even if there is no news, if you could just ring me regularly to say so. Every day at the moment, then once a week. Just say, "I've got no news for you Sarah," and then I'll know that at least you're still there, still doing something.'

'It's my first time as a family liaison officer,' he said.

'Well, I'm sorry, but I don't give a toss,' I replied. 'You're rubbish at it. If I was a liaison officer, I would ring all the people once a week to say "I'm sorry I don't have any news for you, but . . ." and at least they would know I wasn't ignoring them, like you do.'

'OK. I don't know whether they'll let me continue as your FLO,' he said. 'But if I do I will ring you once a week, whether I have anything to tell you or not.'

Would he? I wondered. Only time would tell.

Around lunchtime, I had a call from Paul Cunningham, the chief inspector, to ask if I would be in that afternoon, as he was sending two CID officers round to see me. I was just lurching from day to day at the moment, with nothing planned, so I said yes and agreed a time.

On the dot, they arrived and came into my house. I would have asked Tom to come round, but it was such short notice and he would be at work. I would have to update him later. They seemed friendly and we all sat down in my lounge, me in my Queen's chair and the two of them on the sofa. They started by saying how sorry they were for Anthony's death, so far away and in such dreadful circumstances. They also said they were sorry to hear that Tom and I, as his parents, hadn't had the kind of compassionate support that we could have expected.

'We're here to answer any questions you may not have had sufficiently answered up to now,' said one of them.

'And to explain any procedures that you're not sure about,' added the other.

'Shall we start with something we understand is particularly important to you – the procedures and possible timescale for having Anthony's body brought back to you, so that you can hold a funeral for him and put him to rest in his own home city?'

They both had such a kind and empathetic manner that I felt the whole visit would be very helpful, not least in boosting me up with some threads of hope and restoring some of my faith in the police. They went right back to the beginning, to the examination of Anthony's body by a doctor or medical officer, who writes a report about it. Then they explained that the first post-mortem was a basic examination of the deceased and the first-stage analysis of any illegal substances or alcohol there may be in the body. Since, in Anthony's case, that hadn't yielded any useful information, they went on to do a far more detailed autopsy on the body, taking more specimens of blood and other fluids, as well as more scrupulous examination of any physical anomalies, such as bruises or scratches.

'That's very helpful to know,' I said. 'The Barking and Dagenham police have never explained any of that to me. But is it normal to have to wait longer the second time around for the lab results?'

'Yes, I'm afraid so. It very much depends on what tests the lab is asked to do.'

I learned to my surprise that sometimes it's even necessary to have a third post-mortem, and it might be so in Anthony's case, since there were no explicit instructions about what to look for.

They talked me through the process for interviewing potential witnesses, which had been done with the residents of the flats, and the sorts of questions they would have been asked. They didn't need to say much about Port's charge of perverting the course of justice as Karl Turner had given me and Kate a beginner's guide explanation to all that. I wanted to know why Port had been charged then almost straightaway bailed and why it would be a longish wait for his trial under that charge, so they took turns to explain the usual pattern of such cases.

I realised, from what their chief inspector had told me, that they couldn't at this meeting discuss anything contentious about another police force, so I didn't ask any of my burning questions – the most burning and anguishing of all being why didn't they investigate how Anthony died and who might have killed him. Even though those were the questions that blighted my days and kept me awake at nights.

However, they did not use the phrase 'not suspicious' when talking about the discovery of Anthony's body. Instead they called it an 'unexplained death', which I felt was much more open-minded, like a chink of light, something to hold onto. Although obviously the Barking lot wouldn't see it that way.

CHAPTER 6

Wading through Fog

July 2014, the month following Anthony's death

When the detectives had gone, I felt better for talking with them and for all their consideration but I was totally shattered. I turned on the TV and then I must have fallen asleep, or into some kind of stupor, as I don't remember anything after that until mid-evening.

I came to with a start. It was 8.30 p.m., so still time to call Tom. I spent the next half hour telling him what I'd done and who I'd seen over the past couple of days, bringing him up to date. He never says much but I could tell by his voice that he was pleased we'd made some progress.

'DC Slaymaker rang me too when I got home from work today,' he said. He told me about arresting and charging that man, Port, for perverting the course of justice. That's a step forward, isn't it?'

'But it's the wrong charge!'

'Yes, you're right . . . but at least it will keep him off the streets, out of harm's way.'

'So he didn't tell you Port had been bailed?'

'Oh! No, he didn't. That means we're back where we started.'

Now things seemed to quieten down, with no phone calls from DC Paul Slaymaker, and the only other people keeping in touch were my husband Sami, to catch up daily; Paul, who occasionally called or sent me brief texts to see if I was all right; Anthony's closest friends China, Kiera and Ellie, plus of course Kate, who was my mainstay. But in between, nothing. I now had time to rest – I slept a lot. The other thing I tried to do was clear my mind of all the bad police stuff as much as I could. But often that all crept up on me again and I found myself growing more and more bitter about their lack of any human concern, let alone action. OK, so they'd never met Anthony, but how dare the police just brush him off? They didn't know the little boy who loved lying across my knees while I scratched his back. His eczema drove him crazy and this was his only relief.

When he was young, he was always up to mischief and often embarrassed us. I remember one time, at the airport on the way back from a holiday. There was a long corridor through customs and we had to stand in a queue. As we waited, a sniffer dog went along the line. Everybody stopped talking and you could hear a pin drop.

Anthony loved dogs, so he tried to attract the sniffer dog to come over to us. Whereas I didn't want it anywhere near us, or at least near my suitcase, which was packed full of Tom's and my cigarettes!

'Here doggie, doggie,' called Anthony in his shrill four-year-old voice.

'You can't play with that dog,' I said in a whisper.

'Why not?'

'Because he's working.'

'Why?'

'He's looking for drugs.'

'Have we got drugs?'

'No,' I said curtly, trying to hide my embarrassment. 'It's naughty.'

'But I want drugs. I want to play with the doggie.'

This carried on, to and fro, as we crept all the way along the queue and, as we approached the front, the customs officer kept looking up at me and smiling. I was mortified. Everyone was sniggering as all they could hear was Anthony's voice.

'Can we have some drugs, so I can play with the doggie?'

'No,' I insisted in a stage whisper. 'It's very naughty to have drugs.'

He was still going on as we reached the front so I squeezed his hand and whispered quietly into his ear: 'Ssh now.'

He immediately cried out: 'Why are you hurting my hand?'

As I passed over our passports, the officer leaned right over the counter to smile at Anthony. 'The things they say . . . they would get you shot, wouldn't they?' He laughed.

As he grew older, Anthony turned into a shy, quiet lad in public. I could sense the turmoil in him . . . until he was about thirteen or fourteen, at about the time when he must have realised he was gay. It was quite dramatic the way he totally changed overnight. His hair, voice, clothes, his whole demeanour – everything changed.

His dad always thought he was 'arty farty', and said so to him, but this was because he was developing a passion for fashion – especially fashion design. Somebody gave him the DVD of *The Devil Wears Prada*. He loved that film – he must have watched it at least twenty times.

Unlike most teenagers, Anthony knew from an early age what he wanted to do. After leaving school, he planned to go to the local art college to pursue his dream but, out of the blue and without telling us, he went for an interview at Middlesex University. The first we knew about it was when he told us both separately that he had been given a place to study fashion design there. So he wasn't going to stay in Hull. He would be off to London and the big wide world of fashion in a much grander way. It wasn't just a job he was after, it was glamour, fame and fortune. His aim was to be a top designer with his own fashion house and his name up in lights.

After he left, he would ring up all the time for long, chatty phone conversations. This was now what I missed the most – there was an empty, gaping hole in my heart and in my life where these calls used to be. He could be on the phone for two hours:

'What's going on, Sezzer?' He was just like one of those old women who used to stand at their gates, tongues wagging! He absolutely loved gossip – he wanted to know all the details!

'Go on,' he'd say. 'Who's doing what?'

'Ooh,' I'd reply. 'Guess who's pregnant.'

'Tell me, tell me,' he'd urge with a conspiratorial giggle in his voice, the giggle he'd had ever since he was a toddler.

'You'll never guess.'

He'd start reeling off names . . . and then I'd tell him.

'Oh, my frigging . . .'

'Yes, and that's not the only thing . . .'

I had to ring him at least three times a week because he never had enough money on his phonecard. So he'd text me when he wanted me to call him and we'd go off into all that was going on.

'Come on, Sezzer. What's the latest?'

I'd start telling him who one of his cousins was going out with, or what the next-doors were getting up to while I put the phone on speaker so that I could get some food out of the fridge.

'Take me off speaker,' he'd say.

'I can't. I'm cooking my tea.'

He'd moan so much but he was cheeky with it, so that I had to hold the phone in one hand while trying to cut one-handed as he started telling me all the gossip at his end.

'I've fallen out with Ellie,' he'd say, or other times it would be China, or Kiera, or some other friend. Then the next day they were best mates again. He was such a drama queen.

'Ooh, you'll never guess . . .!' he'd exclaim, as he told me whatever he was getting up to down there.

Or ,'You'll never guess what I did yesterday. What a blast that was! I went into uni early and hid in an empty Ali Baba basket at the back of the room and pulled the lid over my head. When all the others came in and started working, I jumped out screaming and frightened them all to death!'

I could just imagine it – his cheeky grin and his arms flailing about!

It was not so much a mother–son relationship now. Since he'd gone to London, he'd turned into my best friend. We'd become best mates and I loved our chatty phone calls.

'Gi's a ring, Sezzer. I need to talk to you.' Or if I hadn't called him for a couple of days, he'd text: 'Are you dead, Sezzer?' He knew I'd ring him.

A couple of times, after he died, the phone would go and I'd think 'Oh, that'll be Anthony.' It was painful to realise it wasn't . . . and it never would be. I would never hear his voice again.

I felt deeply that nobody understood. How could they? I wasn't even able to go out of the door without seeing the looks on people's faces when they saw me, unsure what to say to me, especially when I told them Anthony had not just died: he'd been murdered. I suppose I don't blame them. They must have thought my protestations were a mother's way of coping.

I knew I was depressed but somehow I was able to hide it from Paul as he had his own place, a job he liked and things he enjoyed doing, so he didn't come round much. When he did, I always put on my 'normal' face and I'm pretty sure he didn't notice a thing.

Now that nothing was happening, the days seemed to merge in a blur of grief and recurring shock.

As I wrote in my diary, 'Grief is a terrible thing. It consumes you.'

I just couldn't think any more. My head felt fuzzy, as if my brain was frozen. Just trying to think of things . . . didn't work. It was a very strange feeling, as if I was in the world but wasn't part of it. Sometimes I would sit there, in my chair, and sit and sit, doing nothing, thinking nothing, not eating, not even watching mindless television. I was catatonic. Then suddenly it was four o'clock and I'd done nothing all day.

71

I was sinking and sinking. I developed chest pains, every day, tightening round me like a vice. I'm sure that was stress. It wouldn't go away, and worsened in those few lucid moments when the bitter indignation and frustration hit me afresh – the time passing and the police doing nothing. I'm a doer – that's the way I get myself out of trouble – but now I could do nothing. I was powerless and that frightened me. My despair crippled me. I sank into a spiral, lower and lower. I was no longer aware of the days or the nights. I was wading through fog. I'd blink and another day had gone. I lost a stone in weight.

Kate says she used to pop in using the spare keys I'd given her but I don't remember. She later told me how worried she had been about me.

She told a friend of ours: 'Sarah's eyes are glazed over, empty, and she looks like a skeleton, gradually dissolving to the ground.'

One morning, about four or five weeks after Anthony's death, Kate came in and found me in a trance, as if asleep but with my eyes open. Seeing the state I was in, she shook me gently. 'Come on,' she said. 'We're going to go and get you some help.'

She took me out to her car and said: 'Right. We'll try the Samaritans first,' and off we went.

A young girl, about eighteen, was sat there on her own. I took one look at her and thought, 'You haven't got any idea, love.' It wasn't her fault, of course, but she was no use to me.

'Why don't you try Cruse or Victim Support?' she said.

So Kate took me to Victim Support. She led me upstairs and we sat down. I sat silently on a chair while Kate explained what had happened. 'She just needs some help,' she said. 'She needs something.'

The woman turned to look at me. 'Sorry, she's not actually a victim, so there's nothing we can do to help.'

I couldn't believe it. How dare she? All I wanted was some help. I silently pleaded: Somebody *do* something to make it better.

'I can't help her,' added the woman.

By now I was more alert and I was fuming at what she'd said. Do you know, I thought, even as a fellow human being, why don't you just make me a cup of tea and listen to me? I would have done if I'd been her. I just wanted her to listen to me. I might have ranted for twenty minutes but I'd have felt better for it. That's human nature. But then she would have had to put herself out.

She gave us the number to ring Cruse, for people whose loved ones had died. We went out to the car, where Kate rang the Cruse number, put the call on speaker and explained all over again.

'We'll take her number and we'll ring her back next week,' said the Cruse lady.

'Phhhh,' I breathed out between my lips, feeling completely deflated.

'In the meantime, you could try Mind,' she suggested. 'They're very good for mental health.' All they were doing was passing me along, like a parcel nobody wants.

So Kate rang Mind and they said: 'Well, if you want to come into the office, we'll see if anyone can come and have a chat.'

So that's where I ended up but they were all going home at the end of the day, so that was no use either.

Cruse did ring me a few days later so I made an appointment and went to see them the following week. A middle-aged bloke met me and showed me into a sort of sitting room where he sat and told me all about his friend who had died and how he felt about it. I wanted to say: losing your friend is nothing compared to this. But I didn't. I just got up and walked out.

It was late afternoon and the two of us sat in Kate's car, completely despairing.

'I just don't know what to do,' Kate said, in anguish. 'No one is interested and I don't know how to get you the help you need.'

She drove me back home and we agreed that I would make an appointment to go and see my GP. So, first thing the next morning I rang and explained how awful I felt and how desperately I needed to speak to someone.

'We have a new relief doctor here today. His name is Dr Chadda and he's very nice. Shall I book you in with him?'

'Yes please.'

So along I went to see him later that morning, with some trepidation. I needn't have worried. Within two minutes I could tell he was the most wonderful man you could ever meet. He just sat there and listened to me rant for twenty minutes. That was our first meeting and I already felt a lot better. At the end of that first session, I told him I couldn't sleep at all – not properly.

'I spend most of my days in a daze,' I explained. 'But I'm always tired and can't really sleep at all. I long for a good, deep sleep, without being woken by nightmares or shaking with the fear that Anthony will be forgotten, his death forever unexplained and justice never achieved.'

'I'll prescribe you one week's sleeping tablets,' he said. 'I don't want to put you on antidepressants yet but ring up in a couple of days to book your next appointment. In the meantime, I'll tell the receptionist to make it the last appointment, so that it doesn't matter how long you're here.'

He was an absolute godsend. A lovely man, genuinely kind and compassionate.

I went back a week later.

'Did the sleeping tablets make any difference?' he asked.

'Not in the slightest!'

'Hmm. I've never in my whole career given any patient two weeks' sleeping tablets, so you'll be the first! I'll give you one more week . . . and that is all as I don't want you to become addicted.'

'How can I get addicted?' I asked. 'They don't even work!' We both laughed. In fact, the second week's sleeping tablets still didn't touch me at all.

He was a real gentleman – more like a friend really. He'd just sit there and listen intently to me while I ranted on about all my torments – all the problems we'd had with the police, trying to get them to do something, even to recognise that they should at least try to explain an unexplained death on their patch. No matter how long I talked, I could see by his gestures and his facial expression that he never stopped listening, concentrating on every word. He looked like he was thinking about everything I told him.

'That is shocking!' he would say.

It was an enormous relief for me to let it all out and know my concerns were being heard. He was from London so, at the end of that long second session, he told me all about it and what it was like to live there.

'Somebody is murdered in our area every week,' he said, shaking his head. 'Every time a family suffers the loss of a beloved son or sibling. But Anthony's case is exceptional in the fact that the police are not even supporting you properly or investigating his death.'

I went to see Dr Chadda every week, always at the end of the day and sometimes for as much as an hour and a half. I used to look forward to it so much. He was great, a lovely man – kind, sympathetic and the best listener ever. He always welcomed me and never rushed me.

After the first couple of weeks, he prescribed me some antidepressants. I didn't like the first batch, so he changed them to a much better type and I stayed on those for a long time. They didn't numb my brain completely but they really helped. He also gave me a chant, a mantra he called it, to help me steer my negative thoughts into positive feelings. I could use that whenever I wanted and it did help a bit.

After six weeks, I decided to go back to work. It was the beginning of August. I could have had longer if I'd wanted but at home I just sat there with my grief and my thoughts every day. That's not healthy for anyone, so I decided to try returning part-time.

The day I went back was good. My boss gave me a hug and everyone was very welcoming. All my colleagues knew, so there was no awkwardness from those who came across to greet me and talk with me, which was great and very comforting. They were just pleased to see me back and that did cheer me up a lot.

There was only one person who didn't come over and talk to me. In fact, she deliberately steered clear of me. It really upset me at first. Her daughter had been killed ten or so years before and I was there for her from day one. I sat with her sobbing on the day of her daughter's funeral, took time to listen to her, sat and kept her company when she was down – a good shoulder to cry on. But now that it was the other way round, she was keeping her distance and turning her back on me.

It's only now that I realise why. The son of one of my friends recently hanged himself and it's a very strange thing but I just couldn't go and comfort her as I would have done before Anthony died. I dreaded having to experience her grief. I did send her supportive messages but I just couldn't bring myself to talk to her about it. . . . It would have hit me like a ton of bricks.

So when this former friend at work blocked me, I was angry with her, very angry. But now, looking back, I understand that it was just her personal coping mechanism, her way of holding back the flood.

Although I was officially back at work, the bosses said I could take days off whenever I wanted. They were fantastic. Some days I'd go in and do a couple of hours and, if I felt that was enough, I could go home. It was good that I'd always talked about Anthony so much, because most of my colleagues felt almost as if they knew him. I'm sure that helped them understand me and the things I was going through. But at home I still had my bad days, full of vacant hours, sitting and staring.

A few weeks later, the time came, as I knew it would, for Dr Chadda to move on at the end of his contract. In my last session with him, he reassured me that I wouldn't be abandoned.

'This is my last week,' he said. 'I have to go back to London next week. But I've spoken to another one of the doctors and I've told him all about your awful situation and how we've been doing this talking therapy each week. He will be happy to continue with you and the receptionist knows that if you need or want to continue coming, she will always book you in with that particular doctor so you won't have to explain every week. I don't want you to have to go through the whole story all over again each time. They'll know who you are and the receptionist will make an appointment for you any time you want one.'

He was true to his word and I moved smoothly on to another great doctor who was also very helpful. In fact, he set me up with counselling too. This was a great release from having to burden my poor sister Kate, or any of my family and friends. I never wanted to offend people or worry them but in counselling I could say what I liked, just as I had done with Dr Chadda.

My counsellor, Nicky, was female, which I think maybe helped in the first session I had with her, explaining every-thing that had happened, or not happened, and how I felt about it all.

'Anything you say will stay within these four walls,' she assured me and I knew I could trust her. She was also a great listener. Every now and then she would say 'really?' or 'how awful', or whatever seemed appropriate, so I knew she was taking it all in. I continued with Nicky for a long, long time after that. At every traumatic stage, she was my confidant and I greatly valued her empathy and understanding. Professional as those responses may have been, they were real and genuine too.

I still struggled, day to day, lurching from one to the next, but having sympathetic people to talk to and good friends at work, as well as continuing on the antidepressants, all helped me get some balance back into my life. But my anger with the police was as raw as ever, fuelled by the complete lack of any contact from them. I was now determined to get back on my bandwagon and make things happen . . . somehow. I wouldn't stop until I claimed justice for Anthony.

CHAPTER 7

Shouting Out Loudest

August 2014, 2 months after Anthony's death

One evening, the shrill ringtone of my phone broke through the numbness in my head. I assumed it was Sami as it was at about the time he usually called me. But no, it was Tom, and I could tell from his voice that something was very wrong.

'This is the last straw!' he said, his normally calm tones rising to an exasperated shrillness. 'I've had a string of awful text messages.'

'Who from?'

'From Anthony's phone!'

'Today?' I was struggling to sharpen my brain.

'Yes, the latest one came today but I've been having them for two or three weeks now.'

'You could have called me earlier.'

'I didn't want to worry you with them at first because Kate told me you were struggling with the overload of grief and everything.'

'Yes, but I'm back at work now and my frazzled brain is gradually beginning to work again,' I explained.

'Nobody else can understand what it's like, can they?'

'No, our lives will never be the same, but for now it's just day to day.'

Tom cleared his throat. 'The texts . . .'

'Yes, what did these awful texts say?' I asked.

'The first one was: "I'm Ed. Anthony loved me, not you." And there were lots more like that but much worse.'

'That's sick!' I was horrified.

'The next one was: "Anthony couldn't stand you." Then there was: "You were just a money-machine to him." After that they got outright abusive.'

'Did you answer any of them?'

'Yes. I tried to ignore the first one but after the second I texted back: "Who are you?" He answered: "I'm Ed. Anthony's boyfriend." That was all. I have to admit, it was quite upsetting.'

'I'd have been distraught . . . and then fuming.' I paused. 'I suppose the freak with Anthony's phone was trolling you because Anthony had you in his contacts as "Dad". But he put me in as Sezzer because that's what he always calls . . . called me.' A knot developed in my throat. 'So whoever has Anthony's phone, and that must be the murderer, wouldn't have known I was his mam, let alone which sex I am.'

'Or, if he had me down as "Tom",' the texter might have assumed I was an old boyfriend.' He paused. 'So you haven't had any text messages from Anthony's phone at all?'

'No. Ellie had a very short text, right at the beginning, but she reported that to the Barking and Dagenham police.'

'Was that when they said they couldn't put a tracker on the number because it was too expensive?'

'Yes, exactly. Nobody would believe it if it was in a film, would they? But it's real life, in Barking.'

'No, not unless it's a film about incompetent detectives like ours.'

'Did you tell the FLO?' I asked him.

'Yes, I called and told him: "I keep getting these bloody text messages from Anthony's phone," and I read the first two texts to him.'

'And what did he say?' I asked.

'Nothing much,' said Tom. 'Just that he'd pass it on.'

'And nobody's rung you since?'

'Not a soul.'

'So much for that bloody FLO's agreement to phone me every week. I'm still waiting! But not any more. Send me all the texts. I don't have to read them, I'll just forward them on to Slaymaker, then call him and see what he's done about it.'

That's what I did.

'So what do you want me to do about it?' asked Slaymaker.

'Track down the phone of course!'

He gave a long sigh. 'Just send a message back, asking who it is.'

'Tom's already done that. The answer was that he was Ed, Anthony's boyfriend.'

'Well, there you are then,' said Slaymaker.

'No! That's what he wants us to think. Can't you see that?'

'Don't make it more complicated than it is,' he replied.

'Look, John,' I used his first name to see if I could get him to take more of an interest, or at least show some sympathy. 'The only person who will have that phone is Anthony's killer. This is your big chance to trace the phone and track down the murderer.'

'And can you not see that anybody could have this phone by now?'

'No!' I said, but in fact, I had actually thought of that. 'Look, it doesn't make sense. If it was anybody else, why would they be sending these nasty, sick messages to Anthony's father of all people? Only a psycho would do something like this. And a psycho would be the number one profile for a murder.'

I could almost hear our FLO thinking: there she goes again, into her imaginative flights of fancy!

'John, whatever you think of me, I don't care. I'm a mother whose beloved son has been killed. Don't you have any compassion for me at all? Can't you try and put yourself in my shoes? Wouldn't you want to bring this killer to justice and stop him from killing any other mother's son?'

'I know you're grieving the loss of your son,' he said. 'But I can't make up evidence for an investigation that isn't happening because this death was not suspicious and your son was not murdered.'

'Paul Cunningham, the chief inspector of Humberside police, sent two very professional detectives to see me not long ago,' I countered. 'And they inferred that it wasn't correct to say Anthony's death was not suspicious. They used another, more open term: "unexplained death".'

'Well, that's the same thing.'

'No, it isn't. Unexplained means that it could have been a murder,' I insisted.

'Look, Sarah, let's try and get on. I'm still your family liaison officer, so how about you take it from me, having talked to my superiors here at Barking and Dagenham, that Anthony's death does not need any investigation as it was clear he had died from a drugs overdose.'

'Oh? Have you had the post-mortem tests back then? What did they show?'

'No, we haven't. If we had, I would have called you. The second autopsy was looking for just the illegal drugs: cocaine and heroin.'

'And?'

'And, OK, I grant you, Anthony did not have those drugs in his blood.'

'There you are then,' I said, triumphantly. 'So what are these extra tests for?'

'They're to find out whether there are any other substances he may have taken that are much harder to identify, so that's why they take longer. We hope to have the lab results sometime in early September.'

'Well, whatever you say, John, I can assure you that Anthony would not voluntarily have taken any substance at all. He was vehemently against all such drugs. And whoever has Anthony's phone and is sending these sick messages must have taken it from him while he was unconscious, or taken it off his dead body. Stephen Port did finally admit when you were questioning him the third time that he was the last person to see Anthony alive, or words to that effect.'

'I'll call you when I am given any further news to pass on to you,' he said and terminated the call.

I didn't think about it at the time but when I went over those words again in my head, later that evening, it almost sounded as if he wasn't allowed to tell us things unless they were specifically passed for transmission to us. Could that be right?

A few days later, Paul Slaymaker called me again. 'This is just to let you know that I talked about it with DS O'Donnell and we decided to call his bluff. I rang Anthony's number and left a message saying "This is the police." After that, we believe the phone was switched off and there have been no further messages.'

'Thank you. But does that mean you are still not going to try to trace where the phone is?'

'That's right. But you could report it to your local police if you want to.' He paused. 'Is there anything else?'

'Yes. Is there any news of when we can have Anthony's body? It makes things so much worse, not being able to have a funeral yet. It's like being in limbo. Can you give us a date, or find out when?'

'I understand that,' he said, with a degree of sympathy for a change. 'But I'm afraid we still can't give you a date. It will only happen after we receive the toxicology results. It really should be soon now but it's not down to us.'

'OK. Thanks. But what about his possessions? Surely you could send them back soon as well?'

'I don't know. I'll have to find out. His possessions are in safe storage and we have his laptop here at the station.'

'Have you gone through that yet for clues?'

'No, that's not deemed to be necessary,' he explained. 'And anyway, as you know, there is nothing to investigate.

We already have Port on a charge for perverting the course of justice and we have sufficient evidence for that.'

'But he was the last person to see our son alive!'

'Yes, so it seems. But that's just a fact. It doesn't add up to murder.'

'Talk about going round in circles!'

'Sorry Sarah, but we just don't have the personnel to go through Anthony's laptop. It's—'

'Let me guess,' I interrupted him. 'Too expensive?'

'Er, yes.'

That was the last I heard from him for a while.

This constant urging the police to act and them not hearing or wanting to hear my pleas, reminded me of my childhood. When I was growing up, I had two brothers and a sister and whoever shouted loudest got seen to. My sister was the oldest, I was the second child and my brothers were the loudest, so I always felt as if I was in the background, always shouting but seemingly not loudly enough for anybody to hear me.

'Listen, listen to this, listen to me: can I have a biscuit? Can I have a choc-ice? I asked first!' But nobody would listen to me. They were all shouting louder than me. I was shouting and shouting but nobody heard. Even I couldn't hear myself against the din the others were making. That's how it was from my earliest memory. So, right from a child, I had to shout out loud to have anything or do anything and my ambition was to have somebody hear me at last.

I told our Kate about this recently and she laughed.

'It was really frustrating,' I told her. 'Because even my younger brothers could shout louder than me, so you or they were seen to and I was always the last . . . if anything was left over.'

Because I grew up having to make myself heard, I haven't lost the habit. I still shout to make people hear me if I have to. Only now it's not over biscuits but for justice and what's right. In fact, if I absolutely believe in something, you would have to beat me to death to shut me up!

I'm a very honest person – honest and law-abiding. I do believe in not breaking the rules but I am quite opinionated. I can't help it. If I've got something to say, I have to say it or it eats me up. I will say it and sod the consequences. That's why I kept on keeping on at the police. If I didn't, who would? And all the time they kept hoping I'd shut up and go away. Not me – they'd got the wrong person.

Life is strange, the way coincidences happen. Just as I was thinking of having another go at the police, my phone rang and it was DC Paul Slaymaker, our FLO.

'I've just called to tell you that the toxicology results have come through.'

'At last. What do they say?'

'They confirm that there were no traces of cocaine or heroin in Anthony's blood.'

'You told me that last time we spoke and it's no surprise to me. It's exactly what we've always said.' Despite my certainty that Anthony hadn't taken any illegal drugs, it was still a massive relief that both the in-depth stages of toxicology proved it.

'Yes,' he agreed. 'But there was something else.'

I went from relief to shock. I could almost feel my blood run cold. 'What do you mean?'

'The deeper analysis showed a substance called GHB. It is almost undetectable so that's why it didn't show up in the two previous lab tests. That's also why it took so long to find out.'

'What is GHB?' I asked, puzzled. 'I've never heard of it. I know Anthony would never have taken it if it was a drug.'

'It's a colourless, tasteless liquid that comes in a small bottle, like the one that was found next to Anthony's body.'

'But that wasn't his,' I protested. I could see what he was trying to do.

'Well, the experts tell us that when we die, our bodies naturally produce a small amount of this drug.'

'Really? I didn't know that.'

'Yes, but if it is over a certain strength it must have been ingested.'

'What do you mean?' I asked, horrified. 'This result must be wrong. It must be the wrong person.'

'In Anthony's case, they found more of it than could have been produced naturally. Quite a large amount, in fact.'

'Enough to kill him?' I couldn't quite believe what he was telling me, even though I knew it must be true if the toxicology proved it. How had this happened? He couldn't have taken it himself. I was certain of that.

'Yes, too much of it can kill,' he replied. 'And that's what it looks like in this case. He must have drunk a fair bit of it.'

'No. He would never have drunk anything but water in a stranger's place. So he must have been poisoned. That proves it was murder!' I almost shouted at him.

I could hear his heavy sigh. 'As I've told you before, there was nothing suspicious about Anthony's death. This sort of thing happens all the time – young lads taking overdoses and dying on the streets.'

'Not young men like Anthony, working hard at his studies and looking forward to a successful career.'

He ignored me and carried on, 'It's a drug that can be bought and used to enhance sex, or so I'm told.'

I could almost see the smirk on his face. He knew Anthony was gay. He was clearly uncomfortable with that, just like DS O'Donnell. In my mind, they were probably all homophobic at Barking and Dagenham police.

'I know Anthony used poppers for that reason but that's because they are harmless. I am absolutely sure he would never have taken anything that could affect his health in any way, never mind the potential that it might kill him. He was a Google freak. Everything he ate or drank, everything he did, everywhere he went – he used to look it all up on Google to make sure it was clean and healthy. He would never have taken this GHB drug. So that proves he was murdered.'

He cleared his throat. 'I'm afraid not, as Anthony was not murdered. Stephen Port told us he took it on his own.' He paused.

'And you believe an excuse of a man who tells you a pack of lies?'

'Yes, the facts are consistent with his final account of the events . . . and I'll keep saying it until you've accepted it and moved on. This was not a crime. So it's no use continuing to ask questions that will never give you the answers you want.'

'Well, I won't give up until justice is done!' Then it suddenly occurred to me: 'I thought you told me the toxicology results were going to come in by 12 September and today is the twenty-first, so nine days ago?'

'Did I?'

'So when did you receive them?'

He paused. 'A few days ago.'

'What? Why didn't you call us sooner?'

'I couldn't call you sooner.'

'Does that mean you didn't understand the results . . . or that nobody thought to tell us? Or that you weren't allowed to tell us till now?'

'Just that I couldn't tell you earlier.'

'Well, whichever the answer is, I'm fuming that you didn't call and tell us. You're supposed to be our liaison officer and you hardly ever liaise at all, and when you do it's late. You did agree to call me once a week . . . but I'm still waiting!'

Silence at the other end, so I terminated the call.

Yet again, although I wanted to be kept up to date, when I was told what was happening – or rather not happening – it ended up in an argument and sent me plummeting back into depression and despair. I turned on the television and just sat there, not watching, not listening, just mulling over bits of my conversation with DC Slaymaker, which made me even more morose. But this time I didn't have long to languish . . .

CHAPTER 8

Yelling in the Dark

September 2014, 3 months after Anthony's death

A couple of weeks after Anthony died, I had signed up on the website of the *Barking and Dagenham Post* to receive newsflashes. Now, one evening, as I sat in front of the television, not watching it, running that afternoon's conversation with Slaymaker over and over through my head, I was jerked out of my semi-conscious state by the beep on my phone. I ignored it at first. It wouldn't be anything important at this time of night. But what if I was wrong? Curiosity won me over and I checked to see what it was. It came from the *Barking and Dagenham Post*, so I idly scrolled down to find, to my horror: 'Newsflash: Third body found – is it linked?'

A terrible sense of dread overwhelmed me. Could this be about Anthony? And two more bodies? I had warned the police so often that some other mother's child might be killed the same way if they didn't investigate who killed Anthony. Now the guilt hit me – that I hadn't done enough, that I should have tried harder . . .

I didn't want to read on but I knew I had to.

It was just a small piece, a potted version of the main points. First, the body of Anthony Walgate (a sharp intake of breath as the shock hit me afresh), aged 23, had been found in Barking on 19 June 2014, outside a block of flats. The body of a young Lithuanian man called Gabriel Kovari, aged 22, had been found by a dog walker in St Margaret's churchyard, just 400 yards away on 28 August 2014. (Why didn't I know about this?) Now, on 20 September, the body of Daniel Whitworth, another young man, aged 21, had been found by the same dog walker in the same churchyard. The journalist pointed out a number of similarities between these three deaths and posed the obvious question: could all three have been murdered by the same man? A police spokesperson said: 'No. All three deaths were drug-related and none of them are deemed to be suspicious.'

That night I hardly slept at all, or only fitfully if I did. I couldn't get out of my head the image of Anthony, his eyes staring into mine, pleading for help. Now two other mothers had lost their boys. Two other families were grieving.

Why hadn't I done more to make the police investigate? And how could they be so obdurate – still unwilling even to contemplate the possibility of murder?

I woke up early and rang work to say I couldn't come in that day. Now I was free to log onto my laptop and went straight to the *Barking and Dagenham Post*'s website. Following the same stark headline: 'Third body found – is it linked?' there were a few more lines of information about the latest death – Daniel's.

The article said that Daniel Whitworth's body had been found with what seemed to be a suicide note. However, it was uncertain yet whether it was Daniel's handwriting so that would be checked with his family, it said. The

note apparently apologised to his family and suggested
that Daniel had been responsible for Gabriel's death. It
had a PS that said: 'Please do not blame the guy I was
with last night. We only had sex, then I left.' But it gave
no clue as to who that 'guy' might be. Well, the cops
might not have the nous to work it out, but I was 100
per cent certain I knew. The report reiterated what the
local police spokesperson had said, that there was nothing
suspicious about any of these three deaths and they were
not related.

Not only was I furious that all this had been allowed to
happen, I was also outraged that my family liaison officer,
who was supposed to keep me informed, had not even
mentioned either of the boys' bodies being found when I
had spoken to him at length the day before. One had died
yesterday, so he should have been able to tell me, and it
was three whole weeks since Gabriel's body was found, so
why the delay? Did they think I wouldn't find out?

At 9 a.m. on the dot, I rang DC Slaymaker. 'I'm in
shock. What the hell is going on?'

'How do you mean?'

'You called me yesterday afternoon about Anthony's toxicology results and we had a long conversation. Did it not at
any time occur to you to tell me there had been two more
gay young men's deaths, very close to where Anthony was
found and with various similarities?'

He was silent for a few seconds. 'I didn't tell you because
they are not related to Anthony's death. There are some
coincidences but nothing much and coincidences don't
make a crime.'

'But you should have told me, instead of leaving me to find out through the newspapers. What is going on?' I repeated.

'Absolutely nothing. One was a homeless guy and the other was somebody from out of the area.'

'But they were all three found so close together and all in the same position – propped up against walls. They were all a similar age, they were all gay and *you* think they all took drugs. The newspapers seem to think they are linked, so surely now you have to investigate all three of them?'

He gave a long, loud sigh. 'No, there is ab-so-lute-ly *no* connection between them.'

'Well, that's really helpful.' I couldn't resist mocking him. 'So the newspapers know more than you do?'

'No, of course not. But we don't go around putting non-news all over the media or the internet. And I didn't tell you because those other two druggies' deaths were just isolated incidents that had nothing to do with Anthony.'

'But what about the suicide note?'

'What about it? These druggies often know each other and this one, Whitworth, wrote in the note that he'd killed Kovari and was killing himself – QED. I tell you, it's nothing unusual. Nothing to investigate.'

'For God's sake, can't you see beyond the end of your nose?' I was fuming. As I wrote in my diary notes later, '*The frustration drove me crazy.*' There was obviously no point in continuing this conversation, so I changed the subject. 'Now that we've had the toxicology results, I assume that you can release Anthony's body to us so that we can have a funeral at last?'

'Yes, as soon as we get the final go-ahead. I'll let you know about that. It shouldn't be long now.'

I rang Kate and she came round so that we could look together at all the info we could find online about the dead boys. We looked at the map of Barking and where the boys had been found.

'Anthony here,' pointed Kate. Then she dragged her finger over the screen and down the road to the churchyard. 'Look how close they were.'

'Just a stone's throw,' I agreed.

As they had been when Anthony's body was found, but even more so this time, the people of Barking were up in arms about the lack of action from their local police. A lot of parents were worried about the safety of their sons, while other contributors to the conversation online were from the LGBT community, scared sick about how to protect themselves from the dangerous maniac who was obviously threatening them all.

That evening, I rang Tom and told him what I'd read about the two other lads' deaths and asked whether Slaymaker had said anything about them to him.

'That's awful,' he said. 'What is the matter with Barking police? No, they haven't rung me for ages.'

'Did they not tell you about the toxicology results?'

'No, I haven't heard anything about that either. I think somebody rang me yesterday evening. I had a missed call but there was no number showing. It might have been the police.'

I told him what DC Slaymaker had told me, with the explanations about GHB.

'I've heard of that,' he said. 'I thought it was a dodgy party drug but I'm sure Anthony would never have taken that. He would have checked it out and seen it was dangerous so wouldn't have touched it.'

'You and I know that, Anthony's friends know that and it's what I told the police too . . . but I don't think Slaymaker believes me. I don't think he wants to believe me. If he would only show that he was listening and taking in what we say, that would be something.'

'Well done for trying but it must upset you more each time.'

'Yes, it does but it also makes me feel better to be doing something. You know me – I can't just sit there and accept what they say . . . If I did that, we'd never get Anthony's body back.'

'That's true.'

'I just have to keep on going. I have to try to stop any more deaths . . . and get justice done for our Anthony, somehow.'

The next morning, I decided to ring our MP, Karl Turner, to see whether he knew anything . . . and to have a moan. It was all I could do. He was a very good listener and always helpful if he could be.

'Hi Sarah. I'm in Westminster today,' he said, 'so I can't ask you round but I've seen the latest about two boys' bodies being found in Barking. Did the police tell you about them?'

'Did they heck! Not a word. I actually spoke to DC Slaymaker, our family liasion officer, after they were found but before I knew about them and he didn't even mention them. When I found out a few hours later, I had to ring back and fire questions at him but it was infuriating. He just wouldn't accept that Anthony's and these other two young men's deaths could be linked. The Barking police just see them as druggies. To Slaymaker, they look like druggies, so they are druggies. And he refuses to even consider the possibility that they might have been killed.' I paused for breath.

'Yes, it's shocking.'

'If these bodies had been girls,' I continued, 'I'm sure the police would have done everything they could, but not for our boys, just because whoever killed them put bottles of drugs next to them, so they must all be 'druggies'.'

'Yes, you're right. I wish I was there so you could come round and I'd give you a hug,' said Karl. 'It's awful, isn't it?'

'Yes,' I agreed. 'The police are being so bloody pig-headed about this. They just won't listen to any of us. China and Kiera, Anthony's closest friends, have tried their best too but none of us can persuade the police to *do* anything. I'm so angry. The frustration is driving me crazy. I feel like I'm constantly banging my head against a brick wall.' I paused. 'But the worst thing of all is these may not be the last bodies to be found. Ever since Anthony died, I've been desperate to prevent any other deaths like his.'

'Murders, you mean?'

'Yes, definitely murders. If we can see it so clearly, why can't the police? I have told them again and again, and pleaded with them, that if they don't act, there will be more innocent young lads dying. These new deaths are my worst nightmare come true. I did everything I could . . . but now I feel so guilty.'

'It's not your fault at all, Sarah,' Karl reassured me. 'You couldn't have done more. It's the Barking police who should be feeling guilty. Not you.'

'Thanks. I'd like to say that helps . . . but it doesn't.'

'No, I understand.'

The thing was, I knew he did understand. Yet even he and his friend Paul Cunningham, the chief inspector of Humberside police, had been unable to exert any influence on the Barking branch of the Metropolitan police up to now.

He asked about the toxicology report, so I explained about the GHB and I also said how upset I was that we still couldn't have the funeral yet but hopefully Anthony's body would be released to us soon. 'But I'm not holding my breath!'

'Well, that's something I may be able to help you with. I'll see what I can do.'

That night, though mentally exhausted, I couldn't sleep. I kept turning over in my mind all the things the police had failed to do and I was desperately sad for the families of those two young men. I, more than anybody, knew how they felt.

I really was yelling in the dark. Would this nightmare ever end?

CHAPTER 9

Anthony's Funeral

October–December 2014, 4–6 months after Anthony died

Following my conversation with Karl Turner, we at last achieved a major goal. It was only our right, of course, but we'd had to fight for so long to reach this point. It was mid-October, four months after Anthony's death, when we finally heard from our FLO that the coroner had released his body and it could now be sent back to us. Finally!

'Will you be sending him in a hearse?' I asked.

'No,' was Slaymaker's quick reply. 'You'll have to arrange and pay for all that yourself. His body can be collected from the morgue at any time from tomorrow morning. Just let me know exactly when so I can pass it on.'

'Oh, right,' I said in surprise. But I couldn't disguise my relief and pleasure that Anthony's body had been released to us at last. I naively thought Slaymaker might catch some of my relief . . . but no. His voice remained at a monotone. 'You'll need to find an undertaker and instruct your driver to take the body there.'

Perhaps he thought he was being helpful but I'd already thought of that. 'Yes, I've spoken to an undertaker who has

been recommended to me. I'll let him know straight away.'
Then I suddenly had a thought. 'Will you send Anthony's
death certificate by post?'

Silence. 'Oh. Don't you have it?'

'No. We've never had it,' I said in surprise.

'Maybe your undertaker has it.'

'We haven't got an undertaker yet. As I said, we have one
lined up and I've had a brief phone conversation with him
but haven't met him yet, so you wouldn't have known where
to send the death certificate. Anyway, we don't just need
it for the funeral. I want to close Anthony's bank account,
but they say we can't do that without his death certificate.'

'Oh.'

'Can you get it sent to us as soon as possible, please.'

'I'll try.'

It was such a liberating feeling to know that at last we
could give Anthony the send-off he deserved. I couldn't
stop smiling as I rang Tom to tell him.

'Phew!' he said. 'That's a milestone achieved, after four
months of pushing for it. Well done.'

'Thanks, but I think it must have been Karl Turner's
intervention that swung it for us,' I explained.

'Well, let me know how much the bill comes to for the
hearse and I'll transfer it into your account.' He paused,
assuming I would do all the arrangements, as I always did.

'Did you realise that we hadn't had his death certificate
yet?' I asked.

'No. It never occurred to me.'

'I asked our FLO when he rang just now to tell us the
news. And he went silent. Do you know what?'

'What?'

'I reckon there isn't one. I wouldn't put it past them. I'll have to chase that up now, on top of everything else.'

'Hopefully they'll get it done soon,' he said. 'Won't it be wonderful to have a funeral for Anthony at last?' I could almost hear him smile.

I spent the rest of the day ringing round the family and friends, including of course Anthony's uni friends to find great relief all round. At last we could commemorate his life and say a proper goodbye. When I facetimed China, I asked her what Anthony's favourite song was.

'Oh, that's easy,' she smiled. 'Every time we went to karaoke, he chose "There Must Be An Angel" by Eurythmics. He absolutely loved that.'

I had called the undertaker to tell him he could now collect Anthony's body, which he did. Then the following evening he came to meet us at Tom's house to see what sort of funeral and coffin we wanted and agree on a date.

There was no tension between Tom and I as we waited for the undertaker to arrive because we were both working towards the same goal – doing our best for our lost son.

'You organise it the way you want to do it,' said Tom. 'And I'll pay for it.' He was always very good about that and I was keen to do it. In fact, I knew it would help me to be doing something special for Anthony.

The undertaker arrived, sat down and got out his paperwork. 'You said you'd like a cremation, Mrs Sak. Is that right?'

'Yes. Anthony wasn't religious at all so we want his funeral to be at the crematorium. My sister Kate has given me the name of a humanist celebrant who she thought was very good at a funeral she attended so I will contact him tomorrow morning.'

'Good,' he ticked something on his sheet. 'Just a standard coffin I expect, and do you have a date in mind?'

'Yes . . .' Suddenly a moment of madness came over me and I started to laugh quite hysterically. Both Tom and the undertaker gave me strange looks, which made me laugh all the more!

'What's so funny?' asked Tom.

'Can you imagine what Anthony would say if he could see us now and hear what we just said?'

Tom smiled, bemused. 'What do you mean?'

'He would be standing there, waving his arms about and calling us "the cheapest bastards under the sun! What are you thinking of, agreeing to a standard coffin? I want diamonds and gold. Don't you know who I am?" He always had fame and fortune in his sights,' I explained to the undertaker.

Tom grinned. 'Yes, you're right!'

We carried on talking through the arrangements. No organist but we'd need the sound system for recorded music. No idea yet how many people would come so better have the bigger chapel – Anthony would kill us if we didn't! We set the date and then I dropped the bombshell . . .

'There is just one problem,' I said to the undertaker. 'We don't have a death certificate because the police have never sent us one. I have requested it, but can't be sure when it will come.'

'No need to worry,' he reassured us. 'It is an unusual situation but there is a way round it. If you are both willing to sign a disclaimer, I will sign it too. It's just a formality to say that the lack of a death certificate is beyond your control and, as soon as you do receive it, you will send a copy of it to us. Will that be all right with you?'

'Oh yes. That will be great,' I agreed. 'Thank you.'

'Yes, thanks for being so understanding,' added Tom.

The next morning, as planned, I phoned the humanist celebrant and fortunately he would be available on the date we had booked.

'I'd like to come and meet you both this afternoon. Would that be possible?'

'My ex-husband will be at work, but I've taken this week off, so yes, that would be fine. Tom said he'd rather just pay for it and leave the rest to me.'

So the celebrant arrived at my house that afternoon, wanting to learn about Anthony and find out what I'd want him to say. He was a lovely guy, mid-thirties, and dead camp. Anthony would have loved that. I answered his questions and told him some of the funny stories about Anthony as a child and growing up. We had a laugh.

'Have you chosen any music?' he asked.

'Yes. Everything was always all about him,' I explained. 'When he was at university in London, I used to speak to him at least four times a week. The conversation always started the same: "Hi Sezzer." "Hi Ant. I need to tell you—" "No Sezzer, you're boring me already. Let's have a talk about me." So we always did, for about an hour – sometimes two. Anthony's life was always about him. He was a typical young lad, thinking the world revolved around him! He always made me laugh. He had such a dry wit.' I paused for a moment, lost in thoughts of happy days.

The celebrant cleared his throat.

'Yes,' I continued, 'this funeral will be all about him, so I'd like the song "All About You" by McFly at the beginning, as his coffin is brought in.'

He wrote it down.

'One of his best friends told me that whenever Anthony went to karaoke, he loved "There Must Be An Angel" by Eurythmics, so I'd like to have that next.' I paused for him to write. 'And for the third one I've chosen "Who Knew?" by Pink.'

'Do you have one for the end as well, when you are walking out?'

'Yes. Anthony used to have a secret crush on Dolly Parton. "Nine To Five" was probably his favourite but I've chosen one of her other songs that he liked: "I Will Always Love You".

'I expect that's more than enough music, is it? Because there's one other song that Anthony loved when he was a baby and a toddler. Whenever I put him down in his cot, I used to sing him to sleep with "You Are My Sunshine". He loved that. As soon as he could talk, he used to say "Sing sunshine song, sing sunshine song!" So I did, and it always worked.'

'You're right that we haven't time to play any more tracks but I could mention that story in my eulogy if you like.'

'Yes, that would be great.'

Once we had all that sorted out, he put on his voice recorder and asked me to give him some more information

about Anthony and any stories I'd like him to tell to all his
friends and family.

First I told him a potted history of Anthony's life and
achievements, including the fun he used to have with his
brother and cousins and his wonderful university friends. I
told him that Anthony always wanted to be rich and famous
and that he had been making good progress in that direction with his fashion shows at uni.

'And would you like me to include an anecdote or two?'

'Oh yes. The only trouble is what to choose, there are
so many!' I thought for a moment. 'I could tell you one
from when he was very young, which would include his
dad, and then maybe something from when he was older?'

He nodded so I carried on. 'When Anthony was about
three, I was at night school at college and his dad was
looking after him. About halfway through my class, a secretary came in and asked me to come to the phone for an
urgent message. My heart sank. "What's the matter?" I
asked Tom. "You need to come home now," he said. I
told him I couldn't but he said it was urgent.

'Apparently, Anthony's tooth had fallen out and you know
how tiny baby teeth are? Well, he said to his father that his
tooth had come out and Tom was cooking at the time, so
he told Anthony to go and put it on the mantelpiece for
the tooth fairy and explained: "The tooth fairy will come
tonight when you go to bed and leave you some money
in exchange for your tooth."

'So Tom finished cooking their tea then went into the
living room. He asked Anthony where he had put his
tooth. "It's in my ear." "What?" asked Tom. "I've put it

in my ear." So Tom asked him why he had put it in his ear. "'Cos I wanted to." Tom immediately picked him up and tilted him to that side, trying to get the tooth to fall out, but it didn't. So then he put a pinch of pepper up Anthony's nose to get him to sneeze and hopefully dislodge it, but that didn't work either.'

I paused for a moment. 'I hope your recorder is picking all this up?'

He looked at it and nodded. 'Do carry on. I want to know what happened!' he smiled.

'So, in the end, I went home and we had to take him to the local hospital. They tried a few things of their own but they couldn't make it budge either. One of the nurses told me that his little tooth was literally resting on his eardrum, so we'd have to bring him back to the hospital the following morning to have day surgery – the only way to remove it. So that's what we did. He had a general anaesthetic and we went into the waiting room while he went into the operating theatre. Finally, a nurse came to take us to see Anthony, awake again in a ward. He was sitting there with his blond hair and big, blue eyes, in his pyjamas on his big hospital bed! Just then, the surgeon came to see him and brought with him a plastic container with some liquid in it and a tiny tooth on the bottom. The surgeon was beaming as he said, "Twenty years I've been doing this. I've taken some things out of some holes, but I've never taken a tooth out of an ear!"

'Anthony just sat there with a grin all over his face, loving being the centre of attention. "I'll take it home and put it under my pillow for the tooth-fairy tonight."

'So I said, "OK, but why did you put your tooth in your ear?" And his little, innocent voice said, again, "'Cos I wanted to." Maybe he thought it would be safe in his ear . . . well, he was right, wasn't he?'

The celebrant laughed. 'Yes, I suppose he was!'

This wasn't an unusual story with Anthony. It wasn't that he was particularly naughty; he just always seemed to be doing the wrong things – experiments and adventures, I suppose.

'And you said you'd like to include an older one as well?' he asked. 'I'm not sure we'd have time for it, because we've got all the music to fit in as well, but we could give it a try.'

'OK. Well, Anthony always seemed to find a way of embarrassing us, without even meaning to. When he was about twelve, we took him on a tour of Italy, then on the way back we stayed in a lovely hotel in Belgium. There had been a mix-up in our booking and they had to find him another room, which they did. I went to check he was OK at bedtime and he was lying in bed, watching TV and drinking a Coke. For some reason, I didn't even wonder where the Coke came from. Early the next morning, I offered to carry his case to the car, but he wouldn't let me.' I stopped for a sip of water, then carried on.

'We had a good trip back to Hull and again he insisted on carrying his case into the house himself, then lugged it upstairs to his room to unpack on his own, which I thought was very strange. I unpacked our stuff, sorted the dirty washing and went back up to get his. I didn't know whether to laugh or to cry when I saw his windowsill . . . crammed full with miniature bottles of spirits! Because he'd not had a children's room, there was a mini-bar fridge in his hotel room and he genuinely thought that everything in this fridge was paid for, so it was his. He'd emptied the mini-bar, and everything from the bathroom as well, and crammed it all into his suitcase. Of course, I confiscated everything and waited in dread for a huge bill to arrive . . . Luckily it never did!'

Finally I told the celebrant about Anthony's passion for fashion . . . and fame. 'It started when he was fourteen and became a real focus for him, designing clothes and looking at materials. He tried sewing something by hand, so Tom bought him a second-hand sewing machine. To start with, he used to mess about with it, trying things out. But soon he started teaching himself to sew things properly. He often went straight upstairs after school to carry on with whatever the current garment was. Even then, he'd often say, "One day I'll be famous!" and I'd say, "Yeah, yeah." And as he grew older, with a part-time job stacking supermarket shelves at weekends, he set his sights on college and something big. "I'll be famous one day," he'd say. "Could you lend me fifty?" Of course, his fabrics weren't cheap – he'd always buy the best. "Go on," he'd plead. "Just till payday?" And I'd say, "For God's sake, you've just had thirty quid the other day!" He smiled his winning smile. "You wait till I'm famous. I will be. Mark my words, Sezzer!" "When you're rich and famous," I'd say, "will you pay me back then?" I knew he'd never pay me back but he was so talented and hard-working that I usually gave in.'

'Would you like to have flowers arranged for you at the crematorium?'

'No thanks. Anthony used to have really severe hay fever so I've decided not to have any flowers at all at his funeral. Instead of flowers, we are going to put his beloved first sewing machine on the top of his coffin, with his picture, bless him. I think he would have approved of that.'

The funeral was going to be on 4 November 2014. As the London people had quite a long way to come, we invited them to come to my house for a meal the night before. We expected five of his university friends to come . . . but twenty-one turned up, including some of his tutors. Luckily my husband Sami is a talented chef and he always cooks enough for an army, so we had enough food. Everyone piled in – twenty-one people in my small kitchen. It was quite a crush, spreading into the lounge. The real problem was finding enough cups and plates for them all. We even shared soup out of a large gravy dish, but we managed to make do, somehow. We sat or stood for hours, talking about Anthony, looking at his old photos and generally getting to know each other.

I had asked everyone to wear bright colours to the funeral. As we arrived in the cortege, I was astonished to see scores, maybe hundreds of people crowding into the chapel. There were more tutors and university friends to add to all those who had come to our house the night before, plus all his old school and art college friends and our extended families. The undertaker's men carried the glamorous coffin into the chapel and placed it down. I walked in behind them, followed by the undertaker himself, carefully carrying Anthony's first sewing machine, as if it was the crown jewels. Everyone gasped when they saw him put it down on top of the coffin, alongside a portrait photo of Anthony.

We all listened to the songs I'd chosen and the wonderful eulogy presented by the celebrant, which really captured Anthony's vibrant personality, alongside the tales of his childhood. As well as all his friends old and new, university tutors and his family, a whole group of Sami's Muslim friends had come up from Essex to attend Anthony's funeral.

It was all very moving. The only reason that I wasn't in floods of tears from the very start was that I was on medication, which dulled my senses on the day. In a way, it was just as well. Everybody who came up to me afterwards said they'd loved the whole occasion as it was so appropriate and true to his memory.

Instead of sending flowers, I had asked people to make donations to St Andrew's Children's Hospice in Grimsby, who were doing a 'buy a brick' fundraising campaign and Anthony's name was written on a brick in their new extension. It's still there today for anyone to see.

We held the wake straight after the funeral, in Tom's friend's pub.

'I'll do you an amazing buffet,' he'd said when we were planning it.

'We'll have to have guacamole,' I said to Tom.

'Why?'

'Because on Christmas Day, when I did a family tea and Sami had made lots of tasty homemade finger-foods with dips, Anthony got hold of the guacamole and all night he kept going up to his cousin Lottie. "You need to try guac

– it's my favourite thing!" He thought guacamole was very sophisticated.'

'Right,' said Tom. 'I think he told me about that.'

'I reckon we can manage that,' said his friend, the pub landlord.

'Anthony used to love these dips and I used to buy him special hams and cheeses. He tried to be sophisticated.' I laughed. 'And he wasn't! He was very much the country boy going to the city. In an effort to save money, he used to go to the Sainsbury's across the road at seven in the evening, when they reduced their prices on ready meals going out of date, and he'd buy a pheasant or a venison steak for 50p and eat it that evening. He thought he was very grand. He did make me laugh when he told me.'

The wake went very well. In addition to the friends I knew and some I didn't, I met and talked to Anthony's head of year and various fashion tutors, who all turned up in beautifully designed, brightly coloured clothes. Unfortunately, they had to leave early to return to London, but it was fascinating to meet them, especially as Anthony used to describe them to me and now I could see what he meant.

While chatting with Anthony's university friends, they mentioned that all he talked about was how cheap Hull was and that he used to go to 'Pounded for a Pound' at one of the Hull nightclubs. So, after the wake, my nieces and their friends took all his friends to see it for themselves. I don't think they believed that you could get into a nightclub free and the drinks would be only £1 all night. Judging by the video messages and photos they sent me, they had the time of their lives. I was really glad about that because I didn't want it to have been a miserable, sad day. I wanted a celebration of a wonderful short life . . . and that's what it was.

Over the next few days I had masses of texts, saying things like: 'It was fantastic,' and 'We had a great time,' and, especially pleasing: 'Anthony would have loved it!' For me, that was what it was all about.

Bringing Anthony's body home had been the first small hint of success in my battle to goad the police into action but, a month later, I still didn't have Anthony's death certificate. When I phoned our FLO, he couldn't, or wouldn't, tell me anything about it. So I phoned my friendly local MP, Karl Turner, and he said to leave it to him. He would phone the coroner and do his best to expedite it.

Sure enough, Anthony's death certificate was finally issued and posted to me and I had to go to the post office and sign for it, two or three days before Christmas.

'It must be important,' said the guy behind the counter. 'This cost a fortune to get it here next day, at this time of year.'

I tore it open, keen to see what they had put for the cause of Anthony's death, but I was disappointed to see just two meaningless words: 'Under analysis'. What a cop-out. Then I noticed the date the death certificate was issued was 18 December 2014, six months after his body was found. The police hadn't even bothered to order it till then.

The weeks after Anthony's funeral had been a terrible anti-climax. And now this uninformative death certificate. I felt completely in limbo. I had worked so hard to achieve the simple privilege, the human right of being given back my beloved son's lifeless body. I had put all my energy and enthusiasm, everything I had, into arranging the best possible celebration of his life, meeting and greeting all his uni friends and tutors, then watching them all go back to move on with their own lives. Finding that the long-awaited death certificate didn't even give his cause of death – that was the last straw. I had been on a high for a few short weeks . . . and now, as the tree lights lit up around the city, I plunged back into the depths of despair. It would be a sad Christmas, an empty Christmas – the first without my fun-loving son . . . and we were still no nearer finding out how and why he died.

That night after picking up Anthony's death certificate – the final proof in plain black and white that he was really dead – I felt at my very lowest. The only hope I had was that the new year might bring a new start. But it was a slim hope.

CHAPTER 10

An Empty Victory

Christmas 2014–June 2015, 6–12 months after
Anthony died

Paul texted me on the afternoon of Christmas Eve and put a kiss and love at the end of the text, which he had never done before. I knew something was wrong so I texted him back saying to come round to my house.

He arrived in floods of tears, looking terrible.

'Mum's here,' I said as I gave him a long hug. 'Stay the night. You can sleep on my sofa . . . and have whatever you like for breakfast.' I paused. 'Do you remember all those Christmas morning breakfasts with Anthony when you were children, when I said you could have anything you wanted?'

He nodded, but without a hint of a smile. Perhaps I'd said the wrong thing but I carried on anyway, trying to cheer him up.

'The first time, you both chose bacon sandwiches stuffed with pieces of Mars bars, with the chocolate melting and oozing out.' I paused. 'Those Christmas breakfasts became a tradition didn't they? You had a lot of fun together. He loved you to bits.'

I made up a bed for Paul on the sofa that night . . . and that's when he had his breakdown. Everything had been building up and building up inside him, so he lay down on my sofa on Christmas Eve – and stayed until June. All those months he stayed on that sofa. He didn't even go back to his flat for clothes or anything. He functioned, but barely. His work place was closed for two weeks over Christmas, so he hardly moved for all that time. When the workshop started up again, he got up, went to work and came back home to my sofa again, day after day, week after week. He just used to lie there and hardly ever said a word. It wasn't only me – he stopped talking to everyone.

I knew he couldn't help it but it did pull me down too. Part of it was that, as his mother, I knew I needed to help him, but I didn't know what to do. I tried to be cheerful, bright and breezy, attempting to chivvy him out of the depths of his depression, even though I rarely felt like it. I still had my own grief to contend with. I couldn't even mention Anthony to him now, although I always wanted to. Needed to. He refused to talk about him, or about anything. It was really hard on me for so long.

Paul has always been one to bury his head in the sand and hope any bad things will go away. So he just watched the telly, in a daze, or occasionally played mindless games on his phone.

Tom rang one day to ask how Paul was doing.

'Not well at all,' I said. 'It really gets me down that I can't find a way to help him.'

'Let me know if I can do anything.'

'OK. Thanks.'

'I've been wondering,' added Tom. 'Shouldn't there be an inquest for Anthony?'

'Yes, that's true. I think Slaymaker mentioned it could happen in London after the third post-mortem, which was a while ago now and nobody has said anything.'

'Should we call and put in a request for the inquest?'

'Yes, that's probably the only way we might get some answers.' I sighed. 'The trouble is, Slaymaker is almost as fed up with me as I am with him at the moment, so I doubt he'd tell me anything. Maybe you could call him this time? I think you'd be more likely to prompt some action. And can you ask him if it can be in Hull?'

On the first sunny Sunday of spring, I had the whole family round and we sat out in the garden. I coaxed Paul to come out and join us, but he sat morosely, keeping his eyes on the ground. Then somebody asked me to tell a story about Anthony. I started to remind them of the time when we all went on a skiing holiday together – Tom, Paul, Anthony and I, with their auntie, uncle and the boys' cousins – and, straight away, Paul shot back inside. He wasn't ready to reminisce yet. I would usually stop if it was just him and me but with the family there I carried on relating one of my favourite Anthony anecdotes.

'Anthony was about thirteen that year. We'd been skiing all day, then somebody had organised a sledging activity at teatime, so we asked the children if any of them wanted a go . . . and they all did. So we paid the money and all us parents stood up the side of the slope to watch.

'At the top of the slope, they had all the children lined up with their "sledges", which were plastic crates, like milk crates, for them to sit on and ropes to steer with. At the bottom was the restaurant terrace, full of tables and chairs outside, where people were having their tea. The supervisor showed all the children how to lie on their crates and explained that they would have to turn quickly and make their crates spin to stop.

'We watched the first child going down, then turning and stopping. Next it was Anthony's go, so he lay down on the crate and launched off, gathering speed down the slope, going fast – too fast as he approached the end of the run and everyone, about fifty of us, all shouted at him: "Stop! Turn, turn, TURN!" . . . and he didn't. As he reached the bottom, there was a slope straight ahead of him, up to the restaurant.

'The people on the terrace saw him coming and jumped back as his "sledge" ploughed on past them, scattering chairs as he went, then on up the slope and straight through the open double doors into the restaurant itself, only stopping when he reached the counter! We all roared with laughter once we realised nobody had been hurt. And, after the initial surprise, all the customers joined in too!

'Anthony picked up his crate and walked out with his head down and his ears red with embarrassment. But then, realising he'd been the centre of attention, which he loved, he said, "Can I go up and do it again?"'

In the garden that afternoon, we all laughed and laughed till we nearly cried at the memory of it. It felt so good to talk freely about Anthony again.

'That was such a fun holiday,' said Kate's daughter, Lottie, and we all agreed.

Talking and laughing about Anthony again was just what I needed, so I was sad when they all went home.

My battle with the police continued. I knew I couldn't let up the pressure, for Anthony's sake. There were some days when I really felt like giving up but then I kept thinking of him and of the justice he deserved. He would have done exactly the same if it had been the other way round. He was the mirror image of me. He would have stood outside 10 Downing Street with a placard if he thought it would help. So I couldn't let him down. Even though I wasn't getting anywhere, I had to keep doing my absolute best or I couldn't have lived with myself.

Each time I spoke to our FLO, he kept repeating all the usual phrases: 'Anthony has not been murdered. There is no evidence that he didn't kill himself, either intentionally or accidentally. He was just found dead . . . and that's that.'

'Well,' I used to reply, 'it's blindingly obvious to us that he didn't kill himself, so I will never shut up or stop pushing you until you investigate his death. Then you'll find the proof staring you in the face that my son was murdered, and the other two boys as well.'

At around this time, DC Slaymaker reduced his contact with me to brief emails, which was even more infuriating. I was damned sure this wasn't in the FLO training handbook of how to support a grieving family.

In January 2015, seven months after Anthony died, Stephen Port had been officially charged with perverting the course of justice and immediately bailed with no conditions. Two months later he was returned to court to plead guilty. He couldn't do otherwise really, as he had clearly given different accounts of his actions and, what the police didn't seem to realise, he must have wanted to plead guilty to this charge to avoid any deeper investigation, which would result in a much more serious charge. This way was the better of two evils for him.

In the third week of March 2015, both Tom and I had calls from DC Slaymaker. He and DS O'Donnell wanted to come up to Hull to meet with us both and to talk through Port's forthcoming court hearing. I was astonished – yet pleasantly surprised and curious to be meeting them at last after so many belligerent and desperately frustrating phone calls, interspersed with such long, hollow silences. In some ways, I didn't allow myself to expect much. But I couldn't rid my mind of a slight hope. . . that perhaps, just maybe, they were going to take some action at last over the three boys' deaths.

Two days later, I went round to Tom's house, as arranged. Waiting for them to arrive, we both felt apprehensive. It would be the first time we'd met DC Slaymaker or DS O'Donnell and I was on tenterhooks.

'Don't get your hopes up,' advised Tom, somehow knowing what I was thinking. 'It will just be a short meeting, a quick explanation and they'll be off again.'

'Yes,' I sighed, knowing he was almost certainly right. 'But what if . . . ?'

'Don't expect anything – you'll only be disappointed,' he continued. 'They haven't budged all this time. They're not going to change their tune now.'

Just then the bell rang.

They were on time, dressed in plain suits, walking into Tom's lounge as if this was just another job to get over with. Even judging by the opinions I had already formed of them, they were disappointing. They had no umph in them at all. They just sat down, with no paperwork – not one sheet of paper, and very little presence. They were there – that was all. They might as well have been insurance salesmen, except that even salesmen would have had paperwork.

After a few seconds, they started to tell us about arresting Stephen Port. It was all very matter-of-fact, which made me angry. There was no mention of Anthony, no sense of compassion or even concern for how we might feel about all this. Tom was right. They just went through the motions. I could already tell they wanted to keep the meeting short and avoid any questions. I would have expected them to respond to our feelings, especially my anguish and frustration, but no.

DS O'Donnell did most of the talking, telling us how Port had been interviewed on three separate occasions and told different stories each time.

'Well, how could you believe any of them?' I blurted out. 'He obviously lied about everything. This was the last man to see our son alive. Are you telling us that you didn't question him about that?'

'We weren't there to question him about anything other than how he had found Anthony's body and what led up to it,' explained DS O'Donnell.

'We had no reason to ask him anything else,' added DC Slaymaker, the man who was supposed to be liaising with us yet hardly ever did, let alone listen to our concerns or support us in any way at all. Even now, face to face, I was shocked at his disinterest.

'Port admitted perverting the course of justice but nothing else.' DS O'Donnell looked at us, explaining with less feeling than telling us a boring weather forecast.

'Right,' I said, getting riled up to confront them. 'We need some answers. First of all, how old is Port?'

'Oh, twenty-eight or twenty-nine,' said O'Donnell with a vague hand movement. He didn't even look it up – he had no information with him. I suspected they were probably way out. I would later be proved right.

I asked more questions and we talked some more about Port's upcoming court appearance, but they wrote nothing down. I thought they were useless. Absolutely useless. When I asked them what exactly 'perverting the course of justice' meant, they gave us a long, rambling explanation that didn't really tell us anything.

'Our MP, Karl Turner, gave me a much clearer explanation than that,' I told them. 'He said that it's like a car crash. One driver rams into another car. The other driver calls the police but the first driver moves his car before the police arrive. That's a case of perversion of justice, isn't it?'

'Er, yes.'

I asked them to tell me what Port had actually said each time he was questioned.

'Well,' began DS O'Donnell. 'First he told us that he'd been coming home from work and just found Anthony already propped up, dead in the street. The second time he said he had been in his flat with him, but he took some drugs he had in his pocket and was sick, so Port put him outside, ill but alive, and rang for the ambulance.'

'And the third time he admitted that Anthony been in his flat, then Anthony took some drugs he had brought with him and died in Port's flat while he was at work. So when he got home he took Anthony's body outside and called the ambulance.'

'Oh no!' I was shocked and appalled, not just at the details of what they told me, but the way they told it.

'There is one extra thing Port told us,' said DS O'Donnell. 'He told us that he was going to pay Anthony for sex.'

Yet another shock, but I was so sure it must be wrong that I confronted them: 'Right. Did Port have any money?'

'No, and his account was overdrawn.'

'So you did do a bit of investigation then!'

'Into this, yes.'

'But didn't it make you even a little bit suspicious that Port had agreed to pay Anthony, when he had no money?'

'No, not really.'

'Couldn't that be a motive for murder, or at least for getting rid of him, so that he didn't have to pay?'

'It just wasn't like that.'

'Right,' I changed tack. 'So you're telling me that Port's saying Anthony took drugs and he was sick all over his flat?'

'Yes.'

'So did you go in and see the sick?'

'No, we didn't.'

I more or less interviewed them about everything they had said. They were the detectives but I was the only one asking questions.

'I must have told you a hundred times that Anthony would never have taken drugs, especially not in a stranger's flat, in an area he'd never been to before,' I said.

'We found drugs in two little bottles in Anthony's digs. In his bedside cabinet.'

'Yes, but they weren't drugs. They were poppers.'

'No, no, no, they're drugs,' insisted DS O'Donnell.

'I'm telling you now that poppers are definitely not illegal drugs. You don't take them or smoke them. You just sniff them to heighten the senses. Anthony told me himself. He and I had a conversation about this the Christmas before he died. In fact it was an argument about whether poppers are drugs or not. He told me he had introduced China and Kiera to poppers and they wanted to make sure they weren't illegal drugs so they looked them up on the internet and they're definitely not. So there you are. Poppers are legal, that's that.'

They refused to believe me so I took yet another angle. 'So, did you have those bottles analysed?'

'No,' admitted DS O'Donnell. 'Not yet.'

'We don't need to,' added DC Slaymaker. 'This case is about Port, not about Anthony.'

I asked when Port's trial for 'perversion of the course of justice' would be.

'On Monday,' O'Donnell said. 'And it's not a trial. Port pleaded guilty, so he's already been convicted. It's a court hearing on Monday for sentencing him.'

'What? This Monday?'

'Yes.'

I was horrified. 'But it's Friday today. Didn't it occur to you that we might want to attend it?'

They looked blankly at me.

'Well, thanks for the notice!' I snapped. 'I could have gone if I'd known, but it's too late now for me to get the day off.'

They still said nothing. No apology or explanation.

'I don't suppose Tom can go either.' I looked at him and he shook his head. 'I'll have to get my husband Sami to be there on Monday. I'm sure China and Kiera will want to go too.' I paused. 'I'm fuming that you've kept this from us till the last minute.'

'Fair enough,' said DS O'Donnell. 'But the hearing is only about determining what sentence he'll get.'

'But we understand that to you perverting the course of justice is a very serious crime,' said Slaymaker, presumably in an attempt to calm me down. But even after all these months, he didn't know me at all.

'It's the WRONG charge!' I yelled at him. 'Can't you see that?'

'It's the only charge,' shrugged DC Slaymaker.

'So you insist on believing everything that Port says now?'

'Well, yeah,' nodded Slaymaker.

'There were two people in that room,' added O'Donnell. 'One's dead and the other won't tell us much, so we'll never know what happened.'

I was appalled. 'But what about the evidence?' I asked.

'What evidence?' he said.

'Exactly. You should have looked for evidence right from the start,' I paused. 'What about Anthony's laptop and his phone?'

'We've been here before,' said Slaymaker, with an undisguised sigh. 'It's too expensive spending hundreds of hours doing that. We've got him anyway.'

They were so offhand about everything that neither Tom nor I could believe it. I'll remember their cruel comments till my dying day.

'Right. We've got to go now,' said O'Donnell as they both stood up.

Slaymaker looked at me. 'I'll give you a ring after court on Monday.'

'Thanks, but Sami and the girls will be ringing me all day, telling me what's going on.'

They shrugged and said a peremptory goodbye as they left. They'd only been there about an hour and it was such a relief when they'd gone. But I was still angry. Tom and I went and sat in his conservatory.

'Absolute bastards,' I said. 'Do you know what? If he hadn't been a copper, I'd have knocked him out for saying that.'

'The two men in a room bit?' asked Tom. 'I can't believe he said that. It was dreadful, wasn't it?'

'At that moment, I could have literally knocked him out. Oh God. I'll never forget it, till the day I die.'

'You know what?' asked Tom. 'I reckon they only came to see us because they had to.'

'Yes, you're right,' I agreed. 'So they got it over as quickly as possible.'

'The whole conversation was very stilted, wasn't it?'

'Yes, they were totally useless. Not at all what I expected. I thought they'd at least have some paperwork with them to help them explain more fully and answer our questions properly. I expected them to be professional . . . but they weren't. It was a shambles.'

'Yes. Very unprofessional.' Tom paused. 'But at least they've got Port on something. That should keep him off the streets for a while.'

'I can't believe they didn't tell us sooner about Port's sentencing on Monday.'

'Yes. I totally agree.'

I was fuming now. I felt totally helpless that I couldn't even attend the hearing, let alone my exasperation at the slapdash way they conducted our meeting. 'Why can't the bloody police get off the fence and ask the right questions?' I almost shouted at poor Tom.

'Perhaps we will never know.'

'No. I do have moments when I think it may never happen but it has to. We can't just let it go. We have to get justice for Anthony. I'm not going to stop till I make them take action and properly investigate his death. And the other two boys as well. If they do nothing, mark my words, there will be more innocent young boys murdered when Port gets out of jail. I can't stop now.'

Sami went to the court on Monday morning and met up with China and Kiera. China kept me up to date with all the details. Apparently the waiting area was packed with people and as they walked in, Sami pointed to a man and said, 'That's him!'

'I asked him how he knew,' explained China. 'He said: "That's him. I'm telling you. That's him. He's evil. I can read people like a book and he's a predator." We were amazed when we found out he'd got the correct person. He was right.'

'Yes,' I smiled. 'He can just look at somebody and know what they're like.'

'Port's really ugly and creepy,' she said. 'Oh, we've just got to go into court . . .'

China and Sami kept me up to date throughout the day and I had a word with Kiera too and thanked them for going to the trial. At the end of the day, Sami called and told me all about it. I was glued to the phone, hoping for a long sentence.

'He is already guilty,' said Sami.

'Of course he is,' I replied. 'How long did he get?'

'Eight months: four in jail and four on licence.'

'I'm glad he'll be in prison but it's a rubbish sentence, nowhere near enough.'

When China rang me she told me what Sami didn't mention. 'Sami really kicked off,' she said. 'You should have seen him. You'd have been proud of him.'

'Why? What did he do?'

'He went straight up to Slaymaker and said: "Right. He's killed my son, so when he gets out, if I kill him I will get eight months as well? It's disgusting!" Slaymaker told him he couldn't say that. Sami asked, "Why? It's wrong." Slaymaker said: "No, it's not." So Sami shouted at him: "I know he killed Anthony. I *know*." Then Slaymaker got stroppy and told him to leave the building.'

'So Sami's been asked to leave because he kicked off at Slaymaker? Oh, I wish I'd seen that!' We both laughed. I suppose it helped to ease the tension.

Sami took China and Kiera out for a meal because it was China's birthday that day. She certainly did something

memorable on her birthday but not something she would
have chosen to do. If only it was all a bad dream and none
of this had been necessary.

A few days later, when I looked at the Barking newspaper online, I almost missed the most important, most
shocking paragraph. The prosecution barrister stood in court
before sentencing Port and said: 'A murder investigation
was launched unnecessarily.'

What? I couldn't believe it. It went on to say, 'There was
no suggestion that Mr Port bore any criminal responsibility
for the death of Mr Walgate . . .'

I got straight on the phone to DC Slaymaker, but he
didn't answer. I tried a few times but it always went to
voicemail, so I left an angry message about what I'd read
and demanded he call me as soon as he returned.

I tried again the next day, and the next, and waited some
more, but he didn't call me back at all. It was just as if he
had blocked me from access to him.

As usual, when I was angry or fed up, I took out my frus-
trations and anguish on Sami when he rang in the evenings. I
knew it was mean of me but I had to vent my fury somehow
and it did help that he always listened to me, when I couldn't
have a rant at anyone else – only Sami and occasionally China
or Kate.

Less than two months later, Port was released, wearing a tag
on his leg. I discovered this not from Slaymaker of course,
but from Karl Turner, who rang to tell me gently as he didn't
want me to see it first in the newspapers. Now my anxiety
rocketed again.

I did the only thing I could do. I rang Slaymaker and this time he picked up the phone. I could tell he wasn't very happy to hear my voice.

'Why didn't you warn me that Port was going to be released so early?'

'Because it doesn't make any difference. He's wearing a tag and will have to report in here regularly.'

'If he's out now, don't you realise he's a danger to your community? Please, please, please look at those three young boys' deaths again and you'll see the similarities.'

'Coincidences,' he replied.

'It doesn't matter what you call them,' I insisted. 'I'm pleading with you to check them out and investigate whatever evidence you have, like Anthony's laptop. Why haven't you checked that yet? And what happened to the inquest we were supposed to have into Anthony's death? Do you remember? It was supposed to be in London but you emailed me that I'd got my wish and it would be in Hull – it should have happened by now.'

I could hear him rustling some papers. 'Ah, yes,' he murmured, then said louder: 'The coroner cancelled it because there wasn't enough evidence!'

'And nobody thought to tell us? After all, we're only his parents!' I couldn't avoid a sarcastic tone, since it was like a repeat of all the other things they didn't tell us. 'So Port's been released and now the inquest is cancelled. Anything else you'd like to get off your chest?'

That night I went to bed feeling as if I might explode with worry – about burdening Sami so much, about how it all affected me and the wider family, about the other dead boys and their mothers and families. But most of all, I worried for all the other unsuspecting boys out there who might be lured in on dating apps, as Anthony was, and probably Gabriel and Daniel too.

I wished I didn't think it, but now that Port was out again, I felt eerily certain that these three deaths wouldn't be the last. If only there was something, anything I could do . . .

CHAPTER 11

The Fourth Body

July–September 2015,
13–15 months after Anthony's death

One fine day, Kate and I decided to take her six-year-old granddaughter, Kaitlin, with us to help weed Anthony's grave. My niece Lottie came along too. We parked the car and walked down to his grave, where I knelt down to pull out some weeds.

Kaitlin stood on the grave, looking down and started to talk to Anthony. 'Hello Anty-Panty,' she began. That was what she had always called him. 'I've come to see you and tell you about my new teacher at school. She's very nice and I told her about you. She said she was sorry you died.' Then she told him about some of her friends.

After a couple of minutes she stopped and listened. 'He's not answering me,' she said. 'Why isn't he answering me?'

She was quite upset, so we tried to explain that he couldn't answer her because he had died, so he couldn't talk any more. To soften the blow, we said he might be able to hear her and that her stories would cheer him up. She just gave me a look and said: 'If he's not answering me, I'm not talking to him either!' and she marched straight back to the car.

That's when I decided to make a memory garden for the children in my back garden. We fixed a date and all the family came together to help make Anthony's memory garden. Even Paul got off my sofa and came out to join us for a few minutes. Everybody brought something to plant or display and that seemed to help Kaitlin as, after that, she was always happy to come and tend the garden when it was needed.

Gradually, over the next few days and weeks, it became a little easier to talk to Paul and even to mention Anthony's name now and then. Until, one day in summer 2015, he was on the sofa and I was on my 'Queen's chair'. I don't remember what we were talking about. He'd had his tea and then he turned to me and said, 'Right, you're doing my head in, so I'm off home. Tarra.' He just stood up and walked off, out of the front door. What a relief that was, knowing he had recovered enough to go back to his own life – a weight off my mind . . . and my mood.

Still the email correspondence with our disgruntled FLO continued, with me asking him at least once a week when Anthony's possessions would be released to us so we could have them back at last. Every time it was the same reply: 'Not yet. I'll look into it.'

Over the past few months, both my physical and mental health had gone downhill with all this constant banging my head against a brick wall. I lost a stone, and I didn't really have it to lose, so I often felt poorly. Meanwhile, Port was still out on licence and had now had his tag removed. Another worrying period that no one seemed to have any control over – least of all the police.

The summer passed me by in a daze. I was still on antidepressants and continuing the counselling that Doctor Chadda had arranged for me. It helped to talk to Nicky once a week and offload my emotions each time but I wondered whether there would ever be an end to this – ever a time when I could accept and move on. It didn't seem likely, which was depressing in itself.

At least my days at work were all-consuming, with so many things to organise or problems to sort out. Many of my colleagues were also my friends and they were all very understanding, letting me talk about Anthony to my heart's content. Sometimes I'd have a moan about the police and they would all put up with it. I even had the chance to clear my mind of everything when we were at our busiest.

But then I would slump again and call poor Sami to have another rant about the same old things and vent my constant, angry frustration. I didn't realise how selfish my grief made me . . . and he took the brunt of it, almost every day.

As Sami's business was in Essex, he could only come and stay with me in Hull every other weekend. The rest of the time he rang me most nights, or sometimes I phoned him. But, without realising it, I was taking him for granted. I quite forgot that he was grieving too, in his own way. He was the quiet, private one, whereas I had to let it all out – at Slaymaker when I could, but mostly at Sami, who found it all very difficult.

In fact, in the year or so following Anthony's death, we gradually seemed to drift apart. Whether he rang me or I rang him, I'd have another of my daily meltdowns about what had happened, or more often not happened, and he was stuck down in Essex unable to do anything about it. So he started calling me less often, not wanting to be upset by my furious rants. Then I grew even more angry because he wasn't ringing me as much . . . So this terrible situation we found ourselves in did affect our relationship. It built an invisible wall between us. In the end, I realised we needed to sit down together and have an honest face-to-face talk about it all and he agreed. So he came up to Hull the following weekend.

The cultural differences in our upbringings had never previously been a problem but now, since Anthony's death, they had come to the fore. As a Turkish Muslim boy, Sami had always been taught to look after and protect his womenfolk. He had been a rock of support to me and tried his hardest to take away my pain, but he was in pain too.

'I just want to make it all better,' he said.

'But you can't. How can you bring Anthony back? That's the only thing that would make it better . . . or at least getting the police to take his death seriously and investigate it properly. That's what I'm fighting for every day and, even though I'm getting nowhere, I have to keep trying. It's all I have.'

I then went straight into a long, angry tirade of the police's faults and everything they had failed and refused to do. Throughout this, Sami sat there on the sofa, saying nothing, looking dolefully at me, with his pain hidden behind his eyes. I should have seen it, but I was too self-absorbed to notice.

Finally he managed to butt in. 'Shout slowly,' he pleaded, in his endearing Turkish accent. 'Because I can't understand you! It's a big BLAAA!'

'How-can-I-f★★★ing-shout-slower? It's-not-the-same-when . . .'

And we both ended up laughing!

'How can I have a good rant, when you don't understand?'

He just sat there with a glazed look on his face as he had no clue what I was saying, once I started shouting quickly at him. But that's what we did, every time. No wonder he was getting fed up with me.

'And while we're on the subject, why do you always swear in Turkish when you're angry with me?'

'I'm not angry with you,' he explained. 'I'm only angry when you shout so fast that I can't understand what you're saying.'

Sitting together in the same room, we just looked at each other and burst out laughing again. That was as much therapy as any amount of ranting. We'd had the occasional spat in the past but, even though this was such a different, alien situation and so much more serious, we never rowed for long. We smiled and hugged, then had something to eat or drink, which is the Turkish answer to everything.

'I just want to make it better,' he repeated. 'I want you to be who you were before.'

'I'm sorry but I'll never be that now. It's changed me . . . forever. Nothing that anybody does or says can give me back that person.'

His deep brown eyes gazed at me with great sadness. But when we had these chats it became a lot easier to understand and cope with each other better.

'I don't know what to say to you,' he said. 'I feel helpless.'

'When I rant and rave at you over the phone,' I explained to him, 'I don't want you to say anything. I don't need your opinion or sympathy. All you have to do is listen to me and, if you really need to say something, say: "There, there." . . . And that's it. I'm not asking you to solve the problem, just to listen.' I paused and smiled at him.

'I don't get that,' he said, using one of my English expressions.

'It's Slaymaker who's done all this to me, so it's him I'm angry at, not you. I'd like to shout at him a lot more, but if I did, he would put his phone down.' I paused. 'Look, when I'm ranting at you, just rest your phone down on the side. You don't even have to listen to me. It just makes me feel better to release all the rage inside me. I have to get it out.'

'But I'm your husband. You are my wife. I must protect you.'

'Just let me get it out my system,' I said again. 'That and a hug are all I need.'

So he gave me a great big, warm hug, like a bear protecting its young.

'Your gold watch is still in the drawer, you know,' I challenged him.

'Yes. I can afford a plane ticket home if you are horrid to me!'

And that set us off laughing together again.

The one thing I couldn't talk to Sami about was the subject closest to my heart. I needed to keep talking about Anthony, even if I was only talking to myself. But any mention of him upset Sami too much. If I tried to tell him something about Anthony, the tears would start trickling down his cheeks.

'Stop crying, pack it in,' I'd say. 'We need to be practical. Now isn't the time for emotion. We have so much to do.'

But he couldn't change his reactions any more than I could. You see, unlike me, he's never been on anti-depressants and, being a man, and a Muslim man at that, he refused even to consider it. Whereas I, with my typical, no-nonsense English upbringing, sometimes saw his attitude as something of a weakness, that he didn't take the tablets to suppress his sadness and keep him soldiering on like me. Above all, though, his protective attitude was one of the things I loved most about him. He always stuck up for me, no matter what, and all he ever wanted throughout this time was to make me happy.

From then on, I tried not to mention Anthony much to Sami. However, to stop talking about him, or to him, as I often did when alone around the house and in bed at night, would be to make him and his vibrant memory dead. So I had to keep his name alive, to keep him near me.

It wasn't just Sami who found it difficult to know what to say. I had to recognise that my loss didn't consume every-one's life as it did mine, and some of the people I thought would be there for me were not. This kind of situation can pull a family apart. In my case, it didn't quite do that because nearly everyone was very caring and supportive, which was just what I needed. However, there was one fracture that I would never have expected – a cold shoulder that not only shocked me, but really hurt me.

While my mam, my sister and one of my brothers had been very supportive, each in their own way, I had a second brother, Andy, to whom I had also been close. When Andy's wife Sandra's mam died, not long before Anthony, I rang her to offer condolences and we chatted for forty minutes. However, although they visited Tom, my ex-husband, to offer their sympathy, I am still waiting for the phone call from my brother Andy.

One day, my mam said to me: 'When it happened, I told Andy about Anthony's death and a few weeks later I asked him whether he'd seen you or spoken to you.'

'Yes?'

'And he said: "No, I can't. I don't know what to say to her."'

Brother, you didn't need to say anything, I thought. Just coming to have a cup of tea with me would have meant the world to me at the time. Total strangers showed me more compassion than you or your wife have done, and that's something Sami and I will never forget.

Conversely, many people were amazing, especially my boss Angela. Many times she cried along with me. There were often days when I just couldn't cope with being at work, surrounded by people and noise, and felt an overwhelming panic – a need to go home to peace and quiet. I didn't even want the TV or radio on in the background at home. I just needed to be alone. She always let me go straight away, with no need for an explanation, knowing I'd be back and feeling a little stronger the next day. I couldn't have done this journey without her support. *Thank you, Angie.*

On Monday, 14 September 2015, while Port was still on licence and I was at work, my phone beeped. I thought it would just be something mundane so I didn't look at it straight away, but when I did, it was a news flash, so I read the headline and the shock sent panic waves running through me: 'Fourth body found in Barking, near other three'. Surely now the police will make the link?

I don't remember driving home but I do recall the desperate urgency I felt to find out more, mingled with that awful guilt. If only I'd tried harder, couldn't I have prevented this? But I'd tried as hard as I could. If I'd been able to afford a private investigator I would have done. On my own, I nearly destroyed myself trying . . . and now, because I'd failed to stir up the police to investigate from the start, another boy had died.

As soon as I arrived home, I looked on the internet to see if I could find the details. Sure enough, there it was. Jack Taylor was this young man's name and he was found propped up against a wall at Abbey Green. I immediately looked at a map of Barking and found this was a place between the flats where Anthony had been found and the churchyard where the dog walker had found Gabriel, then Daniel – not much more than a stone's throw away from each other. A chill ran through my body.

I read the rest of the short article and it sounded so similar: Jack's age group, his slim build, the circumstances, location and even the position of his body, propped up against a wall, in a sitting position. It had to be . . .

CHAPTER 12

All Change

September–October 2015,
15–16 months after Anthony's death

I rang DC Slaymaker first thing the following morning. 'Yes?' He sounded annoyed with me before I'd even said anything.

'I've just seen the Barking newspaper online and read about the fourth body.'

'It's just another death. We have a lot of them down here. Probably a drugs overdose or suicide.'

'But surely you can see the similarities?'

'A lot of young men die like this, all over London.'

'You've got to investigate it . . . and Anthony, Gabriel and Daniel.'

'No. We've told the press and I'm telling you – they're absolutely nothing to do with each other.' He repeated it slowly, syllable by syllable – 'ab-so-lute-ly', as if I was an imbecile.

'You're so wrong!' I yelled and ended the call.

I was exasperated, angry, frustrated . . . – burdened with a sense of guilt and so many other emotions that churned around my brain, which struggled to cope. The anti-depressants I was still taking slowed my senses and dulled my emotions, which had been a good thing. But now I made the decision. I started to wean myself off the pills that night. I needed a clear head, to feel and think clearly if I was going to be able to fight for justice for these four boys. Somebody had to do it and I was willing to take on the world for Anthony and these other three young men, all of them with lives to live, cruelly cut short.

I looked all over the internet for whatever press coverage there was about Jack's death. As I searched and read, it occurred to me that Jack's family were probably doing the same about Anthony's death, then Gabriel's and Daniel's too. I felt sure they would recognise the similarities and I hoped they too would bombard the police with questions and demands, just as I had done. Anyone who looked could have seen what the police chose not to see, or were too uncomfortable with to probe.

Cutting the medication heightened my rage that had built up over the fifteen months since Anthony's death. I had so many more questions, but when I rang my FLO or DS O'Donnell, they didn't want to know. They just blocked me now. If I'd lived nearer, I'd have gone straight to the police station and had it out with them face to face, but I couldn't. And I don't suppose it would have been any more successful anyway. The more I thought about it, the more scared I was by my anger and frustration. It boiled up like road rage. I realised it could get me into trouble, so I poured it all out to my poor counsellor, Nicky.

'You need to channel all this rage somewhere else,' she said. 'Because if you don't, somebody will get it all . . . and that will only add to your troubles.'

I tried to follow her advice and channelled my anger into household chores and digging up the garden. I tried walking too but the city of Hull isn't the ideal walking territory to relieve anyone's stress. As usual, it was long-suffering Sami who bore the brunt of most of my rages. He may not have realised it, but he did help, just by listening and agreeing. He knew me well enough not to try to soothe or stop me. I had to vent my fury and get it out of my system, but I still wasn't considering how much it might be affecting him.

One afternoon at work, the phone rang. This was not an unusual occurrence of course, but I did notice the date and time – 5.30 p.m. on Thursday, 15 October 2015, which subsequently became etched in my memory. I will never forget that phone call as long as I live.

'Sarah. The shit's hit the fan! We need a photo of Anthony immediately! Have you got one?' There was panic in Slaymaker's voice.

'Well, not this minute. I'm busy at work. Ring me back in half an hour.'

'No. I need it *now*!'

'Well, yeah,' I said, catching the panic, but not knowing why. 'I've probably got one on my phone.'

'Right. You need to email it to this guy Duffy. I'll text you his email address.'

'Yeah, OK.'

There was a slight pause, during which I could hear raised voices in the background; it sounded chaotic. 'Send it now and I'll ring you back in five minutes.'

I found the photo I wanted and emailed it to 'Duffy' as instructed. The phone went again almost immediately.

'Have you sent the photo?'

'Yes, but what is it for? What's this all about?'

'Are you sitting down?'

'I'm in the main office,' I replied.

'Well, I've got something to tell you.'

'OK, I'll just go and find a quieter room.' My heart was racing. 'I'm ready now. What is it?'

'We've just arrested Port.'

'Right . . . what for?' This was all so sudden that I needed a minute or two to think straight and listen.

'For four murders—' Just then, somebody in the background called out his name. 'I'll have to go now 'cos I need to get on.'

And that was it. I came off the phone, my head reeling. What? Nothing – no explanation, no 'sorry', no 'you were right all along, for the past sixteen months' . . . nothing at all. I burst into tears, confused, angry, glad, all rolled into one. If they'd only listened to me, the other three boys would still be alive. It hadn't just been me telling them. It was the newspapers, websites, people in the community, our MP and others. It didn't need Sherlock Holmes to solve this case.

I didn't even feel relieved I'd been proved right. It was more a case of *Shit! I was right!* None of that mattered now. My chest tightened, as if someone was gripping me hard. I wanted to go out and find someone to tell, to share it, but I couldn't at that moment. I was on my own and I sat there, sobbing uncontrollably for several minutes. Finally, the tears slowed and I went to find Tony, another manager.

'Whatever's the matter?' he asked as he saw my tear-stained face. 'You look wretched.'

'I need you . . . I have to tell . . .' My breathing was still tight and I could hardly get the words out.

'What's happened?' He paused. 'Is it about Anthony?' Of course, Tony had kept up with the story all the way along, so he knew what I had been through.

'Yes,' I told him in short breaths and he listened till I'd finished.

'F***ing hell! You were right,' he blurted. 'Sarah, just go home. Go on. Talk to your family. Go and do whatever you have to do. Don't worry about coming back till you're ready. We'll share out your work.'

News travels fast. In the time it took to gather my things and leave my office, everyone seemed to know. They were all coming up to me, saying: 'Oh my God, you were right!' 'You were right all along.' 'You always said . . .' Another colleague came to find me as I was about to leave the building. 'You were right,' he echoed the others.

'Didn't you think I was right?' I asked him.

'Well, to be quite honest, it was that shocking, some of the things you were telling us,' he said. 'I thought you were probably delusional, or massively exaggerating, or making half of it up. I thought it was a mother–son thing, you know? But now it's actually come out, it's blown me away. What the frigging hell! You were right!' And he gave me a quick hug.

As I left the building I thought, 'Well of course I was right – didn't you believe me? I always knew I was right.'

I felt a sudden wave of relief as I got in my car and started to drive home but on the way I decided to go to Kate's instead. Sitting alone in my four walls wouldn't help. I needed to talk it all through. It was all running through my brain as I drove. I was in shock. It felt like I was on a roller-coaster, out of control. But gradually I began to feel calmer, knowing that this was a positive move at last.

I arrived at Kate's and found her adult daughter Sophie was there too. Once I sat down with them, it all came out. The panic in Slaymaker's voice, the urgency, the chaotic background noises, everything.

'It must be a whole month since Jack's body was found, isn't it?' asked Kate.

'Yes, a month and a day. But it's been sixteen months since Anthony died,' I replied. 'All that time, the struggle to be heard, the despair and anguish that nobody would do anything, or believe anything I said . . .'

'Yes, it's been a terrible time for you,' she agreed.

'But thank God they've finally got him,' added Sophie.

'What a shock!' said Kate.

'I still don't really know what's going on,' I explained. 'I don't even know why they wanted Anthony's photo so urgently. And what has suddenly made them arrest Port for all four murders?' I was very puzzled about it all, and desperate to know.

'Well, let's see what we can find out on the internet,' suggested Kate and we gathered round her computer.

The first thing we discovered was that Port had been charged in court earlier that day for administering noxious substances and on suspicion of murdering all four boys.

'So Slaymaker was a bit ahead of himself,' said Kate.

'Does noxious substances mean drugs?' asked Sophie.

'Yes. And you're right, Kate,' I added. 'He told me that it was for four murders, not just suspicion of. Well, maybe it's suddenly all moving so fast that we can't keep up.'

'I guess they have to say "on suspicion of" to cover themselves.'

'Judging from the panic and chaos in the background when Slaymaker was telling me, I expect it's all hell let loose and nobody knows what everyone else is doing. They sounded like a bunch of headless chickens. They need a proper boss there to sort them out.'

'Look at this,' Kate pointed to some text on a page she had just scrolled through.

'What does it say? Read it out to us,' I suggested.

'The sisters of Jack Taylor demanded the police scan through the CCTV footage near the station to see if they could identify their brother.'

'That's what I told them to do as well but they wouldn't,' I moaned. 'Although I later heard that it wasn't even working the night Anthony met Port.'

'It sounds as if his sisters are quite feisty,' said Sophie.

'Yes, they'd need to be,' I agreed.

'Well, it says here that the police looked through several CCTV recordings until they finally found one that clearly showed Jack Taylor walking away from the station with a man they later identified as Stephen Port.'

'Wow,' I gasped. 'When did they find this?'

'The thirteenth, it says here, so just two days ago.'

We had a cuppa and chatted about what we'd found out so far. Then I went home to carry on Googling for the rest of the evening. Things were obviously happening fast now

. . . at last. Kate carried on searching too, so we kept ringing each other up and comparing notes about what we'd read.

Finally, around midnight, I found out why Slaymaker had wanted that photo of Anthony. There he was, his smiling face splashed all over a number of first editions of the next day's newspapers, alongside photos of the other three boys: Gabriel, Daniel and Jack. I just sat and looked at them, each one in turn. 'What a waste,' I said aloud to myself. 'What a bloody waste . . . and it needn't have happened to any of them, or at least not the three boys after Anthony.'

Having the day off, I thought I might lie in a bit the next morning, but no chance. The press pack were on a crusade. At 8 a.m. I was woken by a loud knocking at my front door. I went down, bleary-eyed, to find a reporter from the *Sun* newspaper standing on my doorstep, wanting to interview me. I sent her away and said I'd let her know. Then the *Daily Mirror* rang me, swiftly followed by the *Daily Express*, the *Independent* and Calendar, the regional TV people – all before lunch. So I rang Tom at work. He was up to date with the news and he'd had several messages too.

'Thank God they've finally got their act together,' said Tom.

'Yes, all our protests have at last broken through the brick wall they built around their prejudices, their refusal to see the truth staring them in the face,' I said. 'But what I find the most shocking is that it was not until three more boys had been killed by that murderer.'

'Your protests,' Tom corrected me. 'You've never given up.'

'It's Jack's sisters too,' I said. 'They must have pushed the police to follow up on their brother's death as well. And now the press are hounding me.'

'Well, I suppose it's time the Barking police were shown up.' He paused. 'I'll leave you to do all that side of things. Just keep me out of it.'

'Yes, but it's OK though,' I told him.

'What do you mean?' he asked, sounding puzzled.

'Well,' I explained, 'Anthony would have been *mortified* if we'd talked to the *Sun*. But the *Independent* want it now, so we'll be fine! He'd be happy with that.'

We laughed a lot about it. I suppose we needed to break the tension.

'It's got to be the *Independent*,' I continued, 'because that's quite a posh paper.'

'Yes, he'd like that,' agreed Tom. 'He liked to think he was posh.' More laughter – which made us both feel better.

But the press didn't stop there. Oh no! We were both bombarded for a few more days so we told the lot of them to sod off!

Over the first couple of days following Stephen Port's arrest, the story had gathered pace in all the local and national newspapers, adding new revelations each time. On 18 October, Port was up in court again, charged with all four murders and taken into custody. On 19 October, the papers ran the story in their late editions that the Met police (which includes Barking and Dagenham) had referred themselves to the IPCC (Independent Police Complaints Commission) for 'vulnerabilities in their response to the deaths'. I smiled ruefully when I read that. I couldn't help a feeling of triumph. At last.

The press pack were in full force now, looking for new angles to report on every day. With all the publicity, Karl Turner gave me a call to catch up and asked if I'd like to go and see him. As I walked into his office he gave me a big grin. 'Oh my God, you were right! I knew it all along of course but now the whole world knows it too.'

'If I was paid a pound for every person who's said that to me these last two days . . .: "you were right . . . you were right . . .", I'd be able to afford a great holiday.'

'I expect you need one.'

'Yes, but not yet. There's a long way to go with all this before we can really relax, if I ever will.'

'Come on in and sit down,' he said, taking me through to his surgery office.

We sat down and chatted about what had happened so far. Then, having been a barrister, he asked me if I'd thought about making a complaint to the IPCC about the Barking branch of the Met.

'They've actually referred themselves now,' I told him. 'But yes, I have thought about it a lot and I would like to make my own complaint as well.' So he told me what the IPCC is, what it does and how it works.

'You'd need to refer yourself to the IPCC. I'll give you their contact details,' Karl explained. 'And let me know when you've done that and I'll talk you through all the stages.' He paused, with a look of genuine concern: 'Is there anything else I can do for you now?' he asked.

'No, not at the moment,' I said. 'Apparently, the Crime Squad from Scotland Yard has taken over now, so it's all starting to get going, at last. I'm expecting we will all become more involved as time goes on. At the very least, I hope the new detectives will be more professional and also more compassionate.'

'I'm certain they will be,' Karl reassured me, which gave me renewed confidence.

'Good. Well, they couldn't be any worse!'

'You've got my private number, haven't you?'

'Yes, it's in my phone.'

'So just keep in touch and give me a call if there is anything I can help you with.'

In bed that night, I felt such a mix of emotions. I was relieved and happy at the sudden turnaround but it had been so quick that I hadn't yet fully acclimatised myself to it. I also felt guilty that I should feel happy. How could I be pleased when it was about my son's death? It seemed a cruel irony. My mind was racing. I felt in limbo, since I didn't have my old family liaison officer any more but I didn't have a new one either. Would I be given a new one? I knew there must be a lot going on but I didn't know what. Would anyone tell me? Would the new team keep me informed? What kind of evidence could they gather this long after Anthony's death? I was so confused, frustrated and tired that the tears began to run down my cheeks and onto the pillow. That's when I must have fallen asleep, hoping for a better tomorrow.

CHAPTER 13

Looking Both Ways

November–December 2015, 17–18 months after Anthony's death

A few days later, my phone rang. It was an unfamiliar London number, so I hoped it wasn't another newspaper badgering me. But no, this didn't sound like a journalist. It was a new, calm and friendly-sounding voice.

'Hello Mrs Sak, I'm calling to introduce myself.'

I was still wary, but intrigued. It seemed rather an old-fashioned opening line. Who could this be?

'My name is Ian Atkinson and I have been appointed to be your new family liaison officer. I shall be supporting you from now on and will keep you up to date with regular calls. The Serious Crime Squad has now taken over the case. We are managing this whole murder investigation – starting afresh and digging deep. We have already started work on gathering whatever evidence we are able to find. I can assure you that I will keep you up to date with everything we are doing to get this investigation off the ground.'

'Thanks Ian. I'm sure it must be a huge task, after that Barking shower's incompetence.'

'Well, there is certainly plenty to do, Mrs Sak, and we're determined to get the murderer behind bars for life.'

'Thank God for that,' I said. 'Oh, and please call me Sarah.'

'OK, I will. Now the first thing I want to do, Sarah, is to come up with a colleague and meet both you and Anthony's father, Thomas. I shall be ringing him too, after this call. Do you think it would be possible to see you together or would you prefer separate meetings?'

'Oh, together will be fine. We get on quite well when it's anything to do with Anthony. We are both highly relieved that Port has been charged with the four murders. I can't tell you the battle I've had, banging my head against one brick wall after another, and absolutely nothing was done. But now it's a great step forward and a huge boost to hear that you've taken over and that you're all working so hard on the case.'

'Yes, we'll be glad to explain everything to you when we meet, so if you have any questions, do please jot them down and we'll try to answer them all.'

'Yes, I will,' I said with an enormous sigh of relief. 'I've asked hundreds of questions since Anthony's body was found and not one of them has been answered. In fact, both China and I were told by DS O'Donnell to "stop asking questions that will never have any answers". I can't tell you how distressing it was to be blocked every step of the way . . . till now.'

'I can imagine, Sarah. You have had an awful time and, on behalf of the Metropolitan police, I can only apologise.'

'Thanks,' I said with tears filling my eyes. I didn't dare say anything else in case I broke down on the phone.

'But now I can promise you it will be very different and I will answer every question you ask me, as fully as I can.'

On Monday, 9 November 2015, I went round to Tom's after work and we shared our impressions of what was going on and how things might progress.

'I don't suppose they'll be able to find any evidence after all this time,' I said, feeling gloomy, after my initial euphoria at the abrupt change.

It felt like an anti-climax and yet I think we both anticipated this meeting with a degree of curiosity about how good an FLO this Ian would make. However, we were still apprehensive about meeting the new team, remembering how awful the last meeting was with Slaymaker and O'Donnell.

'Hopefully,' said Tom, 'the Crime Squad will do a lot better than the Barking shambles.'

'Well, they couldn't do any worse,' I replied. 'But they've got a huge hill to climb!'

Just then, the doorbell rang and I went with Tom to let them in.

'Mr Walgate?'

'Yes, come in. I'm Tom and this is Anthony's mother, Sarah.'

'I'm Ian, your new family liaison officer, and this is my colleague and boss, Tim Duffield.'

I was shocked . . . in a good way. My first impressions were completely different from the last lot. These two men were smartly dressed in pressed suits and ties. They were both carrying briefcases and they smiled warmly as they came in and sat down. Tim in particular had a presence that impressed me – a sense of *I'm in charge and I know what I'm doing*. Ian seemed very genuine and I could tell straight away that he had the compassion Slaymaker had lacked.

Out came their sheaves of paperwork – again, so different to Slaymaker and O'Donnell, who had brought no paperwork at all. This time, I knew from the start that we were with the professionals. However, in my compulsion to get things right, I launched into a tirade about Slaymaker and O'Donnell: 'It's been worse than the worst nightmare,' I began, hardly pausing to draw breath. 'Right from the start, the whole things was a disaster. They even told Tom that his brother had died, instead of his son. Can you believe it?'

They looked at Tom, who nodded. 'That was awful,' he agreed.

'And from the time Anthony's body was found,' I continued, 'they just assumed he was a druggy and refused to change their minds, no matter what we said. The last seventeen months have been absolute hell. Most of the time, they completely ignored us – his family and friends. We were the ones who knew him best, who knew he wasn't a druggy. He had a great future ahead of him but they didn't want to know about any of that. They refused to listen or to see what was going on. They had a complete lack of compassion. Quite the opposite – absolute indifference and distaste. And, even worse, they refused to investigate anything about Anthony's death, other than the post-mortem, and that was only because they had to do it. They got things wrong all the time, they told us lies, didn't ring me when they said they would—'

'*Woah*, Sarah,' Tim stopped me in mid-flow. 'Trust me. It will all be utterly different now. I have already started up a painstakingly thorough investigation. All my team are completely focused. I will get him. I will even know who he was sat next to at primary school by the time I've finished. Forget them . . . they didn't do what they should have done and now they are being investigated for their failings. We're the elite team and we will sort it. They didn't do their job properly but we *will*.'

'We'll see . . .' I replied. He did sound convincing, very much so, but I wanted them to know that I would keep on their tails, just to make sure.

As the meeting progressed, everything about them gave me confidence. When we asked questions, they consulted their documents, so we knew they must be telling us the truth. They both made notes too, of most of the things we told them. They seemed so caring and genuinely interested in everything we said. Tim and Ian made a good team. They spoke and listened by turns, asking us a lot of questions to help them develop a better understanding of our experiences.

'Did you make a statement to the Barking police?' asked Tim.

'No,' I said. 'But I would have liked to. I kept telling them what I would have put in my statement if they had let me but they never took any notice.'

'Do you know whether anyone made a statement?'

'Only China, Anthony's closest friend,' I said. 'And that was because she went to Barking police station and insisted on making a statement. But I don't think they were bothered about it.'

Tim and Ian began to tell us the details of what had happened and what they'd done so far. 'The big chiefs called me up to Scotland Yard for a meeting,' explained Tim. 'They dragged me in and presented me with my orders.' He paused. 'The boss said, "Sort this mess out," in no uncertain terms. So that's what I'm going to do, and I've got the best team to help me do it.'

'As you know, we've arrested Port,' said Ian. 'And charged him with the four murders.'

'Yes. Thank God for that,' I exclaimed.

'Yes,' added Tim. 'And now we are working hell-for-leather to dig out every bit of evidence we can.'

'Won't that be difficult for the first three boys, so long after the events?' I asked.

'Yes, you're right,' agreed Tim.

'The last lot didn't seek out any evidence at the time,' added Ian. 'In fact, unforgivably, they actually lost or destroyed some of it.'

'So we're going right back to square one and delving into every little detail,' explained Tim. 'It will be much harder than it should have been but I can assure you, we won't miss a thing.'

I looked at Tom and I knew he was thinking the same thing as me – that we really believed they would; if there was anything to find, they would scrutinise it minutely.

'I don't know whether you realise,' added Tim, 'that despite Port finally admitting that Anthony had died in his bed, nobody ever went into his flat, let alone got a warrant to gather any potential evidence or even look for Anthony's phone. So we really are starting from rock bottom.'

Ian asked us about our initial contacts with the Barking police. I told them how I'd first heard about Anthony's death, the awful journey back from Turkey and the main points of my first contacts with DS O'Donnell and DC Slaymaker.

'He was my FLO,' I explained, 'but he was rubbish in the role – worse than useless.' I looked straight at Ian, our new FLO, and he laughed.

We asked Tim and Ian all the questions we had and they answered each one openly, with patience and empathy. The meeting lasted two hours – at least twice as long as the one we'd had with the previous lot. And this time we had gained a lot of understanding and support. At last we felt we knew where things were going.

'Let's swap phone numbers,' suggested Ian with a smile. 'You can ring me any time, and I mean that.'

'We'll be in touch,' added Tim, as they prepared to leave. 'I'll call you in a couple of days.' And I knew he would.

After they'd gone, Tom and I sat and chatted. 'Well, they were a lot more compassionate and professional than O'Donnell and Slaymaker,' I said.

'Yes, let's hope they can do a proper job this time,' added Tom.

'Do you know? For the first time in all these months, I really believe they can.'

Tim did call me two days later as he had promised. And Ian was a fantastic FLO, he really was. He rang me every time there was something new to tell, sometimes daily. Several times in the weeks following, I also rang him with new questions and every time he answered them directly. I actually told him off one day.

'I'm away on holiday with the family next week,' he'd explained on the phone. 'But if you need me, just ring me.' And while he was on holiday, he still rang me to update me on the investigation.

'Ian,' I said. 'You're on holiday. You told me you would be on holiday. You don't need to ring me now. Surely you could switch off and just catch up when you get back to work?'

'But we're camping,' he said. 'So I don't always have a signal and you might be trying to call me. So just ring me whenever you want to and if I don't have a signal to answer straight away, I'll ring you back when I do.'

'Look, Ian,' I told him firmly, in my best school-teacher voice. 'Unless it is life or death, I am not ringing you on your family holiday. So you must stop calling me till you get back. Go and enjoy yourselves.'

Not long after their first visit, Tim and Ian came up to see us again at Tom's, to take our statements for the very first time. I was a bit wary as China had told me about O'Donnell taking hers. He had insisted on writing it himself and when she was given it to sign, she read it through and was shocked to find he had missed a lot out, including some very important things. She had wanted to add to it but he wouldn't let her. However, this was a completely different experience for us, with the new, professional team.

'Write your statements yourselves if you like and take your time, to make sure you add in everything you want to say.'

So I did. I wrote it all exactly the way I wanted it to be. I realised I couldn't write everything – that would be far too much — but I did include all the important points, especially about Anthony and also the gist of my subsequent, woeful contact with the Barking police.

As Tim put our statements into his file, I suddenly thought. 'Will you ask China and Kiera to make statements as well? China did one before, but DS O'Donnell wrote it and left things out.'

Tim looked at a list in the front of his file. 'Is that Miss Dunning?'

'Yes, China Dunning. I don't remember Kiera's surname but China will tell you.'

'I'll give them a ring tomorrow and organise new statements for them too,' he assured me.

'Thanks.'

'Before we leave,' said Ian, 'I just wanted to let you know that we've now been given a provisional date for the trial to start — 23 April next year.'

'But there's a lot to do by then,' explained Tim. 'So it's not definite yet.'

When they had gone, we both said we felt uplifted by everything that was happening and the thorough, conscientious way they worked.

'They really care about getting it all right,' I said.

'Yes, they do.'

'I know it will be extremely difficult for them but I really think we have a good chance of gaining justice for Anthony and the other three lads at last.'

Ian rang me at least twice a week after that and kept me up to date. 'We've co-operated with the local press to get a new invitation out to the local LBGT community,' he told me. 'We want anyone who has info that could help us, or who was snared and survived Port's advances, to come forward, anonymously if necessary, to help with our enquiries.'

'Yes, that's good. There may be somebody who can help.'

'It came out in the local paper yesterday and already we've had some calls and a couple of additional victims' statements,' he said. 'Both of them drugged and raped by Port before Anthony died.'

I found this mind-boggling. My first reaction was anger that they hadn't come forward at the time. If they had, Anthony might not have died. But I was also astonished that all these things were going on and most people never hear about them.

'It's like a secret society,' I blurted out.

'Well, not quite,' Ian replied. 'But I know what you mean. And they've been able to tell us more about Port's methods.'

'Did any of them know anything about what happened to Anthony?'

'No, only what they read in the paper when his body was found.' He paused. 'I don't think many of them had any idea that it was happening to other young men as well as themselves. It must have been complicated for them too, if their families don't know they are gay.'

'It's terrible when families turn against them and make them ashamed of being gay. I knew from his early teens that Anthony was gay but it didn't make any difference to me.'

'He was very lucky to have you as his mother,' Ian said. 'But not everyone has your confidence and tolerance.'

'What's there to be tolerant about?' I couldn't really

understand parents who would turn against their own children for being born with a different sexuality than they expected. To me, it was just a fact of life.

'There are probably a lot more of Port's victims who will never come forward,' he added. 'This story could be bigger than we'll ever know.'

After the Serious Crime Squad took over the case and Port was charged with the murders, I found out that I could now go to Victim Support for some help. I didn't feel any different than I had felt ever since that day in Turkey, the day I found out. Grief had been ever-present, through all my days and nights, but only now did I qualify for bereavement counselling.

So I went along to the same place as before and, sure enough, they were kindness itself this time and allotted me to a lovely young woman called Amna. We sat down together and, as she started to explain her role as bereavement counsellor, this thought kept running through my mind: 'So I'm a victim now, am I? I've been a victim for eighteen months, yet nobody gave a toss. But now I've been proved right about Port, they are all falling over themselves to help.'

As it happened, Amna turned out to be a great listener and a great support to me in my darkest moments, and I still had plenty of those throughout the long wait for the case to go to trial.

My next call from Ian was a bit of a let-down – yet more delay. 'I'm afraid that finding and analysing evidence is proving a mammoth task so we've had to postpone the trial date from April to July. I'm sorry it's so long to wait but we are determined to have as watertight a case as we can.'

'Yes,' I groaned. 'That is disappointing. We won't be able to see an end to our grief and move on with our lives until Port is convicted. We all need to see him locked up for life, to achieve justice for our boys and find closure for ourselves.'

'I do understand how awful this long wait is for you, but—'

'Yes, it is . . . but I know how important it is for you to put together the best case you can,' I sighed. 'So I'll just have to try my best to be patient for longer. At least he's off the streets so no other mothers will have to endure the heartache I've had.'

It was hugely frustrating to have this delay but at least the charge list was growing now, as Ian told me that some of those LGBT victims had agreed to come out to their parents and work colleagues so that Port's crimes against them could also be tried in court. It seemed that quite a few of them were lucky survivors but still traumatised by their experiences. These brave young men's stories now helped the police to piece together what happened to each of the murdered boys. They also helped the police to understand the whole chemsex scene, in which drugs such as GHB are used to enhance sex. This was such a contrast with the Barking lot, who were so homophobic that they refused to admit their ignorance, preferring to stick easy labels on our boys. Out of sight, out of mind.

Thank God we now had Ian, Tim and his expert team working so hard to right the wrongs for each of our murdered sons. I had such trust in them that I actually started to sleep better at night. It wasn't so much that I was ready to step back, but I did feel I could relax more, knowing we had everyone working so hard for us.

But just when things seemed to be going well and the police were motoring on, there was another delay of the trial date. 'Sorry Sarah,' explained Ian. 'But there is still so much to do and every day we find out more. It's quite overwhelming, so we have had to request a further delay. We have to be 110 per cent certain we have everything covered to send him down. The trial is now booked to take place at the Old Bailey, starting 4 October, and is likely to last for up to eleven weeks. This is a firm date.'

'Are you sure?'

'Yes, absolutely.'

'So it will finish in time for Christmas?'

'Yes.'

'That will be two and a half years since Anthony's death!'

'Yes, it's been a long, hard slog for you, hasn't it?'

'And now an even longer wait to endure. I'm going to be a nervous wreck by then.'

A few days later, I had a phone call from someone called Ben Williams. 'Hello Mrs Sak. I'm the officer in charge of the IPCC investigation into the failings of the Barking and Dagenham Police. I'd like to come up to Hull to meet you and Thomas. I could tell you more about the complaints process and answer any questions you may have. I'd also like to take down all your concerns and complaints about the police.'

'That will be a very long meeting then!'

'Yes, we don't want to leave any stone unturned, Mrs Sak.'

'It's Sarah, and my ex-husband is usually called Tom.'

'That's fine, and I only answer to Ben.' He sounded quite formal but in a friendly, caring way. 'I want you to tell me every single thing that you felt went wrong in this investigation.'

'Well, for a start,' I replied, 'there wasn't any investigation.'

'Er yes, that's what I understood,' he said. 'I'll write that down now but please could you make a list of all the things that went wrong following Anthony's death and we'll discuss it all when I come.'

'That will be easy as I've been making notes all along. I've made a case file too, with all the emails and notes about all the phone conversations. I've got pages and pages – a fat sheaf of complaints.'

We arranged a date and time to meet at Tom's a few days later. The meeting went well. He was very efficient and, at the same time, showed concern for all the terrible mistakes the police had made and the effects on us. I gave him all my notes and he put them in his briefcase when he was ready to leave.

'Will we meet with you again?' I asked him.

'Yes, but probably not till the trial. I'll be there with my assistant every day, making further notes to add to our investigation. At the end of the trial, I shall need you both to make a further statement about anything that has come up during the proceedings and how far the trial has met your expectations.'

So now the complaints commission was on a roll and all we could do was wait until it was all over. After all that panic and rushing around since Jack's body was found, and the Crime Squad taking over, and meetings, there was nothing more I could do but hang onto my sanity as best I could, with the great help of my therapist, Nicky, who I talked to at my GP's surgery, and Amna, my lovely Victim Support bereavement counsellor, who used to come round to my house once a month and always stayed a couple of hours.

I was in limbo. I still had panic attacks some days and flashbacks of Anthony every night. It was the longest wait I'd ever had. The anticipation was building, seizing me with apprehension, which turned to fear and dread when I thought about what awful details I might have to hear and endure at the trial, not to mention the appalling prospect of having to see the devil himself. The longer it went on, the more the tension built up. And there was another eight months to wait.

One day I'd feel deflated that there was so long a hiatus, and the next I'd build myself up, then sink down again. I was like a yo-yo.

I don't think I could have got through it but for Ian and his regular phone calls. Our frequent conversations are what kept me going. He had been allotted to us full-time so he kept tabs on every development and updated me every step of the way. He was brilliant. I told him one day that he was born for that job.

'Mind you, I can't imagine you arresting anybody,' I added. 'You're too kind.' We laughed. He reminded me of the friendly bobby on the beat that I remembered from my childhood, always positive, caring and sensitive to my moods and needs – the complete opposite of Slaymaker, my first FLO.

I fervently hoped that Ben from the IPCC would slate him in particular for all his failings. I'd certainly provided lots of evidence. Just the emails themselves were very telling of his disdain and complete lack of action.

If only I had a crystal ball to reveal how it would all turn out . . .

CHAPTER 14

The Wrong Sort of Fame

Spring–Summer 2016,
21–24 months after Anthony's death

'Tell me more about Anthony,' asked Ian one day on the phone. 'I know the facts, like his age and that he was at university, but I don't know much else. I feel I'd like to get to know him better, through your memories of him.'

'Ooh, where shall I start?' It was a rhetorical question of course, as I had so much to tell. It always helped me to talk about Anthony, so I started by telling Ian about him as a small child and how funny he was.

'He was always getting up to mischief,' I said, with a smile. I started by telling Ian about the evening he got his tooth stuck in his ear. Then the day he dug up the dead hamster to show his little friends.

'That conjures up a lovely picture,' said Ian.

'Yes, that was a laugh!' I said. 'I had to wait till after I'd put him to bed, then I reburied it in a different part of the garden, as deep as I could.'

'Like burying a body under the patio?' he suggested, referring to a TV soap's storyline.

'Yes, but this time a much-loved pet.' I paused. 'I don't

know whether any of my neighbours saw me digging in the dark . . . they might have wondered.' We laughed.

I went on to tell Ian about some of the other anecdotes from Anthony's childhood – trying to play with the sniffer-dog looking for drugs at the airport, bringing home the contents of the hotel's mini-bar in his suitcase, sledging straight into the restaurant.

'Anthony's brother Paul is seven years older but his cousins were closer in age, so he often played with them as children and, even in their teens, they were always good company together, except for one time.'

'Oh yes?' asked Ian, always the perfect listener.

'Anthony was about eleven and Kate's daughter Sophie must have been fifteen and a bit chunky at the time, like girls often are at that age. They were just joshing around together and began to argue about something. It got rather heated and Anthony yelled out: "Shut up you fat cow!"

'So she turned and walloped him and he punched her back in the face, so she grabbed his hair and ripped out a fistful. So it finished with Anthony having a bald patch and Sophie gaining a black eye . . . but they were the best of friends again a couple of minutes later, as if nothing had happened.'

'It sounds like Anthony had an eventful childhood,' laughed Ian. 'What about when he was older? Did he know what he wanted to do when he left school? Did he have any ambitions? What was he like character-wise?'

'Well, he was always a funny boy who made everyone laugh. I knew he was gay early on, about thirteen or fourteen, but we never talked about it till he was older. I would have done if he'd said something but he didn't and anyway, I was fine with whatever was right for him. I'm pretty sure he realised it too when he was about fourteen, because he became more confident and somehow happier in himself. This was when he started to take an interest in fashion and drawing designs for clothes. Tom used to say he was "arty-farty" but Anthony never minded. That's when we bought him his first sewing machine, so that he could start to make things out of his designs, but first he had to teach himself how to use it.'

'That young?' asked Ian. 'I'm impressed!'

'Yes, he was so like me in some ways. Once he got his teeth into something, he kept at it and didn't give up. Even at that stage, he used to tell me he would be famous one day. This was his ambition, so he set his sights on college and "something big". He started a course at Wilberforce College in Hull but at the end of the first year he got a place at Park Street, which was the art college. Then, out of the blue, without even telling us he'd applied, he went for an interview for Middlesex University and got a place there to study fashion. He was over the moon.'

'Good for him.'

'Yes, but we were so close, him and me, that I pleaded with him not to go. "Please stay and go to Hull University," I said. "I'm not going to stay in Hull and vegetate," he protested. "If I'm going to be famous I need to go to London. Don't worry, Sezzer. I'll be fine." So off he went to the bright lights he had always craved.'

'He sounds very determined. And yes, that is like you!' Ian laughed.

'He was. He set his sights on fame and fortune. "Mark my words, Sezzer. One day I'll be famous." That's what he used to tell me, time and again.' I paused. 'I took him to the station the day he left for London and watched him go in. I sat in my car and cried – I was so worried. I rang him every day for a month to see if he was OK.'

'And was he?'

'Yes. He made some great friends there and loved every minute. He'd always been quiet and shy as a child – the only time he appeared on a stage was when he was a pumpkin at nursery school. But once he got to university, his confidence exploded. "I can be me. I can be who I like in London," he said. "I'll have my name up in lights. I'll be the best fashion designer the world's ever seen," and he really did think it.'

'So he was definitely ambitious then?'

'Yes, and he worked hard to make it happen, starting with his successful university fashion shows. He sent me a YouTube video of his latest designer outfit being modelled in a Camden show. As well as designing and making the clothes, he had to buy shoes and accessories for the model, so he used to buy them for the show and afterwards return them to the shop for a refund. If the shoes were scuffed, he'd colour any marks in with a felt-tip pen. Once the shoes didn't fit the male model, so Anthony had to lend him his own shoes and walk about among the famous fashion designers in his socks.'

'I hope they didn't have any holes in them.'

'Oh, quite likely! I didn't ask him that. Anyway, it was a good talking point, so when he was chatting to this well-known designer, he asked if he'd like to try on his jacket – one that Anthony had designed and made. The designer agreed and wore it for the rest of the show.'

'Did you ever go to any of his shows?'

'No, I was working and I preferred to go down when we could spend time together. He often used to attend the big, classy fashion shows as well. He knew whose designs he liked best and one of those was Victoria Beckham.

'We used to speak every day on the phone and one day he told me about this one designer – he used to tell me all their names, but I didn't know them, not being into that world. He'd go "Hiya" and wave to the designer and, thinking he must know him, the designer waved back. I said, "Yeah, OK. Why?" and he replied: "Well, they don't know me from Adam now but in five years' time, when I go for an interview with them, they'll feel as if they know me." I couldn't help laughing at his audacity. "OK," I said to him. "There's method in your madness."

'Throughout his four years at uni, he had a great time with his friends. He had a room, sharing a flat above a second-hand clothes shop in Golders Green. He often used to buy clothes in there and alter them to fit him. He loved Golders Green – absolutely loved it and the people were very friendly.

'Anthony's celebrity-chasing wasn't just about designers and models. He rang me once to tell me he'd had a "moment" with Michelle Collins. He spotted her in the supermarket. Apparently, she was buying lemons and he was buying oranges "and we locked eyes," he told me.'

'I suppose there's not much chance of celebrity-chasing in Hull?' asked Ian.

'You're not wrong there!' I laughed. 'Anyway, eventually, he began to lean more towards designing menswear and he set his sights on going into Savile Row tailoring with his sleek new designs. I think he could have made it too.'

'It certainly sounds as if he was going in the right direction,' agreed Ian.

'Yes.' I paused, wistfully. 'I always used to laugh when he told me he was going to be famous but he was right – he is famous now, but for totally the wrong reasons.'

'You've painted a lovely picture of your talented son,' said Ian, somehow sensing that I was welling up. 'It's a terrible thing that his life was cut short so cruelly, with such a promising future to look forward to. But he was obviously greatly loved and admired and I almost feel as if I know him myself now. Thank you for telling me about him.'

Later that day, Paul popped in to cut my grass and I told him Ian had asked what Anthony was like. He didn't mind so much talking about his brother now and I'm sure it did him good not to have to block him out any longer. After he'd finished, we went into the kitchen to get him a drink and we actually started laughing about Anthony and his funny ways.

'I've got to go and have my hair done on Wednesday,' I said. 'Can you imagine how Anthony would have liked me to have it?'

'He'd have said "Don't you dare show me up, and I mean it!"' added Paul.

'Yes. "Get your hair done and some new clothes. And wherever you go, if there's a camera there, don't show me up!" God, he was such a giggle, wasn't he?'

'Yeah,' agreed Paul.

'If he was here, he'd get me to video the clothes I was going to wear so he could have a look to see if they were all right. Then he'd say: "You're not wearing that!", wouldn't he?'

'Oh God, yeah,' exclaimed Paul, laughing.

'He was such a snob for clothes and hair and accessories. Do you remember he'd say "They're cheap clothes," and "Didn't you look at yourself in the mirror?"?'

'Yeah, he'd have driven me nuts!'

It was good to laugh about Anthony with Paul. They say laughter is the best medicine, and it certainly was that day.

Now that things were moving on, with a firm trial date on the calendar, Karl Turner rang to see how I was doing during the waiting period. I told him that Ben from the IPCC had come up to Hull and taken down all my complaints.

'That's good,' said Karl. 'Is there anything I can help you with?'

'Yes, I forgot to ask him what happens now. Is it something he will work on all the way through, until after the trial?'

'Yes. I expect he'll be attending the trial, probably every day.'

'He said he would be and he will want to take Tom's and my statements after it's finished.'

'Right, so he'll be going through everything now in minute detail – all the correspondence, mostly emails these days, the daily records, the call-logs and any other documents they can find. He'll also contact all those non-police people involved, such as the coroner, the London Ambulance Service and anyone else and take statements from them if appropriate. His job is to be meticulous in his investigation, down to the smallest detail.'

We talked a bit more about that and about the way the solicitors and barristers work in the run-up to a large trial such as this, with twenty-nine separate charges. He asked me what the other charges were, so I explained about Port's rape, assault and poisoning victims.

'Lucky survivors, by the sound of it,' he said.

'Yes, that's what I thought.' I paused. 'The most upsetting thing for me is that two of those survivors were attacked before Anthony's death. If they'd only gone and reported Port's crimes then maybe Anthony would be alive now.'

'Yes, that must be hard to take. I'm quite surprised that they haven't charged Port with attempted murder of all the others. I don't see why they haven't.'

'I think the police decided they have enough on him already to make sure he will never get out.'

'Mmm. Well, they're probably right. The Crime Squad know what they're doing. How long do they expect the trial to last?'

'Eleven weeks.'

'Well, that's probably another reason why. The poor jury would never get back to work if it went on longer than that.'

'I don't envy them their jury work,' I said. 'It's going to be tough to get through.'

'That's true. Well, don't forget to give me a ring if there's anything else I can help you with.'

Karl was very good and always meant what he said.

★

I carried on going to work and I think I did pretty well at staying focused on all the varied tasks and challenges that came up day by day. But at home it was a different story. Despite the Crime Squad working so hard on the case, I could not clear my mind of the need to prove my son was murdered. Now at least the killer was in prison and, it seemed, likely to be convicted, but I was very aware that it was not a foregone conclusion, with so many opportunities missed and so much potential evidence lost.

It totally consumed my every waking hour. I wasn't sleeping well, even for me, and I had not managed to sleep through the night even once since the day I heard Anthony was dead, two years before. Every time I went to bed, my brain kicked in again with flashbacks and nightmares. I tried everything from sleeping pills to herbal remedies, to writing down my thoughts before bed. But nothing worked.

As my nightly notes, written at that time show:

As I'm writing this, it's getting nearer and nearer the trial. I chant to myself sometimes: 'Keep going, you're nearly there, you can do this and see it through to the end.' And I will do, even if it breaks me. I have to, for Anthony.

CHAPTER 15

Gross Misconduct?

August–September 2016,
26–27 months after Anthony's death

With only eight weeks to go, I checked my emails one Tuesday morning and was surprised to see the name Ben Williams. It was a familiar name, but for a few seconds, I couldn't remember who he was. Then it struck me. Of course. He was the lead investigator for the IPCC.

I clicked on his name and a very long email came up. He started by explaining that he was writing to update me on their progress so far. Well, this was the first IPCC update I'd had so, although I was at work, I immediately started reading through the email. He explained how they'd been in regular contact with the Homicide and Serious Crime Command and had recently spent several days with them, trawling through literally hundreds of documents and statements which were assisting them in processing their investigation.

Ben said he was gaining a clearer picture of what had or hadn't been done following Anthony's death. He then went on to say: 'We have taken the view that a number of officers may have acted in a way which may justify them being subject to disciplinary proceedings.'

I took a deep breath. Had I read it right? *I* knew it, but it was the first time I had ever seen such an admission in black and white – I was positively euphoric with triumph and relief, that they now showed their recognition in print of what I'd been telling them all along. Finally, after two long, dark years, here was proof that my complaints were justified. I could have jumped for joy and done a dance with anyone . . . but I was at work, in my office, so it didn't seem quite right.

I was counting down the time now, during these last few weeks – counting down with very mixed emotions. On 4 September 2016, my phone beeped and I saw that I had received a text from Ian. My jaw dropped as I read: 'Devil has pleaded not guilty to everything!'

I really did feel as if my heart dropped into my stomach. What did this mean? How could he . . .?

I was just about to look online to see if it had come up on the newsfeeds yet when the phone rang. It was one of the newspapers, and that was only the start. Several others called and tried to persuade me to do an interview with them but I was in no mood for that, so I stopped answering the phone. Luckily, though, I did notice when it was a familiar number and I picked up that one.

'Did you read my text?' Ian asked.

'Yes, I was horrified,' I said. 'And that's not all, the press have been badgering me all morning. What's going on? I thought you had put together a watertight case? How can Port plead not guilty to everything?'

'I know it sounds worrying, but please don't let it get you down as it's just a ridiculous attempt by that devil to claim innocence, against his barrister's advice.'

'But surely it raises doubts. Suppose he manages to persuade the judge and jury? Isn't there a danger that they might believe him?'

'No, not at all. There can be no doubt that he is, at the very least, actively involved in the deaths of Anthony and the other three boys.'

'I know that really but I can't help panicking.'

'OK. I'm going to clear my diary tomorrow and come up to see you so that I can explain all the details and we can talk it all through.'

'Oh,' I breathed a small, tentative sigh of relief. 'That would be great.'

'Can you take the afternoon off?'

'Yes, that's no problem.'

'I'll contact Tom too and see if he can join us.'

Although, at first, I had felt slightly comforted that Ian was coming up specially to explain this new situation, as soon as I put the phone down I felt sick. As I wrote in my diary that night:

This does not sound good. I don't think I'm going to sleep tonight . . . It is now 02:02. I've been in bed reading for hours and trying to get to sleep. I have to be up at 6 a.m. for work. So I've given up and gone downstairs for a cuppa. I'm so tired. My eyes are actually sore. My mind won't stop playing scenarios of why he is driving from London to Hull to speak to us face to face . . . This has been my life for over two years.

Waiting for Ian to arrive at Tom's house that afternoon, to say we were anxious would be an understatement. But we didn't have to wait long. Ian sat us down with a professional yet calm and sympathetic manner.

'I'm sure you must have a lot of questions,' he began. 'But first, let me tell you both what actually happened. As with most charges of murder, the judge had a video-link with the prison, so that Port could be guarded in an interview room there, while the judge explained that he would read out each of the twenty-nine charges in turn, including the four charges of murder.

'"I will read out each charge in full," said the judge. "And each time I will ask you whether you plead guilty or not guilty to that charge. Do you understand?"

'Port nodded, shrugged and said an almost inaudible "yes".

'"You will need to speak up so that I can hear you clearly."

'"Yes," he said, a little louder.

'The judge then read out the charges. To the first murder charge, which was your Anthony's, Port pleaded "not guilty". The judge was astonished as Port's own defence barrister had previously said the accused would be pleading "guilty" to all four murder charges. So he asked Port to repeat his plea, which he did, louder and clearer. He said the same for Gabriel, Daniel and Jack as well.'

'Do you think there's a danger that anyone will believe that?' I asked.

'I cannot predict what any individual will think, especially the men and women of the jury, but I honestly believe that once all the evidence has been presented there can be little if any doubt he killed them all.'

'But is killing the same as murder . . . or manslaughter?'

'That's a good question, Sarah, and it may be an important one for the jury to explore and discuss, but don't forget that the judge will provide them with both oral and written guidance on every relevant point. He will also instruct them to send him any unresolved questions they may have so that he can advise them accordingly.'

'So, was that Port's final word?'

'Well, let me just explain that the judge discussed this unexpected situation with Port's barrister, who affirmed that he had strongly advised Port to plead guilty, as this might carry with it the possibility of a slightly shorter sentence and would cause the families of the victims less distress. For that reason, he asked Port to have another discussion with his barrister, after which Port should be brought into the court to plead a second and final time, directly to the judge.

'His barrister duly made another trip to the prison and explained all the reasons why a guilty plea would be preferable, not least that, despite the delay in starting the investigation, the evidence against him seemed irrefutable.'

'So then what happened?'

'He was taken into court by his guards to make his pleas face to face with the judge. But first the judge reiterated all the reasons why it would be advisable for Port himself, as well as better for the families, if he pleaded guilty. But I'm afraid it made no difference. So his not guilty pleas still stand.'

'So will that make any difference to the trial itself?' I asked.

'Not as much as it might have done.'

'What do you mean?' asked Tom.

'Well, it should normally mean that Port would call as many witnesses as he wished to speak in his defence, which would extend the trial to take up at least the full eleven weeks set aside for it, but, in this case, as far as I am aware, he doesn't have many friends or relations to call on. Worse than that for him, though he doesn't seem to realise it, is that he appears to be making up his own fantasies to relate when it's his turn to speak for himself, just as he did to the police following Anthony's death. He will know all the evidence against him by then, so he'll probably make it up as he goes along. Although I can't deny there might be a smidgeon of doubt, I'm sure that most or all of the jury will see through that straight away.'

Ian went on to give us some examples of the stories he was weaving and the excuses he was making. After a cup of tea and a few more questions from us relating to the trial itself, it was time for him to go.

As Tom closed the front door, we both still felt deflated but less pessimistic. We now knew how the not guilty pleas had happened and were heartened by Ian's confidence and his more positive view of it all. As I wrote in my notebook that evening:

I've just returned from meeting DI Ian Atkinson, my FLO, and feel much better than last night, as it seems the devil has just fitted his defence around the evidence, and certain of his excuses are laughable. Ian said he came up to see us out of politeness as some things need saying face to face, rather than over the phone.

Ian is everything I would have expected a family liaison officer to be.

A week later, I went up to York to meet the prosecuting solicitors who were preparing for the trial. They explained their role in the proceedings, which was mainly gathering evidence and briefing the prosecution barrister. They explained that they wanted me to have the opportunity to ask any questions at all about the case. I suppose the idea was that it was better for me to be fully briefed regarding what to expect during the different stages of the trial. I certainly came home with a greater understanding and a little more optimism but still full of qualms about how I would cope with the trial itself and all that it would reveal – perhaps things I didn't yet know – and with even more apprehension about how it would all turn out.

All this time I had been building up a fear of how I would cope with my emotions during the trial. I had been on antidepressants for much of the time since Anthony died and I felt more confident that I would be able to handle it all if I started back on medication to dull my reactions and feelings. But another part of me knew that my brain would be dulled and my memory affected too. So would I need to keep a clear head, regardless of how I felt? Or should I start back on the medication straight away, to build up some emotional immunity? Every day that brought the trial nearer, my anxiety grew, which decided the dilemma for me and I gradually built up to my previous dose, which felt like having a security blanket wrapped round me.

At the last moment, before I left for London, I received another long email from Ben Williams of the IPCC. It stated that the IPCC's investigation had identified 21 officers in total who, in Ben's opinion, 'may have behaved in a way that would justify the bringing of disciplinary proceedings'. However, by this time, two of them had retired or left the police force, so that left 19, 'nine of whom may have breached the standards of professional behaviour'. Ben went on to explain that, 'these failings, if proven or admitted, could amount to gross misconduct, which has the potential ultimate sanction of dismissal'. The other twelve officers had received notice that 'their conduct is indicated to amount to misconduct'.

My first reaction was shock, because I'd only had dealings with Slaymaker and O'Donnell and I had no idea that there would be so many other officers involved, let alone that so many had failed us and the other families. It seemed like a whole police force of detectives.

My next thought was the fervent hope that the powers that be – the higher rankings – didn't make the lower ranks take all the blame for what they themselves had failed to do.

After a fuller update overall, Ben explained that this shocking indictment of the Barking and Dagenham police would not be released until the day after the trial had finished. So it only had to stay brushed under the carpet for a little while longer . . . and then it would come out. I could only imagine what the press would make of that. It gave me plenty to think about but, after my initial triumphant euphoria, I set it aside for the time being, to focus on getting through the next few days.

Nicky, the therapist from my GP's surgery, had been with me throughout the two years since Dr Chadda had left and she had helped me prepare in the long run-up to the trial. Every week, I would unburden onto her whatever was happening, or not happening, and now was no exception. She was heavily pregnant and her maternity leave was due to start the day after the trial began, so this would be my last session with her. Almost every time, I would arrive and immediately start blurting out to her whatever was bugging me that week.

'Do you know?' she said. 'As soon as you come in and sit down on that chair, I'm on tenterhooks, thinking: "What's been happening to her this week?" Honest to God, nobody else makes me feel like this. It's like reading a crime novel!'

It was true. She had been with me from straight after Anthony's funeral to the beginning of his killer's trial. I was sorry she had to go now but I was getting a new counsellor when I returned home from London. I'd have to learn to cope through the trial itself.

At the end of that day, on the eve of my trip down to London, only thirty-six hours before I would step into that courtroom for the first time, my brain was spinning and my heart thumped relentlessly, shortening my breaths. As I tried to sleep, the last thing I was conscious of was Anthony's smiling face, egging me on, like he used to do when he was a child. I hoped I could do him the justice he deserved. 'I'll do my best,' I said and smiled back at him through my tears.

CHAPTER 16

The Day Before

3 October 2016, 27 months after Anthony's death

I woke up early, with my insides feeling as if they had all been twisted and tied up in knots. My head was spinning with the realisation that this penultimate day had finally dawned. It wasn't a wish or a hope any longer . . . it was about to become a reality.

It was 3 October 2016, the day before the long-awaited and much-needed Old Bailey trial was due to start. Today was the day that could be the beginning of the end of my life of desperation, frustration and two years and four months of unending stress and heartache as I battled the police – the immovable giant that had for so long seemed to be laughing at me.

I knew these feelings would continue to dog my days, at least until the end of the trial, but from now on I would no longer be in control. All I could do was to go and watch and listen. It was bound to be highly emotional at times . . . and I wasn't sure how much emotion I could take.

Yes, I hoped the antidepressants would help to distance me from all the worst traumas but, as well as dreading the details of how Anthony and the other boys died, I had to face the devil himself. I also feared not being alert enough to understand and deal with the ups and downs of the trial. Would I cope better in the midst of a woolly cloud? Or should I stop the medication and open myself up to the horrors and pains that may come with a full understanding of both the lies and the truths? Perhaps the best option was to wait and see.

I felt totally lost and helpless all morning, my bag packed, watching the clock and waiting to leave. It seemed such a huge step to take, out of the security of my own house and into the total unpredictability of a criminal trial that I hoped would finally answer all my questions but might leave me with a whole set of new problems to learn to deal with.

All the way to London, I just wanted to turn around and go back home. I felt so vulnerable. Kate had come with me and tried her best to keep me calm.

'What are you worried about most?' she asked.

'I'm terrified of coming face to face with him – the devil.'

'You mean Port? You know he's just a piece of garbage, don't you?'

'Yes, of course,' I agreed. 'But that doesn't take away the fact that he took my son's life in one of his sick and murderous games. I wish I didn't have to see him at all.'

'You will see him but you don't have to look at him,' she said. 'You can look at the jury, the judge, the barristers, Ian and Tim, the court staff, even the floor – all of them much more interesting and important than that louse.'

Kate did her best to calm me down. She tried everything she could to get me thinking about something else but my emotions were all over the place. 'I feel sick,' I shouted, as

I ran to the toilet. In fact, I was sick three times during the train journey and I felt my chest would explode with the stress of it all. I had waited two and a half years for this.

As we approached London, I thought back over the time since Anthony's body had been found. If only I could turn the clock back to 3.30 in the afternoon in that hotel in Turkey, when I was happy and carefree with Sami, oblivious to anything but relaxing, swimming and enjoying meals or drinks in the warm evening sun with our friends. But I couldn't pretend. Too much had happened since then.

'All the fighting I did with the police at the beginning,' I said, thinking aloud to Kate. 'To get them to do something. All the emails, the phone calls, battling in vain to try to get them to investigate Anthony's death. . .'

'But you didn't give up,' replied Kate. 'Most people would have given up years ago but you're made of stronger stuff.'

'I don't feel it.'

'Well, I'm sure I'm not the only one who can see it. You've got guts. I think it's called courage, and that's what kept you going.'

'I'm glad I contacted our MP. Karl dropped everything to listen and to help.'

'Yes,' agreed Kate. 'He's a good mate, very down to earth, and I suppose that's what makes him such a good constituency MP. He understands ordinary people like us and he always listens.'

'But then, when each of the three other lads' bodies were found, I felt more and more guilty that I couldn't make the police do any investigation,' I paused. 'If only I had made them do something – see the similarities, the links . . .'

'But it must have been at least partly because of you that Jack's sisters were able to add their pressure and that made all the difference.'

'But he needn't have died,' I said in anguish.

'None of them need have died but that wasn't your fault.'

'No . . . but if I'd done more the other three would still be alive.'

'You have to try and block all that out now,' suggested Kate. 'It's all in the past. You have a job to do now, at the trial and afterwards, to make sure it doesn't happen again, to anyone else.'

'Yes, you're right.'

After another short silence I reached a decision that immediately lifted a load off my mind. 'I was planning to be in court to listen to all four of the murder cases,' I said, 'but now I realise I should just go to Anthony's part of the trial – the days when the prosecutor is presenting his evidence.'

'OK?'

'I can't take on all the sordid details for the other three murders,' I explained. 'I can't take on all that as well as everything else. I think my brain would melt. You're right. I can see that now. I couldn't have done any more than I did. I have tried carrying on all this time, pushing and pushing. It was a long, heavy struggle and it very nearly killed me. Then, thank God, Ian and the rest of the Scotland Yard Crime Squad took over and everything changed.'

'It certainly did.'

'So now I have to leave it up to them – the Crime Squad, the lawyers, the judge and the jury. I'll just attend on the days that focus on Anthony and leave the rest to the other boys' parents.'

I felt better for those last few minutes of the journey. But it was a strange thing. As we pulled into King's Cross Station, I stood up and felt so dizzy that I had to sit down again. Kate helped me off the train and the fresh air strengthened me as we made our way to the hotel where we had booked to stay. However, as soon as we arrived at the front entrance, I started shaking, visibly shaking.

'Stand still and take a deep breath,' she said, putting her arm round my shoulders to steady me. She got out her bottle of water. 'Here, have a swig of this.'

That helped.

After we had checked in and taken our stuff to our rooms, we met up with Tom and his friend Graham, who had come to keep him company. By this time, I was so jittery again that we all four went to a local bar for a drink to calm me down. I hadn't had an alcoholic drink for more than two years . . . but that night I just had to have something to relax me.

Ian rang to see if we'd arrived and he said he'd like to come to the hotel to meet Tom and me. 'I'd like to talk to you both before you go to the court in the morning.'

So we arrived back at the hotel just a few minutes before he turned up and went up to my room, away from the bustle in the hotel lounge bar.

'I've been looking through Port's defence,' he said as we sat down, 'and it's laughable.' He smiled. 'He has no witnesses at all, except himself.'

'Really?' I asked, shocked . . . in a good way. 'But what about his sister? I thought she was going into the witness box?'

'Yes, she is,' he replied. 'But she will be speaking for the prosecution.'

'That really is surprising!' I was amazed . . . and yet perhaps she knew him and the things he got up to. 'I'm quite heartened by that.'

'Yes,' agreed Tom. 'Me too.'

Ian leant down to open his briefcase. 'Now, I've brought some things to show you, to prepare you for tomorrow and especially for the evidence the jury will see.'

He took out some stapled typed documents and a thick A4-sized bound document. 'All the families will be given a copy too, so I thought it best you have the chance to see what's in it. This is the Jury Pack,' he said, opening the bound folder at the first page. 'But first, here are Port's statements and those of other people, like his neighbours, who knew him. He didn't seem to have friends as such, just passing acquaintances, with whom he often had abusive sexual relationships.' He leafed through these typed pages.

'And the Jury Pack has all sorts of things in it, like loads of copies of emails, texts and transcriptions of his phone conversations.'

'Including the Joe Dean one with Anthony?' I asked. 'Remember? Joe Dean was the false name Port gave to Anthony when they arranged on the phone to meet?'

'Oh yes,' Ian nodded. 'Well, it's all here. We don't have time to read it all now but you'll be given your own copies tomorrow, to follow what the jury are seeing.' He turned each of the first few pages, then several at a time to show the variety of inclusions. I noticed some maps and diagrams, plus photos of the graveyard and a building flip by.

'There are several sections,' he said, 'and some of it is arranged in the same order the evidence will be presented in the trial.'

Just as he stopped speaking, the pages opened out and the shock hit me. The air left my lungs and my heart turned to stone. I burst into tears, gripped with horror. There it was, lurid on the open page, a photo of Anthony's dead body in the street, propped up against a wall. His face was blacked out, but I knew it was him.

Ian instantly shut the book and apologised profusely but it was too late. I had seen it. It was one of the four photos on that page, done to show the similarities in the way they were positioned. I desperately wished I hadn't seen it. I was traumatised after that, although I suppose it was better that I saw it for the first time privately in my hotel, rather than in the full courtroom the following day.

As he left, Ian warned us about all the press and media that were bound to be outside the Old Bailey when we arrived. 'This is a high-profile case,' he explained. 'They're like gannets, looking to pick up whatever titbits they can, while filming you for their news bulletins. So only talk with them if you want to but I suggest not on the first day.'

Ian needn't have worried. I had no intention of talking to the press, at least not till after it was all over.

When Ian left, we went and found Kate and Graham and all went into the restaurant area for dinner. I didn't feel hungry at all but the others did and I didn't want to sit on my own in the bar or my room so I joined them. We all ordered something off the menu and I told the others about the Jury Pack and the shocking photo of Anthony.

'Oh no,' gasped Kate. 'How awful for you.'

When dinner came, the others tucked in but I had no appetite at all, so I basically had the odd nibble and pushed the rest around my plate for a bit. How could I eat after seeing that image? I felt sure it would be etched on my mind for the rest of my life.

As we parted on the stairs, I had another phone call from Ian. 'Would you be willing to meet the other boys' families tomorrow?'

I hesitated.

'I think it might be helpful for you all, so that you can share your impressions of what's going on . . . and only they will understand how you feel, and vice versa.'

'OK,' I agreed.

I hardly slept at all that night. I tossed and turned, full of apprehension and dread. Tomorrow I would have to look at that devil when he entered the dock. This was the culmination of everything that had occupied my mind and my days since I switched on my phone in Turkey in June 2014 to hear the worst news of my life.

Countless questions and worries filled my mind but worst of all was that horrific image of my beloved Anthony, lying dead like dross in the street.

CHAPTER 17

The Trial Begins

4–7 October 2016, the first week of the trial

The day that I thought would never happen had finally arrived. Tuesday, 4 October 2016, the beginning of the first day of the trial of Anthony's killer. Kate came with me to meet China and Kiera, both of whom wanted to attend that first day with me. I was really pleased they could come but we were all very nervous – and not just because of the trial; even the thought of entering the Old Bailey was daunting.

As we walked round the last corner, the whole street was a mass of press, media, their cameras and microphones . . . all ready to pounce on us.

I froze. Then I did the only thing I could think of. I called Ian.

'Morning Sarah. Are you on the way?'

'Yes, just round the corner,' I said. 'You were right about the press.'

'Best thing is just to ignore them if you can. Just walk straight past them.'

'How do we get in?'

'The entrance is about halfway down the street that's called Old Bailey. It's quite a small entrance for such a large building but that's so they can security check everyone who comes in. I'll meet you there.'

So the four of us walked down the left-hand side pavement, pretending we were just members of the public. It was very stressful, trying not to catch anyone's eye and weaving our way between them. Luckily, that first day, most of them didn't yet know who we were, though a few of the reporters had obviously done their homework and recognised me, coming closer with their mics. I just ignored them and walked right past.

We slipped inside the narrow doorway, past the first guard and showed our IDs, then put our bags down to be searched and scanned as we walked through a glass security pod. Next we were asked to show our IDs again and explain why we were there – which case and court number and who was meeting us. Finally, through another narrow area, past another security guard, we were through. I thought all this was gruelling but they told us we would soon get used to it.

Once through, we found a smiling Ian waiting for us at the bottom of a wide stone staircase. My first impression was of a cool atmosphere, echoing and steeped in history, There was cold grey stone and dark wood panelling all around us as we reached the right floor. It was quite overwhelming. Ian pointed to the far end: 'That's where Court 16 is, but first I'm going to take you up to meet the other families. I'm sure you will see quite a lot of each other over the next few weeks.'

Daniel's father and stepmother were there, together with Jack's parents and his two sisters. We all said hello, trying to cover our anxiety with nervous smiles. Of course we'd read about each other in the press reports but it felt good to meet them at last. Gabriel's family lived in Slovakia, so they weren't able to be there. In a way, I almost envied his mother that she would not have to go through all this trauma but then I knew I had to do it. It was what I had worked so hard for, finally coming to fruition.

Ian then took China, Kiera, Kate and me to a side room, with Tom and Graham, to tell us some of the important procedural points so that we'd have a better understanding of what was going on.

'You've got Judge Openshaw,' said Ian. 'He's one of the best.'

'Oh good,' I replied, trusting Ian's judgement.

'In court, things are always done a certain way,' he explained. 'I expect you'll think that rather archaic to start with but it works and you'll soon get used to it. The jury benches will be empty this morning as the jury selection is still taking place.'

'How long will that take?' I asked.

'Well, it may take longer than usual,' he answered. 'Because it's going to be such a long trial, up to eleven weeks, it will take longer to pick them. For example, some may be sole carers or have young children, while others may have serious illnesses needing treatment, or precarious work situations, or protected jobs, such as teachers or doctors, whose absence for so long might cause harm to children's education or patients' health.'

He explained that he and Tim would be there for us every day, supporting me, and Tom too, whenever he could come.

However, like Sami, Tom would only be able to attend occasionally. Fortunately, my bosses were very supportive of my taking leave throughout the trial.

Next, the witness protection people came to see us and explained their role. A Met press officer from Scotland Yard also came in and recommended how we could best cope with the inevitable media crush outside and any approaches they made to us for interviews. 'Just refer them to me if you like,' he suggested. 'And let me know if they're making a nuisance of themselves so that I can make sure it doesn't happen again. They know I'll move them on if they do.' He smiled.

'Right,' said Ian, getting up. 'Are you ready? It's time to go.'

'Yes,' I agreed. In fact, ready or not, I had to do this. If only my head didn't hurt so much or my heart thump so loudly, or at least, that's how it felt.

'We'll be in Court 16,' said Ian, walking alongside as we approached the throng waiting outside the closed courtroom door. 'The court staff won't open up until ten thirty on the dot.'

We joined the gaggle of people standing near the doors, most of them smartly dressed, some of them talking to each other. Standing a little away from them were two men in gowns and wigs and some other men in suits, carrying sheaves of papers and talking amicably together.

There was a large open area outside the courts with lofty ceilings, marble floors and upholstered benches between low pillars. The men and women sitting here or standing over by the tall windows seemed quite relaxed.

'They're the press and media,' said Ian. 'That group over there is from the BBC.'

Just then, a woman in a black gown opened the door and stood aside for us all to file in. At this point we were separated. As family, Tom, Kate and I were directed to the seats on the floor of the courtroom, while Anthony's friends, China and Kiera, plus Tom's friend Graham, were shown upstairs to the public gallery, which quickly filled up. The lawyers took their places and the journalists theirs, either on the press benches, adjacent to the jury benches, or at the back of the room, facing the judge. I spotted Tim across the room and Ben from the IPCC sitting down at a desk with a colleague, both of them writing notes already. The jury benches were empty but I tried to imagine what it would look like with the jury in their places. It wouldn't be long before we would see them.

I looked around and saw the barristers in their wigs and gowns with the solicitors sitting alongside them, facing banks of lever-arch files stretching the lengths of their desk. The courtroom itself was surprisingly modern for such a venerable building but probably more practical than some of the older courtrooms still awaiting renovation.

There was a hush as we waited, though I wasn't sure what for. Ian was sitting next to me to guide me through everything and make sure I was OK. He leant across and whispered to me: 'Brace yourself. They're bringing Port in. Just look away if you want.'

I did brace myself because I was going to see him for the first time, live: the evil scum who took my baby. But I deliberately didn't turn away. I intended not just to see but to look at this evil creature, to make him look at me, to see my pain.

Raised up along the back of the courtroom was what looked like a long glass box, floor to ceiling. A door at the far end slowly opened and I held my breath. I'd seen Port's photo in the newspapers as well as online. I'd seen his apparently youthful but sickly face and thick blond hair, which I discovered was a toupé, but I wasn't prepared for what appeared through that doorway – a pitiful, shambling, ugly bald man, who looked far older than his pictures and his real age of forty-one. He came in, handcuffed and held by two prison guards who took him to his seat and sat either side of him from then onwards, throughout the trial.

I couldn't believe how ugly he was – not just his looks but as a person. He was ugly right through. It was like facing the devil, albeit stripped of his malicious powers.

I stared hard at him, trying to penetrate his evil gaze, willing him to turn and look at me. All I was thinking was: 'Look me in the eye, you bastard. Look me in the eye.' But he never did, not once. He just sat there, impervious to his victims' families, with a weak smile on his face, as if he was sitting on a bench in the park with not a care in the world. Maybe he saw us merely as an audience.

Just then, the court usher, another woman in a black gown, entered from a door in the far corner of the platform which held the judge's bench.

'All rise!' she said in a loud, clear voice and we did. Through that door came the judge himself, in his wig and full regalia and sat down on his throne. Well, it wasn't really a throne, but it might as well have been.

We all sat down again and the judge, looking down at his papers, read out the title of the case and listed all the charges in turn. Then he explained that, because selection of the jury would take all day, the court would be adjourned till 10 a.m. the following morning.

By this time, it was nearly lunchtime so, once we could leave the courtroom, after the judge had gone, we all went down the stone stairs and outside to face the press again. Somehow, we'd forgotten since our arrival that we would have to get past them again. All of them pointed their cameras at us, hungry for something to put on the evening news.

So China, Kiera, Kate and I put our heads down and went off in the opposite direction to look for somewhere quiet to go. But some of the journalists followed us and every time we tried to go into a cafe or bistro, they stalked us. They hung out, looking in through the windows, hoping to persuade us to talk when we came out. That first day was awful, so we ignored them as best we could and walked away from the area.

Day two wasn't any better. In fact, it was just as daunting as day one, from the persistence of the media crush at the front, to going through security, then into court again. The procedure was just the same as yesterday's but of course, this time we would be joined by the jury. After Port had been brought back in, the woman usher on the door led the jury in, one by one in single file, right through the courtroom, past Port's glass cage and the press benches, to file into their seats on the jury benches. There were two empty rows to fill and I was desperate to see them, who they were, what they looked like, how they dressed, their ages – everything I could glean about them.

As the jury sat down, I studied them intently – ten women and two men. I was really glad there were ten women. I don't know why. I suppose I thought it would make a difference. Maybe women are softer and would be more sympathetic to a mother's plight, I thought. But I'm sure they were given strict instructions by the judge before they came in to make sure they kept a clear mind and not let their judgement be clouded by their feelings.

I watched their expressions as they sat down. It was terrible having to put so much trust in strangers. I reckoned their ages ranged from early twenties to mid-sixties or more and they were all shapes and sizes. They had a wide variety of hair colours and styles; some wore glasses, some wore lots of jewellery and others very little. They really did look like any random group of people you might see walking along a street. And that's what they were – ordinary people put into an extraordinary situation for a concentrated period. The rest of the time they were somebody's grandma, somebody's husband – just Joe Bloggses getting on with their own lives . . . until the jury service letter arrived through their letterboxes.

The judge explained to the court that each of the prosecution and defence barristers would make their opening statements, starting with the prosecution. I tried to focus my thoughts so that I could listen and take note of all the different strands of evidence Scotland Yard's Crime Squad had been able to find.

The prosecution barrister opened by reading and briefly explaining each of the twenty-nine sickening charges. It was all rather lengthy and complicated, though it sounded very well reasoned. The horrors of Port's alleged behaviours piled up into a mountain of revulsion before we'd even got to the end of the murder charges.

I turned my head to see Port's reactions but he just sat there, disinterested and glazed over, as if they weren't talking about him at all. He showed no emotion whatsoever. I turned back to look at the jury and noticed that several of the female jurors had their hands to their mouths in shock and disgust. I was glad it was already affecting them so much as it showed they could now already feel some of what we had felt. No doubt they were already forming their own opinions about this squalid individual.

It was hard to listen to some of the sordid things the prosecutor had to include, so I zoned out at those moments. However, I worked as hard as I could the rest of the time to follow his arguments, though I found it mentally exhausting – listening while I tried to watch the jury. I just couldn't take it all in. I wondered whether that was because of the antidepressants, numbing my senses. Of course, that was what I had intended them to do . . . but now I was not so sure.

On the third day, Thursday, 6 October, again we had to run the gauntlet of reporters and cameramen. They had worked out who we were by then, so the cameras were on us every time we appeared. During the lunch adjournments, we didn't have very long but we were desperate to get away from them all. So Tom and I found a cafe that we thought might be safe for a relax and a drink but a producer had followed us and came in. She introduced herself and, before we could even tell her we didn't want to speak to her, several reporters who had followed her burst in and then we discovered two more who had earlier sat themselves at the table next to us and listened into our conversation without us realising who they were. Luckily we weren't discussing anything to do with the trial or it might have been splashed all over the front pages within hours. So we couldn't even get out of the Old Bailey for fifteen minutes of peace and quiet.

We knew then that we would have to be ultra-careful, so we had our coffee breaks in the family room in the witness suite, where the other families were gathered and we soon got chatting to each other. To start with, while we were still getting to know each other, it was all quite polite: 'How are you?' 'Are you OK?' 'Did you come by train?' and all that sort of thing. Then it became more about our shared experiences, the awful time we'd all had, the barristers and, of course, the journalists. Before long we were quite relaxed with each other.

We gave all the jurors nicknames, such as 'curly-haired lady' and 'girl with big boobs' and started to become obsessed with them, their reactions to everything, how they looked, what they wore and looking out for their facial expressions.

'What do you reckon the teacher one was thinking?' or, 'Did you see curly-hair's face when she looked at the photos?' or 'Spiky-hair looked stony-faced.'

One of the police officers said to me: 'You can never tell what the jury will decide by looking at them. You might think, seeing their different reactions, that no way will they agree about anything . . . and then they come back with a quick unanimous verdict. You just can't tell.'

We did light-heartedly speculate about the jurors and what their normal lives might be like but in the courtroom they were the VIPs to me – twelve people who could change my life, one way or the other, forever.

The prosecution barrister continued his opening statement over the next two days. To start with, I listened as intently as I could but I found it very difficult to sustain my concentration, which was disappointing because I could tell it was all very positive for us. It was clear that his continuous speech was just a way of life to him. He took it all in his stride and delivered it faultlessly. I did find it frustrating – all the stopping for adjournments and restarting again. I just wanted them to get on with it. However, I think it would probably have been even more difficult to follow what he was saying had we not had regular brain-breaks, so I suppose they knew what they were doing.

The prosecutor's opening statement took three days to complete, ending on the Thursday afternoon. From what I had taken in, it seemed thoroughly convincing to me. How could the defence barrister possibly counter that?

The judge announced the court would not sit on the Friday. This news was well received all round and even the jury members were having trouble concealing their smiles, so I went off to Sami's for a long weekend with him and our friends at his restaurant, well away from all the court rigmarole and stress, which gave me a very welcome break and my brain a much-needed rest.

But the apprehension was still there – the fear that somehow the devil would wriggle out of it. I could only hope and trust that the prosecuting barrister's case against Port would be as convincing as his opening summary.

CHAPTER 18

Shock Revelations

10–14 October 2016, the second week of the trial

Now it was the turn for the defence barrister to present his opening statement. Again, we dutifully sat and listened as he went through the arguments he was going to make and the evidence he would present. As Ian had mentioned, there were no witnesses at all for the defence . . . other than Port himself. Judging from his face and his demeanour, not to mention what we knew of his lies when he was convicted for perverting the course of justice, I didn't feel too worried about his own testimony.

I sat and listened as the barrister started off, knowing that even he had strongly advised Port to plead guilty. He listed some facts and signposted which way he would go with his questioning in this case. But the more I heard, the more anxious I became. This barrister was clearly skilful and very persuasive.

The judge adjourned the proceedings for a coffee break and to have a meeting with the two barristers. As we all filed out, I turned to Ian and voiced my concerns. 'When the prosecution finished his opening statement, I was 110 per cent convinced the devil was going to prison. Then the defence began and now I'm panicking.'

'That's a totally natural response,' he replied. 'But don't worry – we've got him.'

When we were let back into the courtroom again, we all sat down and waited, as usual, for Port to be led back up from the cells and into the glass dock and the jury to file back through and take their places on the benches. Finally the usher called 'All rise' and in came the judge. There was a moment's hush, then the judge nodded to the barristers who both stood up. He then announced to everyone present that he and both the prosecution and the defence barristers had agreed that, in the absence of any other witnesses for the defence, the prosecution had only the defendant, Stephen Port, to cross-examine. Therefore, to shorten the trial and thereby reduce the distress of the victims' families, the schedule for the rest of the trial would be realigned.

I looked up at Port to see whether that provoked any reaction in him but he was his usual, impassive self, as if he hadn't understood the importance of what the judge had said. Perhaps he didn't, or perhaps he wasn't even listening, but there was no discernible reaction at all. Of course, we and all the other families were quietly jubilant, smiling at each other in our joint relief.

However, it only took us a few minutes to realise that, even if the case for the defence would be quite short, it would still be harrowing to listen to the prosecution witnesses going through all the sordid things that happened to our boys, and the other survivor-victims, all over again.

The defence barrister picked up his papers and continued to read on through his opening statement. He finished at lunchtime, at which point the judge announced that, to allow the barristers time to adjust to the new plan, the court would not sit that afternoon. This meant that I could now go back to Sami's to spend some time with him and our friends at his restaurant. It was indeed a great antidote at this stage before all the real traumas began. Assuming that the prosecution would work its way through in chronological order, I worked out that Tuesday would be taken up with the cases of Port's first survivor-victims, so that meant Anthony's case would probably start on Wednesday.

I booked the travel and hotel for me and Kate for Wednesday and was happily relaxing with some of Sami's customers at lunchtime on Tuesday when my phone rang. It was Ian to give me a run-down of what had gone on in the morning and tell me that they had moved faster than expected, so Anthony's case was due to start after the lunch adjournment, in about an hour.

'Oh no!' I exclaimed. 'We didn't think that would be until tomorrow.' I paused. 'Is China there?'

'Yes, she'll be the prosecution's first witness this afternoon.'

'Oh no,' I repeated. 'I'm so annoyed with myself for getting this wrong. Will you please tell her I'm very sorry I can't get there in time and I'll be thinking of her. I'm sure she'll do very well and I hope one of you will tell me all about it later.'

'Yes, of course. I expect both of us will.'

'Thanks Ian. You're a star.'

I did look up the trains online to see if I could get there from our distant part of Essex, but it was impossible to make it in time, so instead I watched the minutes tick by till two, thoroughly annoyed with myself that I was missing what I most wanted to be there for.

Ian phoned me first, straight after the afternoon session had finished.

'Hi Sarah, China's going to call you later about the details of her session in the witness box but I've rung first to give you a quick update on what has happened so far in Anthony's part of the proceedings.'

'Thanks. I wish I'd been there.'

'Are you planning to come to court tomorrow?'

'Yes. Why? Will that be too late?'

'No, I was hoping you'd be here as there is still quite a lot about Anthony to get through, so at least the morning and possibly more. OK, I'm going to start by telling you what you probably already suspect—'

'That it was all quite upsetting?'

'Yes, and there may be some information that you didn't know so please forgive me if I cause you any distress, but I feel it's important that you know it from me and China before you see it splashed across the front pages or on the TV news.'

'Yes, I agree. I'm at Sami's at the moment, so I'm not alone.'

'I think you knew that Stephen Port had previously been a gay male escort?'

'Yes. Very sleazy.'

There was a brief silence. 'Well, China took the witness stand and the prosecuting barrister asked her to tell the court how she knew Anthony, did she know him well and for how long? So she explained all that and said he was the best friend anyone could have. Next he asked her to talk about him, what was he like. So she described how funny, loyal and bright he was, how well he was doing at university and what a great future he had. She also said how careful he was about strangers and always checked everything out as thoroughly as he could before going to meet anyone new.'

'Well, that's all true,' I agreed, proudly.

'Then she answered some more questions, mainly about whether he took any drugs, what they were, when and where and so on.' He paused. 'You already know that, don't you?'

'Yes, he was always very open about the poppers he took and the cannabis he smoked only with his university friends. Was there anything else?'

'Nothing much,' he replied. 'She said he'd tried ecstasy too, but no hard drugs.'

'That's pretty well what I thought,' I agreed.

'Then the barrister asked her to explain what happened leading up to the evening he went to meet a man in Barking,' Ian continued. 'She told them what you already know, about Anthony telling her and Kiera he was going to meet a guy called Joe Dean and he showed them the man's photo on a gay dating app called Grindr that he had on his phone. The barrister asked if it was a clear photo and she said it was. So then China was asked whether she could see that man in the courtroom. She said "Yes," and pointed at him in the dock. That was a key moment. "He had thick blond hair in the photo," she explained, "but I think he was wearing a toupé." Then she went on to tell the court what Anthony said when he arranged to meet up with them again two days later and gave them this man's contact details, not knowing they were false, and he actually said the words: "In case I get killed."'

'Yes, that's all as she told me, straight after it happened.'

'But there is one thing that I believe she may not have told you.'

I went cold. 'What do you mean?'

'There's no easy way to say this, Sarah . . . the man Anthony was going to see had promised to pay him £800 for sex and staying over that night, as a male escort.'

'WHAT?' I exploded at poor Ian. 'China had told me about the money that particular night, but I assumed it was a bribe offered by that beast — a one-off, a kind of lure from that devil to get Anthony into his clutches.' I stopped to try and think more clearly. 'No! That's preposterous. Anthony wasn't a sex worker, a male escort or whatever you want to call it . . . that can't be right. He would never do that as a job — it's too demeaning, too dangerous. You must have misunderstood.'

'I'm afraid not, Sarah. The barrister asked China several supplementary questions to clarify that. It's probably best if you ask China herself about it.'

'I certainly will.'

'Well, the rest you already know. China will tell you all the details.' He paused. 'I'm sorry to have upset you. I'm sure talking with China will help you to understand everything much better.'

'Yes, thanks Ian. That is hard to take on board but I know you were right to tell me yourself, so I appreciate it.'

'Are you still aiming to come in first thing tomorrow?'

'Yes, but I can't pretend I'm not anxious.'

'Yes, I know. It might be equally hard to take,' he fore-warned me, 'but I'll be with you all the way.'

'I know. Thanks.'

I was aghast – completely in shock as I put down the phone.

I worked out roughly when China would get home so that I could ring her when she could talk privately. But she beat me to it.

'Ian phoned me earlier,' I said.

'Yes, he told me he would, to give you a quick update.'

'Most of what he told me we'd talked about a few times before. But there was one thing . . .'

'And I know what it is, and I'm sorry it had to come out like that. I should have told you before that Anthony sometimes worked as a male escort. To be honest, I didn't want to upset you unnecessarily and I didn't realise it would be important as far as the trial is concerned. I'm sorry.'

'You did tell me about the money but, as I told Ian, I always assumed that was just a one-off that night and I know Port didn't have enough money to pay Anthony anyway, which should have rung alarm bells with the police . . . I tried to make them see it, but that's history now.'

'Well, the thing was, I didn't think Anthony would have wanted me to tell you.'

'Yes, I know China. You were only being a loyal friend to him, keeping his confidences so that they could go to the grave with him . . . except that they couldn't. But I can't help being shocked about it. Did he actually call himself a male escort?'

'Yes. He'd done it about ten times before, always being very careful to check out all the details to protect himself to the nth degree. You know what he was like.'

'Yes. But why? Why did he do it?'

'He needed the money. His student debt after four years was over £40,000. He was always making up his new designs for models to display at fashion shows and then there were all the accessories to buy. And he was so busy with all that, he didn't have time to take on a regular student job.' She tried to reassure me: 'It's so usual, being an escort. It's just the norm in London. Quite a lot of students do it,' she explained, in an effort to put it into context.

I said nothing. I didn't know what to say.

I arranged to meet China where I was meeting Kate the following morning, to go into court together and we ended the call.

But as I put down my phone, everything in my head changed. I was furious with Anthony for putting himself in so much danger, having sex with strangers for money. That's what sent my mind into a turmoil. If it was anybody else, I would have said it was a mercenary, sleazy thing to do. But how could I put or even accept Anthony as being in that category? He wasn't. He couldn't be. Was it really quite common for students to earn money as escorts? Surely not, I thought, with so much risk involved. It seemed completely shocking to me but maybe it wouldn't be quite so awful if it could be regulated.

At no point had Anthony's sexuality ever bothered me . . . but this? I was in emotional overload for several minutes until Sami came and found me. He took one look at me, tears running down my cheeks, and gave me a big, warm hug – just what I needed most.

The following morning, we all met as planned and walked through the throng into the now familiar security circuit inside the Old Bailey, then up the wide stone staircase. The public gallery was packed that morning and there were several journalists in the courtroom. It was all rather daunting.

Ian told me it would be the pathologist's turn to take the witness stand. I was very apprehensive about this and almost ducked out of the morning's session altogether but I knew I had to hear the truth. My antidepressants were doing a good job of numbing my mind and dulling most of my emotions but I feared how I might react when it came to the details of Anthony's body. Ian sat down one side of me and Kate the other, with my sister-in-law, Sue, next to her. I suppose Ian could see or sense my increasing anxiety.

'If it gets too distressing and you want to leave at any time,' he whispered, 'just go and I'll come with you. OK?'

'Yes.'

The pathologist stepped into the witness box, introduced himself and stated his qualifications, then explained his involvement in Anthony's case. He read from his own notes most of the time, after which I assumed the prosecution barrister would ask him questions to elicit more detailed analysis. I thought I'd probably cope for the first part, so I sat back and listened, trying hard to concentrate as he began with a dateline, followed by Anthony's details – height, weight . . . all that sort of thing. So far, so good.

'Can you tell the court,' asked the prosecutor, 'the state of Anthony's clothes when his body was found?' He then referred the jury to the page in their pack where I'd seen that terrible photograph, the night before the trial started. The jury all turned up the page number, showing various expressions of shock or dismay. The pathologist gave them a few seconds, then began his answer, telling the court what items of clothing Anthony was wearing, and how he was wearing them: 'A loose T-shirt, several sizes too large for his slim body . . .'

Well, I knew for a start that the T-shirt could not have been his. My son would only wear skin-tight T-shirts. He hated anything baggy. Even as a child, he had been pedantic about that.

'Also, the T-shirt was rucked up at the front.'

'What does that suggest to you?' asked the barrister.

'That he was dragged along the ground.' That gave me a shiver.

'His underpants were on inside-out and back-to-front.'

'Did that surprise you?'

'Yes, it did,' said the pathologist.

'Can you tell us, in your experience, what that suggests to you?'

'It strongly suggests to me that somebody else had dressed him, very quickly and without any concern for his welfare.'

I shuddered, and there was a collective gasp round the courtroom. I looked at the devil but he was expressionless. Members of the jury, on the other hand, had a range of expressions that showed they were clearly processing that news.

This was something the police had passed on to me – the way his pants were when he was found – but without any judgement of what it might mean. I had protested to

Slaymaker at the time, I remember, that, as a fashion student, Anthony was always very particular about his clothes and how he wore them but he had just shrugged and said nothing.

'And can you tell me about your examination of Mr Walgate's body at the time of death?' asked the barrister.

Oh no, I thought. I really didn't want to hear this, but I had to.

'His body was found in the early hours of that morning,' replied the pathologist. 'He was pronounced dead at the scene by the doctor who attended with the ambulance crew and was then taken to the mortuary. It was here, a few hours later, that I was able to examine him.' He paused to turn the page. 'At this point, I should say that the doctor's report, included herein, states that Mr Walgate had been dead for about eight hours, judging by the stage of rigor mortis setting in.'

That shocked me. Why hadn't anyone mentioned it before? I'd had no idea he'd been lain there so long . . . then I realised that perhaps he had died in Port's flat and, eight hours later, been taken out to the street. I tried to remember what version of Port's lies the Barking police had first accepted. I thought they had said that the scum had found him still alive in his bed, but ill, or was it the version where he said Anthony had been ill when he left for work but was already dead when he got back from his eight-hour shift? Yes, I thought that was it, but I could easily confirm it with Ian later.

Now things became even more uncomfortable as the barrister asked the pathologist whether there were any marks on Anthony's body.

'Yes,' replied the pathologist and read from his notes. 'There were fourteen marks on Mr Walgate's body.' That was when I got up and ran. Kate tried to follow me, but I'd pressed her arm down, wanting her to stay and tell me later what I needed to know. She got the message but Ian came after me and caught up with me outside the court. I wanted to scream but I knew I couldn't. Ian put his arm lightly round me and directed me up to the family room where I slumped in a seat, filled with horror at what I'd just heard.

'I asked them about that,' I blurted out to Ian as he sat down in the chair next to mine. 'Slaymaker and O'Donnell. I asked them both when they came to see Tom and me. Bare-faced, they both assured me that there were no marks on Anthony's body. "No marks at all," repeated O'Donnell. That has given me such reassurance over these past two and a half years . . . and now this. Fourteen marks. Were they bruises, or scratches, or open wounds? Had he been physically attacked, stabbed or whatever?'

'I suppose they thought it easiest for them just to tell you what you wanted to hear,' suggested Ian.

'Or get me off their backs, more like!'

'Yes, I'm not making any excuses for them. It was very wrong to tell you a lie like that.'

'You're telling me. One of the many lies they told me. I'm fuming. From day one they assured me he didn't have a mark on him . . . and now . . .' I was almost speechless with rage.

At this point, the lovely witness support ladies came over with a hot, sweet drink for me and one for Ian too. I can't remember whether it was tea or coffee but it did calm me down a bit. But then the pain hit me – the horror of all those body marks.

'Did you know about this?' I asked Ian.

'Yes. I'm sorry. I would have told you months ago but I thought you already knew about it – both the clothing and the marks.'

'It's not your fault,' I reassured him. 'You've been a wonderful FLO and marvellous at explaining things. I don't blame you for any of this. Quite the contrary.'

'To answer your questions,' he continued, 'no, Anthony wasn't stabbed or injured deliberately in any way. The marks the pathologist was talking about were all to do with the way he was lifted or moved and positioned. So, for example, he had bruises under both his arms where Port held him by the armpits and dragged him along the floor, perhaps knocked him against a door surround, then outside, over the front doorstep and along the concrete out to the street. What a policewoman who attended the scene first noticed and described as a 'footprint' on Anthony's chest was almost certainly not a footprint at all but a pattern of bruising that can be present after someone has stopped breathing for a while – in this case, eight hours.'

'Oh, well at least he wasn't deliberately attacked, but I shall never forget the shock of finding out, only now, that Anthony's body was not unblemished, as I had been led do believe.'

I didn't go back into the courtroom that morning. I couldn't. Kate later filled me in on what I had missed but fortunately there was nothing as shocking as that. At lunchtime that day, we all went out through the press scrum and off in a different direction, in search of somewhere more private. That's when we turned a corner and there, in the middle of London, found a pub with a walled beer garden. We sat ourselves down with our drinks and snacks, talking everything through – relatively quietly, but without having to look out for listening ears or telescopic lenses.

I noticed Kate and Sue in deep conversation at the far side of the garden but they stopped when they saw me looking, so I asked them outright what they were talking about. They looked a bit embarrassed and unsure what to say.

'It's just about this morning,' started Kate. 'We wondered when we should tell you how Anthony got those bruises and scratches . . . or whether it would upset you too much to tell you today.'

'Oh, that's all right,' I assured them. 'I know you were just being protective but I asked Ian and he told me.'

'I've written some notes about it as well,' said Kate. 'I'll let you have those later if you like.'

That pub garden became our haven over the next few weeks, whenever we attended court, despite increasingly chilly weather and the occasional drizzle. I had intended to stay on for the rest of the week but now I knew it would do my head in, having to hear any more right now. I'd had enough, so I went back to stay with Sami for the rest of the week. I needed the hugs and the normality of being there and I knew Ian would continue to update me, before I had to read it on the internet or the news hoardings.

It was just after this, while I was taking a break at Sami's, that I had a call from someone called Daniel Clark-Neal, *This Morning* presenter and Rylan's husband, asking me whether we could meet and discuss the possibility of my doing a documentary with him. Knowing who he was and having seen him on TV, I rang him back and agreed to meet the following evening. I wasn't keen to do any media interviews at this stage, but this seemed a bit different and I felt I should at least find out more about it before saying no.

'I've been wanting to do this as a TV documentary,' he explained when we met. 'Ever since I first heard about the Grindr killer. I want it to be a documentary about gay dating sites and the dangers of using them,' he explained.

I had been undecided up to that point, but now that he had told me what it would be about, I knew I had to do it, to warn young men and women. I wanted to tell them: 'You are not indestructible. Stay safe. Don't put your families through all this.'

'What do you think?' he asked me. 'Are you up for it?'

'Yes, I am,' I said. 'I want to help these young people, whether they're gay or straight, to learn from what happened to Anthony and the other boys. I don't want any other mothers to have to go through what I have had to face and struggle with over these past two and a half years.'

'Great!' he said with a grin. 'Let's set up some dates for filming.'

'When?'

'As soon as you can fit it in,' he replied.

So we booked some days in a week when I didn't particularly want to be in court. It was when all the other survivor-victims' cases would be heard and Ian had warned me that might be heavy going for me, what with everything else I had to focus on. I had felt bad about that at first because every one of those young men mattered as much as those who were killed. But Ian was right. I couldn't take on all the worries of the world. I already had enough of my own.

It was during those few days away from the Old Bailey that I made the decision to wean myself off the antidepressants. I wanted to be able to think more clearly again, to focus better and to gain a fuller understanding of everything that was going on, instead of lurching from one difficult thing to another, blurred by a medication-induced fog.

But was this wise? I still wasn't sure.

CHAPTER 19

Too Much to Bear

17–21 October 2016, the third week of the trial

This trial was so sick and sordid at times that, to avoid being unnecessarily stressed or upset, I was now carefully picking and choosing the days when I'd attend. Ian always told me which parts of the trial would be happening the next day or week so I could plan my life round it.

Out of curiosity, if nothing else, I definitely wanted to be there on the day the devil's sister, Sharon Port, would be in the witness box. So, on this particular Thursday, Kate came with me and we met up with China and Kiera before braving the press and media to enter the relative sanctuary of the Old Bailey . . . or so we thought.

Today was supposed to be all about the second boy killed by Port – Gabriel Kovari from Slovakia. None of his family could attend so I had the feeling that somebody should be there to represent them. In fact, members of all three of the UK boys' families also attended court that day for the same reason. As usual, I sat with Ian beside me and Kate on the other side as the proceedings began. After a brief statement from the prosecution barrister, he called Sharon Port to the witness stand.

I had been curious to see what she looked like but there was little family likeness between her and her evil brother, though of course he was quite bald and looked spooky, whereas she had thick, long dark hair and looked quite ordinary, except for the puce-coloured flouncy top she was wearing.

I had to remind myself of this unusual situation in which she was not a witness for her brother's defence, as might have been expected, but a witness for the prosecution, giving testimony that could potentially help to convict her own brother of murder and put him in prison for a very long time – hopefully for life.

'How often did you see your brother?' asked the prosecution barrister.

'Rarely,' she replied.

'How often is rarely, would you say?

'No more than once or twice a year.'

'And how often do you speak with him on the phone?'

'Only occasionally. I suppose it would normally be once every few weeks or months.'

'Thank you,' he said, picking up a sheet of paper and scanned it for a date.

Meanwhile, she brushed a loose strand of hair back from her face and shot a glance at her brother in his glass cage. He gave her a hint of a smile, as if he really didn't understand the seriousness of his situation, of her testimony being for the prosecution. It seemed as if it was all a game to him. I shuddered at the thought.

Next, the barrister established that the record on Port's phone showed the date as 27 August 2014 when they had spoken on the phone. 'Was this correct?' he asked.

'Yes, as far as I can remember.'

'And who rang who?'

'He rang me.'

'Who is "he"?'

'My brother, Stephen Port.'

'Was this usual?'

'No, it was usually me ringing him. But when I saw his number and picked up the phone, it wasn't his usual voice.'

'What do you mean?'

'He seemed stressed, so I asked him what was the matter. He didn't want to tell me at first but eventually he told me there was a man in his bed who had stayed the night after taking some drugs and now he couldn't wake him up. I asked him what he meant.'

'And what exactly did your brother say next?'

'He hesitated and then said: "There's a dead body in my flat."'

Despite the fact that Ian had forewarned me about all this and all the families expected it, I couldn't help the flicker of horror that shot through me at the way she said it, as if it was an ordinary, everyday occurrence. I turned to the other boys' families and we exchanged glances, assuming this was Gabriel's body he was talking about.

'And what was your response?'

'I was sick with worry and asked him how long the body had been there. He didn't seem too sure, so I told him to call an ambulance and report it to the police.'

'And did he?'

'I rang him a few days later,' she explained, 'and asked him if he'd been to the police yet and he said "Yes".'

'Is that all?'

'Yes, I left it at that.'

I looked across at Daniel's stepmother Mandy and Jack's sisters Donna and Jenny, as if to say: 'What the f**k? If your brother rang you and told you "there's a body in my flat," wouldn't you ask more questions? And why on earth wouldn't you go there and tell the police yourself to make sure?'

The barrister had another look at the document in his hand, then looked up at her again, clearing his throat. 'Did you know about your brother being charged with Perversion of the Course of Justice?'

'Yes, he phoned to tell me before he went to court.'

'That was in March 2015?'

'Yes, I suppose so.'

'And what did you talk about then?'

'He told me it was nothing to worry about. The police just didn't believe him.'

'Anything else?'

'Yes, I asked him what had happened about the dead body in his bed the previous August. Did he find out who it was? And he said I'd got it wrong and it hadn't happened in August.'

I gasped. This was a new turn of events. We all glanced at each other with unspoken questions.

The barrister continued: 'Can you tell the court what you mean? And what exactly your brother said?'

'He said the conversation we had in August was not real time. It was to do with something that had happened two months before.'

I caught my breath and leant forward, suddenly alarmed. If this was true . . . or was it another of the evil scum's fantasies?

She continued: 'He said there was a dead body in his bed in the June. It was a Lithuanian boy.'

Lithuanian, I thought. What was that all about?

'Did he tell you the name of the Lithuanian?' asked the barrister.

'Yes, I think he said it was Anthony.'

Another shockwave. 'My Anthony?' I whispered to Ian. 'But Lithuanian? What? . . . Why . . .?'

He leant towards me but, before he could answer, the barrister asked Sharon Port whether she knew why he had changed his story.

She thought for a moment, then shrugged. 'I don't know,' she replied.

Having come to the end of her questioning, she turned to leave the stand and looked up at her brother in the dock, who gave her a big smile.

I had a strong urge to go up there and punch him. But even worse, I was infuriated that she had been so useless. Why didn't she call the police herself? If she had, she could have saved three more lives.

The court adjourned for a coffee break, so Jenny Taylor and I went to the toilet, chatting as we went about the useless Barking police who'd never investigated any of the evidence we'd heard so far that morning. As we walked into the ladies, still talking, there was a female press reporter there, so we both stopped talking, made an exasperated face at each other and went into our cubicles in 'radio silence'.

As we came out of our cubicles, this woman was still there, looking at herself in the mirror and playing with her hair, obviously hoping to listen in to our conversation. We gave her a 'death stare' and she scarpered. We laughed out loud as soon as she'd gone but it was a serious problem. That was what it was like. It was so stressful for us all, with the press listening round every corner. We couldn't even pee in peace.

We decided to retreat to the family room upstairs, where we would be safe from media snooping while we had our coffees and chatted openly. We all talked about Sharon Port's testimony and how incensed we were, both at the muddle over whose body this was and, secondly, at the lack of action from Sharon Port.

'Doesn't that woman even realise that she could have saved lives if she'd only contacted the police herself?' I asked the rhetorical question.

'Whether the body was Anthony's or Gabriel's, or even one of Port's fantasies, she only had to report it,' agreed Jenny.

'It's so exasperating!' I blurted out. 'And did you see his creepy smile at her?'

'Yes!' agreed Mandy, Jenny and Donna in unison, all as incensed as I was.

Back in court, we knew that the next witness would be Barbara Denham, the poor dog walker who first found the body of Gabriel and then, three weeks later, the body of Daniel, both in the same graveyard, in the same spot, their bodies sitting propped up against the same wall.

She looked nervous as she took the stand and started to describe how she always walked her Border collie on the same route through the graveyard every morning. But one day she was shocked to discover a young man in an untidy state, propped up against a wall. At first she assumed he must be 'sleeping off a heavy night'. But something niggled at her, so she went over to make sure. She touched his leg and found him 'unresponsive and cold to the touch'.

'You mentioned his untidy state. Could you please describe what you saw?'

'His top was rucked up, revealing his midriff. He was on a blanket and had two rucksacks of clothes and stuff next to him.'

I remembered asking Slaymaker about the blanket and whether they'd tested it but he said they'd just tossed it over the wall as it was obviously a drugs overdose. So they didn't even keep it, but had they tested it, I felt sure they'd have found Port's DNA on it, a sample of which they apparently already had on their database, so they could have matched it. An unforgivable lost opportunity.

Next the barrister asked the distressed dog walker about the second discovery.

'I was terribly upset by finding the first body but the police told me it was an overdose and I tried hard to put the experience behind me. I decided to keep doing the same walk as it could surely never happen again . . .'

She broke down at this point and I felt terribly sorry for her. The barrister waited patiently as she tried to regain her equilibrium, as much as she could. Finally, she spoke again, haltingly, sobbing as she forced the words out.

'I was horrified,' she said. 'I thought to myself, please God. Not another one. And then, please let it be a boy who's in a drunken stupor, not dead. I went to shake him but he too was stiff and cold.' She paused and took a few short breaths, still overwrought. 'It was another body in exactly the same place as the first, with his T-shirt rucked up as well, just like the first, showing his stomach. This young man was also sat up leaning against the same wall in exactly the same position. This time he was on a blue bed sheet.' She paused again. 'I could see that he was holding some sort of note or letter in a plastic folder but I did not touch that.'

She broke down again, in floods of tears, and by this time I was crying with her.

The barrister said he had no more questions for her and beckoned a court usher to help her out of the witness box and away from the courtroom. As I watched her go, I recalled that the police had kept the blue sheet but, despite being asked by the coroner to have it tested, they never did. When the Crime Squad had it analysed, they found Port's DNA all over it, as well as on Daniel's clothing.

The prosecution barrister turned to the judge and jury and added: 'As we know, this was purported to be a suicide note and will be admitted as evidence during tomorrow's proceedings, when more will be said about it.'

It had been a harrowing day, so I was happy to be going back outside for some fresh air while walking China and Kiera to the Tube station. However, just as we were making our way up the street, I became aware of a TV presenter hovering behind us, trying to listen to our conversation about the way the first lot of police had missed so much evidence. I stopped talking as soon as I noticed him. But then he caught up and stopped me.

'Hello Sarah. What do you know about how the IPCC are getting on, in their investigation of the Barking police failings? What went wrong?'

I was very polite and told him: 'I'm sorry. I can't talk about it.'

But what I really wanted to say was: 'You knobhead! Right now, who cares? Four dead lads . . . and all you're interested in is what the police did wrong? The police failings need to be shelved until this trial is over. Only then will we go forward with that.'

I just turned away and walked faster. I was so angry. That was the second press intrusion in one day – a day that would have been difficult enough without it.

By the following morning, I had built up quite a head of steam and strode into the Old Bailey fuming about the press and all set to blow my top at somebody. I went straight to find Ben Williams of the IPCC, as I thought he should know how intrusive and threatening the press pack were, and I also wanted to make an official complaint. However, he and his team had been let into the courtroom early that day so I had to wait until the lunchtime adjournment. Meanwhile, there was to be more evidence given about Gabriel and Daniel, the second and third deaths.

The 'suicide note' was one of the items under discussion. It appeared that the Barking police 'took it as face value', as a Scotland Yard officer explained. The jurors were directed to the page in their Jury Packs and given a few moments to look at and try to read the handwritten note. Then the prosecuting barrister read out the typed transcription to the court.

The main points of the note were the claim that Daniel had unintentionally taken the life of Gabriel, blamed himself and couldn't live with the guilt so was now killing himself. He apologised to his family and at the end of the letter made a strong plea: 'Please do not blame the guy I was with last night . . .' and finally added that he'd lost his phone.

I suspect most people present had read it before, as Kate and I did online, just after Daniel's body was found. Several witnesses, all friends and family, were asked about Daniel's mental state and all of them insisted that he would never have taken his own life, no matter what. He was a keen young chef with a promising career.

The barrister then made a statement that the Barking detectives neither fully investigated Daniel's movements leading up to his death, nor the identity of 'the guy I was with last night'. In both cases, if they had, they would have found Stephen Port. Even worse, they had only given a copy of a very small section of the handwritten note to Daniel's father and stepmother to verify his handwriting. But they told the Barking police they couldn't tell from such a small piece. They asked to see the whole letter but the police refused. It was thereby assumed, by the police, to be Daniel's handwriting.

It was not until Scotland Yard took over the case that they compared the note to a sample of Port's handwriting and found it to be a perfect match. The other omission of the Barking police was not to have the blue sheet analysed. When the new team took over, they found Port's DNA all over it, as well as the plastic wallet, the note itself and Daniel's clothes.

I was so cross on behalf of Mandy, Daniel's stepmother, sitting along the row from me. All four of the boys had been overlooked, presumably through what the newspapers called the Barking police's homophobia. If they'd only done one or two things for any one of the boys, they would have got their man . . . But they chose instead not to investigate the deaths at all.

Thank God for Ian, Tim and the rest of the Scotland Yard team, that our sons can finally have a hearing.

At lunchtime, I was all fired up again and ready for the fray as I made a beeline straight for Ben at the back of the courtroom, where the IPCC team sat.

'Come and sit down,' he said, turning the empty chair beside him.

'I'm fuming,' I told him and explained about the hovering TV presenter listening into our conversation the day before. I told him what we'd been talking about and what he asked me. 'I understand they need a story,' I continued. 'But this is all so hard for us already, without having to cope with the press intrusion. It's too much to be stalked and confronted like that!'

'Yes, it is hard for you. And we don't want them interfering with our investigation either. Could you make some notes about it for us?' suggested Ben. 'And we'll deal with it after the trial is over.'

'Is there nothing we can do to stop them harassing us like that?' I asked him.

'In this building, yes, but not out on the street, I'm afraid; not unless they're physically obstructing you. But you could go and ask the witness protection officer to look into it if you like.'

The afternoon was made up of more witnesses, reporting on various details relating to Gabriel and Daniel's lives and deaths, but nothing particularly uncomfortable. It was more about telling the jury what they were like and what their futures might have held for them, just as had been done for Anthony to begin with.

The following day, Friday, I had decided not to attend the trial. In the morning, Daniel's pathology report would be read to the court. Far, far worse was that it would be followed by a disgusting video Port had made of himself violently raping unconscious young men.

Ian had explained to me well in advance that when Scotland Yard had taken over from the Barking lot, they had checked Port's phone for the first time and found eighty-three of his sordid, sleazy homemade videos, all of them of him having brutal, drug-fuelled sex with the unconscious bodies of young gay men. I couldn't bear even to think about it. Apparently this was Port's fetish, that they had to be unconscious, which was why he used the colourless, odourless GHB in their water or soft drinks to knock out the young men so he could do whatever disgusting things he wanted to do with them.

Out of the eighty-three, they had chosen just the one video to show, but even that would be nearly twenty minutes long. I couldn't imagine how any of the jurors, especially some of the older women in particular, could possibly endure having to watch it all, which they would be required to do as it was part of the evidence.

To start with, I had intended to go to all the murdered boys' sections of the trial, mainly through solidarity with the other families. But, after all my heavy, uphill struggle over the past two and a half years, and my frightening swings between depression and anger, I just couldn't carry on attending the worst days – especially the pathology reports and certainly not the video. China had bravely offered to stay in the court while it was being shown so that she could watch the jury's and Port's reactions and tell me about it later.

I was on the train home to Hull when she phoned me. First of all, she explained that none of the families or the people in the public gallery could see the video screen at all, as it was mounted high on the wall opposite the jury, where it could only be seen by them, the judge, lawyers, journalists and Port himself.

'Because I couldn't see the screen, I was able to watch everyone else,' she said. 'Most of the jury sat there with their hands to their mouths in shock and kept diverting their gaze to Port, who was actually *smiling* throughout! Sometimes he even giggled at himself and obviously enjoyed seeing himself as the star of his sleazy, squalid video . . . but nobody else did.'

'Please tell me the jury saw him,' I said.

'Yes, several did. I watched them and Port constantly, to and fro – it was like watching tennis!' she exclaimed. 'But not at all entertaining.'

'How did some of the older jurors react?'

'One of them had her hand over her face and just looked out between her fingers. Another tried to look down a lot of the time but forced herself to look up now and then as this was evidence of his disgusting acts and the judge had instructed them beforehand that they must keep watching. It must have been awful for them. Even one of the barristers had to turn away.'

'How distressing for them all,' I said. 'I hope it doesn't traumatise anyone for the future, but it sounds like it might.'

'And,' continued China, 'while Port was smiling and enjoying himself watching it, even the poor guards around him sat staring at him in shock.'

'I'm so glad I didn't go,' I told her. 'I could not have sat there quietly as he was smiling. What a sick, perverted excuse for a man.'

CHAPTER 20

Away Days with a Film Crew

24–28 October 2016, the fourth week of the trial

This was the week when every day the prosecution would cover all the other charges of surviving victims' poisonings and rapes, culminating in Port talking about Port, no doubt revelling in the telling of all his disgusting activities and abuses. It made me shudder just to think of the poor jurors who had no choice but to watch and listen to every sordid detail. This surely would be the most traumatic week of all for them.

In the early days of the trial, I had realised how graphic some of the procedural episodes would be, as they delved into the tawdry details, so I would often zone out for a while. I used to sit there, trying to think up possible professions for each of the jurors in turn, or guess their ages, or how many children they had – anything so that I didn't have to listen to all the evidence about Port's lies.

One thing I knew from the start was that I would not go into the court when Port himself took the witness stand. I couldn't bear the thought of having to listen to his voice. I'd never heard it and don't ever want to hear it. I don't want his voice in my head. It may seem strange and I know that his voice is all over YouTube – the videos on his phone and all that – but I just don't want to listen to it or watch it.

Tom said he would go the court instead of me, so he was there for the start, but he didn't last long as it upset him too much.

I was glad to have a completely different week planned, back home in Hull with the BBC film crews. I had asked Tom if he wanted to take part but he wouldn't do anything like that so he just left it all to me. I was usually the talker, whereas he didn't want to have to talk about his feelings or even to think about them. He's a private person and I think he found it more comfortable not to go over what happened to Anthony.

When Paul popped in at the weekend, we stood in the kitchen while I made us coffee. I was just remembering a conversation I'd once had with him about Anthony's passion for fashion when Paul laughed out loud.

'What's so funny?' I asked.

'Oh Mam, I was just thinking back to how Ant was with you, commenting about your clothes and your hair.'

'I was just thinking of that too!'

'Do you remember, whenever you were going to do something special, you had to show him on the phone what you were going to wear and how you had your hair?'

'Yes, and it was never good enough. He always thought I had rubbish fashion sense!'

'Just think what he'd say now, with you going on the telly and all. He'd say: "You can't wear that!"'

'Yes,' I laughed. 'And he was usually right . . . though I didn't say so!'

★

The following Monday, I'd agreed to do an exclusive interview with the *Daily Mirror* for a double-page feature they wanted to do on me and my fight for justice and Anthony. I thought it would be one hour talking to the feature writer with a hand-held camera and that would be it. But no . . . it was the feature writer with a voice-recorder and a camera-man with two huge bags of camera paraphernalia for the whole day.

'Thanks for a lovely day with you, and for the sandwiches. I hope it hasn't been too harrowing for you to go over all of Anthony's story again?' said the journalist as they gathered their stuff to leave.

'You do remember that this interview can't be published in the paper until after the trial is finished, don't you?' I asked.

'Yes, that's fine. We'll have it all set up and ready to print.'

'What do you think the headline will be?'

'Well, there will be different sections across the two pages, but I should think one of the headlines will be something like 'I warned them twelve times' about your warnings to the police about the likelihood of other killings if they didn't investigate Anthony's. And how right you were!'

Dan Clark-Neal arrived on his own the next day, the first day of his film's preparation, to talk through everything and look through some of Anthony's photos so that he could decide what to film and in what order. He's a lovely man – I know Anthony would have liked him.

On the second day, the crew spent a long time setting up all the cameras, lighting, microphones and all that, just to film me being interviewed at my house, which, even with a few retakes, we managed to do in one day, with just a bit extra the next. Then Dan asked if they could visit the graveyard and film Anthony's grave, which went well. Once they had all they needed, they went off to the studios to do the long job – the editing.

Another presenter and film crew arrived later that week to do another documentary, this time from a slightly different angle, which went equally well, so it was a good week, all aimed at trying to raise awareness of the dangers of dating apps. Dan's was made for BBC2 and the second one was for BBC3, where I hoped more young people would see it.

The whole week was a much-needed break from all that terrible trial trauma. Even with all the film crews' disruption, moving furniture and all that, it felt like I was doing something positive . . . and completely different. As they say, a change is as good as a rest. And it certainly was for me that week.

Every evening I had phone calls from Ian or China to update me. The most significant day, as I suspected, was the day Port took the stand.

China was the first one to call me that day: 'When Port was brought into the glass dock this morning, he was grinning. He even gave a little wave at his defence team, who looked embarrassed, before he sat down between his guards. I'm so glad you didn't have to sit through any of it. You would never have recovered. I don't think anyone who was there will ever recover – we'll probably all suffer nightmares tonight and I should think most of the poor jurors will be traumatised for life.'

'I hope you didn't just stay on because of me?'

'Well, yes, I did, but I was doing it for Neenee too. He wouldn't have wanted me to miss a thing.'

I was pleased to hear China calling Anthony Neenee. It was comforting to hear that she was still using her nickname for him.

'The prosecution barrister took Port through all the details of each charge, asking him to describe how he drugged and raped them. It was all horribly sordid and sleazy. Items of evidence included an applicator and lubrication. Port actually seemed to take a pride in showing and explaining exactly how he would spike his victim's drink with GBH and sometimes other drugs as well and, when they fell unconscious, he used the applicator to inject the lubricant gel into their anus to make it easier for him to rape them. He gleefully told us that he usually took a smaller dose of drugs too, to give him a high. Then, one of the ushers handed the applicator to the jury foreman, who passed it round so that every one of them could have a good look and see how it worked.'

'Oh, how did the jurors react?'

'With disgust, is probably the easiest answer. They all reacted in their own ways as they had to handle this applicator and listen to all his sordid, detailed descriptions of how he used it to penetrate his victims, treating them like rag dolls as he raped them, how he loved tying people up and having sex with them, or sex in foursomes . . . and how excited he felt when it was what he called "good sex".'

'Oh no! How squalid. Don't tell me any more.' It was terribly upsetting to hear about all this and I couldn't prevent myself from imagining how awful it must have been for Anthony.

'But remember, Sarah,' China added, clearly realising how my mind might be working, 'Anthony would have been unconscious the whole time, so he almost certainly had no idea what was happening to him.'

'How long did the devil go on talking like this?' I asked.

'Oh, more or less all day, although the judge did give longer adjournments today,' she replied. 'I expect that was for the jury's sake, even more than for the families and the public. The jurors were horrified. They couldn't close their eyes like everyone else could. They couldn't let their concentration drop, because all this depravity would be part of their discussions when they had to reach all twenty-nine verdicts.'

'I can't imagine how they coped,' I said, genuinely concerned for them all.

'I don't think some of them did,' replied China. 'They had to take notes quite a lot but some of them put their heads down for a few seconds every now and then, while others fidgeted with their hands or their jewellery. One of the older ones put both her hands over her face but mostly with her eyes open, looking between her fingers. Most of them looked shell-shocked.'

'I'm not surprised.'

'I know you didn't want to hear Port's voice,' said China, changing the subject a little. 'But most of us couldn't hear it, or at least not what he was saying. He mumbled very quietly, in a sort of monotone – no expression in his voice at all and hardly moving his lips so it was almost inaudible at times. Sometimes he paused for a long time before answering and then he would gabble his words so quickly that nobody could tell what he was saying. Both the judge and the barrister constantly had to ask him to speak louder and clearer, or often to repeat himself.'

'Somehow, that doesn't surprise me.' I said. 'He's a psycho. He must be to do what he's done. He obviously doesn't have any feelings . . . and probably very little intelligence, by the sound of it.'

'Yes, I expect you're right. His answers were rarely full sentences and he runs his words together all the time. There were one or two interesting interludes this afternoon, if you can call them that. The first was when Port tried to make out that the only reason his handwriting was on Daniel's suicide note was because Daniel had dictated it to him to write. From the surprised expressions of the jury, it didn't look to me as if any of them believed that.'

'I'm not surprised!' I said. 'He's not very bright but he was bright enough to get away with it at the time and now he's probably thinking he's hoodwinked everyone again with his new version of his "truth". Everybody else can see it so why couldn't the cops? Obviously, they weren't very bright either!'

'Well, that was the other stand-out moment, when the judge challenged him that he had given two different versions of the same event, so one of them must be a lie. "Why did you lie?" asked the judge. There was a long pause,' explained China, 'with everyone waiting for his answer.'

'And what was his answer?'

'Almost a whisper − "I'm not sure." The judge's jaw dropped at that.'

The next day's feedback was briefer but still very disturbing. China told me the prosecuting barrister asked Port supplementary questions across each of the poisoning charges, using the evidence given earlier in the trial about the effects of different drugs and amounts of them on the human body. Then he asked Port about the doses and mixtures of drugs he gave to his different victims.

'Whatever he was asked, he kept changing his story,' commented China. 'It was all a big fantasy to him. In fact, the highlight of this afternoon was when Port was asked why he told so many lies.'

'And what did he say?'

'He took quite a while to think about it, then, for once, he gave his answer in full sentences. This is exactly what he said: "I didn't tell the truth because it looked like a lie. So I told a lie because it sounded more like the truth."'

After my week at home, away from it all, I felt mentally stronger again and ready to go back down to the Old Bailey and catch up with the other families.

Ian had updated me on Friday's business in court: 'It's nearing the end of the defence evidence, which should be completed by Monday lunchtime, so the judge has told us the court won't sit on Monday afternoon.'

'Port won't be called to the witness stand again, will he?' I asked, suddenly on edge.

'No, he's done his worst now,' Ian reassured me. 'And, if you remember, there are no other witnesses for the defence, so I expect Port's barrister will just be talking things through for the jury's benefit, linking the various strands of the case for the defence.'

'Do you have any idea what will be happening after that?' I asked him.

'Yes. The judge suggested an outline timetable for the whole of this week,' said Ian. 'I'll type it up and email to you. It's only a guide as it may run on a day or two but we'll be able to adjust it as we go along.'

'Does that mean the trial itself will end this week?' I asked hopefully.

'No, not that soon, I'm afraid, but probably only another two weeks before the judge turns it over to the jury. How long they will take is anyone's guess.'

CHAPTER 21

The Jury's Out

31 October–25 November 2016,
the final four weeks of the trial

On Sunday, Kate and I took the train back down to London and checked into our usual hotel. In court, the first few days of the week more or less followed the plan Ian had given me, with the judge advising the jury about the various points of law that they must take into account while listening to the legal summing-up. Several of them took notes until the judge told them they would each have their own copy of this document.

Next it was the tedious task of listening to the prosecution barrister, who took nearly three days to summarise the many witness testimonies and all the evidence that had been revealed for every single charge. Although it was all important for giving our four boys justice, I think we all found it quite difficult to maintain our concentration, so every adjournment break was very welcome.

How the jurors managed to keep up with all this, day in, day out, I'll never know. These twelve ordinary people were faced with an extraordinary and traumatic task. During the session after lunch one day, I noticed one of the older women with her head down, her face in her hands and her eyes closed. She didn't move for a number of seconds – at least half a minute. I was getting worried about her. Had anybody else noticed? What if she was ill? Should I do something, or tell somebody? But suddenly she shook herself and sat up again in a valiant effort to keep herself alert.

The following day, Thursday, 3 November, the prosecution summing up was becoming more and more harrowing to sit through. By now, I knew most of it . . . but I still couldn't bear being subjected to it yet again.

By the end of the afternoon, I'd had it. The last straw was being hassled by the press as we left the building. I felt stressed enough without that; I hated the press, I was sick of the trial, sick of our hotel and sick of London. I didn't want to be there any more. I'd had two and a half years of anguish and I'd had enough. I needed to get away, so I jumped on a train with Kate and went to see Sami in Essex. All I needed was a good hug.

Sami was wonderful. He hugged me and fed me . . . and then he told me I had to carry on.

'You will never forgive yourself if you don't,' he said. And I knew he was right. I had to carry on. I did go back to the court the next day and didn't abscond again. Instead, Sami came up to support me as often as he could in those last few days.

After the prosecution summing-up came the defence barrister's turn and another two days of sitting down, for six or seven hours a day, listening to poor excuses for Port's depths of depravity. It was hard enough for us sitting there listening day after day but at least we could get up and leave the courtroom if we wanted or needed to. The jury couldn't.

It was so frustrating to hear the same things rehashed over and over again, or that's how it seemed to me. I used to say to Ian: 'For God's sake, why has the judge gone over that for a third time?'

'Sarah,' he replied, 'he needs to be 150 per cent sure that nothing is missed, that there's no need for a retrial.'

Other days were so frustrating because nothing seemed to be happening. Sometimes the barristers and the judge would go over a point ten times.

'They have to do it,' he explained. 'The judge has to go over that point again and again and the barristers have to reply to it. They have to do everything correctly. Port doesn't seem to see or understand how bad all this is, so he'll probably appeal. There must be no omission or lack of clarity. Nothing should be said or seen that could potentially be an excuse for granting a retrial. Nothing must go wrong.'

Finally, on Friday, 11 November, it was time for the judge's summing-up – the last session before handing over to the jury. As well as summarising the case, the judge was very particular in going though the document he had prepared for them, entitled 'Further Directions upon the Law'. They would all have their own copy of this to keep by them and guide their deliberations. All those present in the courtroom were also given a copy.

These further directions were specific to this trial and to Port himself. For example, the judge gave very clear guidance about how to consider the lies that the defendant used for the first time under oath during the trial and which

differed from any of the explanations he had previously
given when interviewed by the police, also under oath.

The judge further directed the jury that: 'If the facts on
which he now relies were true, he could reasonably have
been expected to mention them during the course of the
interview and, as he did not do so, you may conclude that he
made them up later, so as to accord with the evidence called
against him, or because he believed that his account would
not stand up to scrutiny.'

We came back bright and early on the morning of Monday, 14
November to try to avoid some of the media scrum. Everyone
assembled in Court 16 for the judge to talk to the jury again
about procedural issues. Then, as I wrote in my diary:

> *The jury retired today. That was it. No more to be done. Twelve*
> *complete strangers have to decide our fate.*

It felt very disconcerting, after all the intensity of the
previous weeks (and years), all the horrors and heartaches
of the evidence, the ups and downs of emotions, that now
we had to let go. We had no role. The battling was over.
All we could do was to fade into the background while
these assorted strangers had all the power, to make or to
break us, to redeem our boys and give them justice, or . . .
Any other option was too unpalatable to think about, but
the fear remained.

Once the jury and the judge had gone and Port had been
taken out and down to the cells, I heard that several of the
police and journalists were laying bets on how long it would
be before they came back with their verdicts.

'Ten minutes,' suggested one young officer. 'What is there to discuss?' More reasonable guesses were anything between two days and two weeks.

God forbid that it should be two weeks, I thought, as I crossed the marble floor outside the courtroom with the others and went up to the witness suite. Sami was with me, and Kate, China and Kiera. We joined Daniel Whitworth's and Jack Taylor's families to start the wait.

'Make sure you listen out for any announcements,' Ian advised us. 'Though I don't suppose it will be for quite a while, maybe a few days. After all, they don't just have your sons' deaths to decide on, but all of the twenty-five other charges.'

'What if we want to go out?' I asked.

'If you do, you must make sure your phones are fully charged and have them out ready, in case we call you. You would only have twenty minutes' notice of the jury returning and the judge won't wait for you if you're not back in time. So don't go far.'

'That's a challenge,' I said. 'I'll go stir-crazy if I have to sit in here all day, every day, just in case . . . but of course, none of us wants to miss the verdicts.'

'How late in the afternoon would we have to wait until it's OK to leave?' asked Kate.

'Good question. Every day, whether the jury are ready or not, they are called back into the court at 3.30 p.m. sharp and we can all be there too. The judge will have been told whether or not they have decided on all charges,' he explained. 'And, if not, the jury will be sent home, with the warning that they must not speak to each other or anybody else outside the jury room, not even in their own homes.'

'That must be hard for them,' I said.

'They'll be storing up mental problems for themselves after this is over,' added Kate.

'They will all be offered counselling after a trial like this,' said Ian.

'Oh good,' said Jenny Taylor.

'They'll need it for sure,' added her sister, Donna.

'Is someone keeping Gabriel's family in Slovakia informed?' asked China.

Ian nodded. 'Yes, they have their own family liaison officer and translator.'

'That's good,' said Mandy Whitworth.

The witness care ladies were a great support. They knew we were probably going to be waiting for the verdicts for at least a few days so they were very attentive and did their best to help us pass the time and keep as calm as we could. They made sure we had drinks when we wanted them and chatted with us, telling us stories of funny or strange things that had happened to them while working in the witness suites over the years. They listened to our moans about the press, our journeys to court, our families and everything. They also told us the basic details of some of the other trials going on that week. Of course they didn't tell us anything they shouldn't – they were well trained in confidentiality – but we all knew from the TV and newspapers that the MP Jo Cox's murderer was on trial this week. We saw her family in the witness suite during adjournments and I recognised both her husband Brendan and her sister from the earlier TV reports. It was awful to see other families' distress because I knew exactly how they felt. But nothing could take away all this, we had to go through it, and for me it was Anthony who silently goaded me to keep on going.

The witness care people watched out for us every day, ready to sympathise and reassure. It really was a calm, safe haven in there.

We three families really got to know each other well during this time, as we sat there day after day, waiting and waiting. On one occasion, we all joined in a discussion about our boys and the other survivor-victims. We compared our boys' heights and weights. It occurred to us that one of the differences between the survivors and our four boys was that our four were very slim – 'twinks' as Port had referred to them in the witness box. So maybe the slimmer, lighter ones died, while the others were able to survive the same-sized dose.

We talked about our experiences with the Barking police. Jenny told me she had heard or read somewhere that I had made numerous complaints to the police and to the IPCC about the Barking police's failures and their offhand, homophobic attitudes. Although Jenny and Donna and their parents had only had to endure a few days of this treatment before the Crime Squad took over, it nonetheless made Jack's sisters very angry. We compared notes and I found out that they had also complained to the IPCC. I had now started to look into finding the right barrister who might be willing to help me sue the police, which was exactly what they were doing too. In fact, when I told them the name of the barrister, Leslie Thomas, that I'd had recommended to me as 'the best' for this sort of thing, they too had picked this name out and had made a preliminary approach to him. We agreed to join forces once all this was over and look into taking a joint action.

Occasionally, we were called to court at odd times of the day and we hurried down there, full of nervous expectation, only to find it was just that the jury wanted to ask the judge a specific question or to request to see an item produced as evidence, as they did on one occasion when they wanted to see how the lubricator worked. This caused some consternation, purely because the judge opened several packets to check them, only to find they were incomplete, before he finally found one with its plunger intact.

At 3.30 each afternoon, we all dutifully filed into the courtroom. The jury would come in and sit down, all of them except the one juror who'd been chosen by them to be the forewoman, to chair their deliberations. Each afternoon she stood and was asked whether they had reached any verdicts yet which were unanimous.

To begin with, every day the answer was, 'No, not yet.'

'In that case,' said the judge, 'we will adjourn until tomorrow morning at 10.30.' And out they would all file again, till the next day.

Sometimes, during these days in limbo, China, Kiera and I decided to snatch a quick break outside the Old Bailey altogether and get some fresh air, but we didn't stray far and always put our phones on and ready in case we were called to return to court.

It was agonising, all this waiting, and, after five whole days of it, we were ready to go home for good. But of course we didn't want to miss the vital moment.

On the Friday afternoon, after a late lunchbreak at the pub with the garden, we had to almost fight our way through the press pack outside the Old Bailey as we came back to the court, only to find, yet again, that the jury were still not ready to declare any unanimous verdict on any of the counts.

My anger rose when I realised that one of the cameras was filming me. I turned my face away and said to the girls: 'I wish they would all f**k off.' Then I realised they had probably recorded my voice as well. I felt very stressed at the time but later on we had a laugh about it. At least, with the expletive in it, I could be pretty sure they wouldn't put it on the *Six O'Clock News*.

The waiting seemed endless and every time the Old Bailey's archaic announcement system crackled into life and we strained to hear what it was saying, the tension was terrible. It was only rarely for us, and then we all trooped back into court, our hopes and fears rising, only to find the jury just had another question for the judge to answer. These ups and downs were difficult to deal with so we tried our best to stay calm by chatting about other things and making fun of the dreaded press.

The best escape for me was going back to Sami's every evening at this end stage – back to normality, encouragement and hugs. Whenever he could, Sami would come up to the Old Bailey with me, which helped while away the time, but we still had no idea how long it would be. My own fear was ever-present in my mind, like a mantra – *I hope they don't get it wrong. Please God, don't let them get it wrong.*

★

At 3.30 p.m. on Tuesday, 22 November, we were all gathered in court as usual to see the same question as every other day put to the forewoman of the jury. She stood. The usher asked: 'Do you have any unanimous verdicts?'

'Yes,' she replied.

There was an immediate gasp of tension across the court – almost a sense of shock that finally, after all this waiting, something was about to happen. We all sat up and fully engaged our brains to hear what would come next. The anticipation was almost tangible. But we didn't expect what happened.

'Good,' said the judge. 'We will hear them at 10.30 tomorrow morning. Court is adjourned.'

There was a collective intake of breath across the room. We, the families, all exchanged glances of surprised exasperation.

Another sleepless night; perhaps the worst of all the nights since the trial began. Not knowing is the most wretched feeling, when it could go either way. My brain said he would be found guilty but my gut was warning me that he might not be. I couldn't really conceive that he'd be let off entirely, yet now even my brain started to play tricks on me. 'What ifs' abounded. I tossed and turned with all the scenarios rattling around my head and hardly slept at all.

The next morning, 23 November, Kate, Sami, China, Kiera and I met round the corner at the Tube station, earlier than usual. 'Right,' I said. 'Straight faces for the press,' and we walked together down the street, through the greatest throng of media we'd seen, and into the relative sanctuary of the Old Bailey. Of course, there were plenty of journalists inside its hallowed walls, many more than usual, but at least they respected our feelings that morning and kept their distance. We met with the Whitworths and Taylors in the witness suite, then went all together into Court 16.

The jury filed in. I tried to read their expressions but couldn't gauge anything. Perhaps they'd been told not to give us any clues.

'All rise,' declared the court usher and we stood up as the judge came in and took his place. You could have heard a pin drop as the usher stood in front of the jury and asked the forewoman to give their verdicts.

'We shall go through each count in numerical order,' explained the judge. 'Answer either "guilty" or "not guilty" if you have been unanimous in your decision or "undecided" if not unanimous on any count.'

I was all keyed up to listen out for Anthony's name, and the names of the other boys. But it wasn't as easy as that.

'On count one,' began the usher. 'Have you reached a unanimous verdict?'

'Yes.'

'Do you find the defendant guilty or not guilty?'

'Guilty.'

I wrote it down on my notepad but I was completely fazed. Who and what was count one? I looked up at the others and we all exchanged glances with the same baffled expressions. We hadn't realised it would be like this.

'On count two . . .'

What the hell were counts one and two? I panicked. Ian was sitting beside me but I didn't have time to ask him as I had to listen and write it all down. He was writing it down too.

'On count three, have you reached a unanimous decision?'

That was also a 'Yes' followed by 'guilty'.

'On count four, have you reached a unanimous decision?'

I recalled that number four was the murder charge for Anthony and I held my breath. It was probably no more than two seconds but it seemed like an age.

'No.'

I froze in shock. 'Does that mean they've said "not guilty"?' I whispered to Ian.

'No, just not unanimous.'

I tried to keep up, frantically writing down all the other numbers and answers, so my mind shut down for the duration, but as soon as the twenty-ninth count had been completed, I collapsed into a torrent of tears. I could see from the jubilation on the other three families' faces that Port had been convicted unanimously for the murders of their boys and I was torn in two – part of me delighted for them but the rest of me was completely distraught about Anthony. Was this right? How could it possibly be?

The judge retired the jury again with the instruction to try to reach a ten out of twelve verdict for the counts that were not unanimous.

I walked out in a daze, supported by Kate and Sami, then turned to the Whitworths and the Taylors and congratulated them. 'I expect you'll be going home now,' I said.

They all looked at me with surprise. 'No,' said Jenny. 'We're all staying here with you until Anthony's murder verdict comes through.'

'However long it takes,' added Donna. They all nodded their agreement.

I could have cried with happiness that they were going to stay with me to the end. To us all, it had always been about the four boys and we had stuck together throughout on that, so now they were following through in solidarity, giving me their full support.

We all went back upstairs to wait . . . again. As I sat down, I suddenly realised that I wasn't even sure what the other verdicts about Anthony had been. Had the jury not even been unanimous about his poisoning? I rang Ian's number in a panic and he came within a couple of minutes.

In his calm and kindly voice he explained. 'There were three counts for Anthony. Count four was murder, count five was manslaughter and count six was administering poison. If you remember, we put in the manslaughter charges for each of the boys, just in case the jury could not agree on murder. So, the jury were not unanimous regarding murder, but they were unanimous about both manslaughter and poisoning, so he will be convicted of those two for certain and we'll have to wait a little longer to see whether they reach an agreement about the count of murder.'

'So they were unanimous that Port killed Anthony?'

'Yes. They were.'

'Oh, so that's not so bad.' I breathed a sigh of relief and began to calm down. 'I could live with a manslaughter verdict. In fact, I'd be just as happy with manslaughter as murder. I just needed him to pay for Anthony's death.'

However, as soon as I thought it through again, I did feel defrauded. I knew Anthony was the first, or probably the first that Port killed, so perhaps the jury thought it was only then that Port would have known a dose of GHB could kill. But surely there was enough evidence on his laptop and in other ways to show he didn't have a care as to whether Anthony was alive or dead and that he had lured him there on false pretences and in fact knew he had killed him. It was all for the devil's own squalid pleasure.

Yes, I realised, I did need to have the validation of a guilty verdict that Port had murdered Anthony but would the jury be able to agree? Would that verdict ever come?

CHAPTER 22

The Final Verdicts

Late November 2016,
over 29 months after Anthony's death

It was nearly 3.30 p.m. on the day the jury had returned their unanimous verdicts, but not Anthony's. We had popped outside for a cigarette when my phone rang. It was Ian.

'Get in here quickly! They've got all the verdicts.'

I dropped my cigarette and ran, closely followed by China and Kiera. We rushed through the doors like madwomen and threw our bags under the scanner. The security guard gave us a quizzical look.

'Quick,' I said. 'The verdicts are in!'

He knew us well enough by now and let us straight through. We ran as fast as we could to the court and finally sat down, out of breath. As it happened, we needn't have worried so much as we sat there for three or four minutes before the jury filed in. I counted twenty-five members of the press in the court and they were all watching me. One of the Taylor girls squeezed my hand and I grabbed China's hand in the other.

As the judge came in, we all leant forward to make sure we could hear his softly spoken voice. Then, finally, it came. It felt almost like slow motion.

'Count four,' said the usher. 'Guilty or not guilty of murdering Anthony Walgate?'

I held my breath.

'Guilty, by a ten-votes-to-two majority.'

Everyone jumped back in their seats. It was surreal. I'd done it – 'GUILTY!' After two and a half years of telling everyone who would listen, of fighting even when it seemed hopeless, I should have been ecstatic, but I wasn't. I was relieved and pleased but it was what it should have been. I didn't feel ecstatic because it didn't change the most important thing. I had lost my baby.

The judge thanked the jury for all their hard work in such a demanding case over the fifty-one days it had taken from the first day to the last. He also told them that, because of the traumatic nature of some of the evidence, they would all be excused from doing any other jury service for the rest of their lives. The court could also provide them with counselling.

I felt like applauding or thanking them or at least waving to them as they left the courtroom. These twelve people had been so important to me throughout this trial and now they would leave my life forever. I didn't even know their names.

As we were about to leave the court for that day, Ben Williams of the IPCC found me and asked me to come and make a short statement to him after the sentencing on Friday to round off their report of the trial and how it had been from my perspective. 'I'll be in touch in a few days to arrange for myself and a colleague to come up to Hull and take a fuller statement from you and Thomas for our report, about everything, from Anthony's death till now.'

'Yes, that will be fine,' I said, relieved that he didn't want to do it then and there. I wanted to go outside with the others.

Leaving the Old Bailey, we were surrounded by press and media from all over the world, it seemed, so we couldn't escape them this time. We kept hearing the words 'Grindr Killer' and we'd already seen this used in the newspapers and online, long before he'd even been convicted. We put up with them filming us, but Port hadn't been sentenced yet. We'd be coming back for that on Friday, so we didn't want to talk to any of them till after he'd gone down for good.

Kate was going back home to Hull so we had a drink with her near the Tube station and did a kind of debrief of the day – the swings and roundabouts of the verdicts and our reactions. 'It was all horrifically interesting,' said Kate, which could have described the whole trial as well.

China had a call from her stepmother, Claire, who worked in a large, open-plan office in the city, about five minutes' walk from the Old Bailey. Claire knew Anthony very well, so she'd been keeping tabs on what had been going on throughout the trial and she'd been telling all her work colleagues too. Though because it was on the TV, internet and newspapers nearly every day, most people were already aware of it.

On that day of the verdicts, Claire had been on tenter-hooks all day, sitting, waiting by her phone, to know what was happening. So, when China rang to tell her about Port being found guilty on all three counts relating to Anthony, her colleagues all stopped and waited in silence, till she shouted it out across the office and about five hundred people cheered. When China told me about that it really choked me. None of these people, apart from Claire, had ever met Anthony but they were all rooting for him.

Sami and I took China and Kiera back to his restaurant in Essex that night and we got so drunk. The last time I was drunk was Christmas Day 2013, Anthony's last Christmas. It's a long-standing family joke that when I'm drunk, I think I can really sing. Well, I really can't. That Christmas I started my usual singing to Anthony – always the same songs. So I sang them at Sami's restaurant and we all had a great night, in memory of Anthony and in celebration of nailing that devil down for all his known crimes.

I don't really remember much else but I know I slept well that night – better than I'd done since before the trial started, perhaps even since before Anthony died.

The following day, as well as waking up with a hangover, it all began to sink in. My overriding feeling now was guilt. How could I be so happy that my son's killer had been convicted of murder when it couldn't bring Anthony back? I felt bad to be rejoicing, to feel triumphant, yet I wanted to celebrate the vindication of my long struggle, the end of the turmoil and uncertainty of everything.

Tomorrow, we would be going back to court for the very last time, for sentencing. I was just thinking about that when Ian rang me.

'Before sentencing, it's usual for one of a murder victim's loved ones to read out a brief impact statement, to show how badly all this has affected you and your family. It's your chance to speak to the criminal directly, saying just a little about the effect this has had on you and your family, or how all this has changed your life. Do you think you could do that?'

'Yes, of course,' I said.

'However, because there are four families of murdered sons, the prosecuting barrister will read all four out on your behalf. If it's too long, he may edit it so that they are all about the same length.'

'OK, I'll do it this afternoon.'

So I explained to the others what I needed to do and went off to find a quiet place with my thoughts. What to write wasn't difficult. I knew what I wanted to say, but choosing the words took me some time, changing it round and substituting others, then cutting it shorter until I was happy with it. This is what I wrote:

You, Stephen Port, have devastated our lives. Not only have you taken Tom's only child and Paul's only sibling, you have taken my son, my baby. Anthony was a funny, clever, talented young man with a bright future . . . and you have taken that away from him − and from us all.

As we gathered outside Court 16 for the final time on Friday morning, Ian and the other family liaison officers brought each of us letters.

I opened mine while we were waiting. It was a long official letter from Stuart Cundy, Commander of the Metropolitan Police, Specialist Crime Investigations. Why? What was it about? I didn't have time to read it now, as the usher was approaching to open up the doors, but I quickly skimmed the first two lines:

Dear Mrs Sak, I wanted to write to you to say how truly sorry I am for the murder of your son, Anthony Walgate. The loss of a loved one is devastating and the circumstances in which Anthony died must make it all the harder to bear. . .

I'd have to read the rest of it later, so I tucked it away as we all went in and sat in our places: China and Kiera upstairs in the packed-to-bursting public gallery; the Whitworths, Taylors, Sami and me in the family area. The press area was packed too but the jury benches were empty of course – their work was over. But what was happening? The court usher led a line of people in through the outer door – it was the jury. They filed into their two rows of benches in exactly the same order as they'd been in throughout the trial. I looked at Ian. He shrugged, with a smile. I was smiling too, as were the other families and, for the very first time, so were the jurors themselves.

Every member of the jury was there, despite the fact that they were no longer needed and we should probably never have seen them again.

'Do juries usually come for the sentencing?' I whispered to Ian.

'No, it's almost unheard of.'

I could only imagine they'd come back to hear what sentence Port would get . . . and maybe, just possibly, to show their support to us. I was very heartened to have them there – it was very fitting really, as they'd been with us throughout and it was particularly pleasing to see them with happy faces, instead of alternating from shock to disgust to incredulity as they had done every day of their jury service.

'All rise,' called the usher as she opened the door and the judge walked in.

The court sat, at which point the prosecuting barrister stood, then turned to face Port.

'Each family of the four murdered victims has written a short impact statement,' he said. 'I will now read these to the court.'

First he read out mine and I kept my eyes on Port, who didn't flicker once – totally unperturbed. What a heartless brute.

While I was happy with the wording I'd chosen, I felt it would have been a more powerful message if I had been allowed to read it. I would much rather have read it out myself.

Next the barrister read the statement from Adam, Gabriel's brother, who hadn't been able to attend any of the trial. Following this came Daniel's father's and finally Jack Taylor's family's impact statements. They were all heart-wrenching but the devil seemed impervious. Oh, how I hoped he would get life.

The prosecution barrister took his seat again and Port's defence barrister stood up to speak in what purported to be mitigation: 'Port had descended into a "vortex" of drug-taking, where gratification of his sexual life was central. His fetish for sex with drugged young men had graduated to fixation, and from fixation to compulsion . . .' Then he sat down again.

A hush descended across the court as the judge, Mr Justice Openshaw, picked up his carefully prepared speech. I glanced briefly again at Port, the convicted murderer, surrounded in his glass box by three guards today. Above the level of the courtroom itself, but straight ahead of the judge, the devil sat impassive. He looked as if he were waiting in a supermarket check-out queue rather than for what he must surely have realised would be a long prison sentence.

Clearing his throat, the judge addressed himself over the heads of all the legal and police staff in the body of the court, across to the murderer himself:

'Stephen Port, I accept your intention was only to cause really serious harm rather than death but you must have known and foreseen there was a high risk of death, the more so after the death of Anthony Walgate, the first victim.

'The murders were committed as part of a persistent course of conduct, surreptitiously drugging these young men so that you could penetrate them while they were unconscious. A significant degree of planning went into obtaining the drugs in advance and in luring the victims to your flat. Having killed them by administering an overdose, you dragged them out into the street in one case, or took them to the churchyard in the other cases, and abandoned their bodies in a manner which robbed them of their dignity and thereby greatly increased the distress of their loving families.

'Furthermore, your attempt to cover up two of your murders with a fake suicide note was wicked and monstrous.

'I have no doubt that the seriousness of your offending is so exceptionally high that the whole-life order is justified; indeed it is required. The sentence therefore upon the counts of murder is a sentence of life imprisonment. I decline to set a minimum term. The result is a whole-life sentence and you will die in prison.'

The judge stopped, as if he knew what to expect. There was a collective intake of breath – a silent 'Wow!' across the whole court. It lasted only a couple of seconds. Then the whole court erupted into loud cheers and applause. We all joined in the rejoicing, including members of the legal teams and police, the journalists and the whole jury, who stood and clapped and cheered along with us, clearly almost as delighted as we were. The public gallery too applauded loudly and enthusiastically.

Suddenly, above all the jubilation, a loud voice rang out from the public gallery. It was one of Jack Taylor's friends, who shouted out: 'I hope you die a long, slow death, you piece of shit.'

I looked at the judge, expecting him to be cross. It seemed such an extraordinary break with convention, but he just let it happen, as he sat there and smiled. In fact, he waited good-naturedly, right through until the noise stopped spontaneously, up to ten minutes later. Then, finally, he made his closing statements, which reflected on the part the police played in the investigations:

'It is not for me to say whether the seeming bizarre coincidence of these gay young men being found dead so close together might have given rise to suspicions that these deaths were not the result of ordinary self-administered drug overdoses but that is how their deaths were treated at the time. The competence and adequacy of the investigation will later be examined by others.

'Police had accepted the death of Port's first victim, Walgate, at face value. Whether the police were right to do so, in the light of what they knew or ought to have found out, is for others to decide, having thoroughly enquired into the matter, which has not been appropriate for us to do in the course of this criminal trial.'

I was grateful for these closing remarks, knowing they would help us in our case against the Barking and Dagenham branch of the Met police. The judge left, Port was taken away and the journalists rushed out to be first with the news. We too were now free to go.

I went over to Ben of the IPCC and gave him a quick statement.

'I'll let you know when I can come up to Hull, probably in a few days' time,' he said. 'To take your full statement.'

Then I went over to join the others as we went round saying our goodbyes and thanking the staff, especially the lovely ladies in the witness suites who had made our experience much more tolerable than it would otherwise have been.

'Right,' said Detective Inspector Tim Duffield as we prepared to leave the building. 'I'll meet you all in the pub on the crossroads in half an hour.'

As we left the entrance of the Old Bailey for the very last time, we were besieged by the press. With our heads up and the solidarity of walking out together, we managed to get past most of them undisturbed. I did hear Tim, who led the successful Scotland Yard investigation, telling the BBC News crew: 'These evil crimes have left entire families, a community and a nation in shock.'

Yes, I thought, and hoped it would go out, just as it was . . . Hours later, I saw that it did.

Meanwhile, once we could see past the media mega-scrum, I noticed a group of people across the street, looking in our direction and waving . . . then I recognised their faces. All twelve members of the jury had waited for us to come out so that they too could say goodbye to us. I could have cried that they were still there – I was so touched. We went over and talked with them. I know it's weird but when they were on the jury benches, it was easy to forget that they were ordinary people, just like us, and they'd been through this extraordinary experience with us.

'I haven't slept for nine weeks,' said one of the women to me. 'This trial has really traumatised me. I don't think I'll ever fully recover.'

'Yes, I must have been very innocent before,' said another. 'I had no idea there were such depths of depravity.'

One of the men came and told me: 'We didn't know who any of you were to begin with. But after a while we could work out who you all were and which family was whose. That's when I realised you were Anthony's mother.'

'We were all rooting for you,' said the forewoman.

'You know when we had to give the undecided verdict about Anthony?' asked the man I'd been speaking to. 'Well, I saw your reaction and I felt awful for you. I wanted to shout across "Don't worry love. It'll be alright, you know. We can get ten out of twelve!"'

'Oh really? So I needn't have worried?'

'No.'

'I wish I'd known that.'

'So did we but we couldn't tell you. We weren't even allowed to make eye contact with you.'

'Why did it take all day?'

'Because there were several other counts that were not unanimous and some of those took a lot more discussion before we could decide about them.'

'Yes,' agreed another juror who had joined us. 'We got really wound up and stressed on your behalf.'

'And we were all concerned about you as well,' I replied.

Finally we all dispersed and they went back to their normal lives and we all went up to the pub. It was still only mid-morning so I just had a cup of tea. We sat there and compared notes about Port, then decided he wasn't worth wasting breath over, so we changed the subject after that. The euphoria had taken us over. It was all about being together and sharing our joy that justice had been done and the streets of London would forever be a safer place with that devil locked up for life. We could all rest at ease.

That night, I slept like the proverbial baby. I felt as if Anthony was finally at rest and I could relax at last. I'd forgotten what a good night's sleep could feel like.

But of course, that wasn't the end of the story . . . we had another mountain to climb.

CHAPTER 23

The Aftermath

December 2016–December 2018,
2–4 years after Anthony's death

Immediately after the trial was over, the IPCC issued an update to the press, confirming that: 'Seven Metropolitan police officers have been served with gross misconduct notices, advising them their conduct is under investigation. A further ten officers have been served with misconduct notices. The officers range in rank from constable to inspector.'

Back in Hull, the morning after this statement was issued, I went with Kate, her daughter Sophie and her grand-daughter Kaitlin, then aged nine, to Morrisons to do some shopping. At the end of an aisle, Kaitlin spotted a familiar photo below the headline on the front page of the *Hull Daily Mail*. 'That's my Anty-Panty!' she called out excitedly. So we went across to see. Even as we approached, people were picking up copies of the paper off the pile. I picked one up and so did Kate.

'Mam,' asked Kaitlin, 'what's a serial killer?'

So here was the proof, if any was needed, that those last seven weeks in another world, called the Old Bailey, had all been real . . . Both the Metropolitan police and the IPCC issued comprehensive press releases straight after sentencing so when we checked online, the story was everywhere.

Various newspapers, radio and TV stations rang me asking for interviews but I refused them all, except my favourites the *Daily Mirror* and the *Sunday Mirror*. I did give them an interview and they did an excellent double-page feature the following day. I was also asked by BBC, ITV and other TV channels to do documentaries for them. I told them all that I would think about it.

After the initial euphoria of the murder verdict, I was suddenly hit by the numbness of deep fatigue. It must have been the anti-climax. I stepped up the antidepressants again and they gradually helped. The trouble was, of course, that although the murder trial was over and justice had been done, we had more hurdles to jump over the coming months and there would be so much build up to those as the time drew nearer. The antidepressants and more counselling would be a must in between.

When I had first returned to Hull after the trial, I tried to pick up my 'normal' life but nothing would ever be normal without Anthony. However, Paul was pleased to have me back at last, so that he could pop round at the weekends for a meal or a cuppa and a chat. I had unintentionally neglected my only surviving son over the seven weeks of the trial while I was fighting for Anthony, so now I needed to give Paul some love and attention too.

Then, one day in early December, I received a phone call from Dan Clark-Neal, who had done the first BBC documentary with me.

'Are you free on Wednesday?' he asked.

'Er, yes. Why?'

'I've got you and the other families a slot on *Victoria Derbyshire* this Wednesday. She wants you to tell your story about battling with the police, about what seemed like their homophobia and how it affected their ability to handle the case, as well as the LBGT and chemsex aspects of Port's crimes.'

So it was that on 7 December, Daniel Whitworth's step-mother Mandy and Jack Taylor's sisters Donna and Jenny appeared with me on the *Victoria Derbyshire* morning show on BBC2.

'Do you know it's live?' asked Victoria.

Well, that was it – I was petrified. Mandy was great though. She kept making me laugh. 'I just sound like Farmer Giles,' she said. 'Like, "ooh arr, tractorrr". You sound like a rough northern bird,' she told me, then pointed at Donna and Jenny – 'And they sound like *TOWIES*!'

That got us all laughing. I kept thinking of what she'd said and it did a great job of relaxing me for the programme. It all went well and the best thing is that we're all still in touch. Partly because of the joint action legal case against the Metropolitan police, which means we meet from time to time with the solicitors and all that. Our chosen barrister, Leslie Thomas, had agreed to take us all and we did some crowdfunding to put towards his fees. But also because we've become such good, supportive friends. Only we can understand what each other has been through. It's a bond like no other.

★

Later that month, finally, after two and a half years of asking, Ian rang me to say he'd be bringing Anthony's possessions to me the next morning. I was so excited that I wanted to open the boxes and unpack them straight away, but I didn't want to do it alone, so I asked my niece Lottie to come over and help me. As soon as Ian had gone, we lifted off the lid of the first storage box . . . and my hopes were dashed.

All Anthony's clothes were fusty and covered in mould. Every box was the same. He used to collect ornaments but they were all broken. I could have cried. I'm sure I would have done if I hadn't had Lottie with me. Then we found a box of papers, including some of his designs and university work. It was heart-breaking to see his beautiful drawings and his assignment notes all dotted with spots of mould as well. He had put so much hard work and talent into these things and now they were not even fit to keep, or very few of them at least.

Finally, we found Anthony's laptop, which we connected and logged on to. Fortunately, it still worked well and this was the one positive that afternoon – to find all Anthony's photos, including some of his catwalk designs and clothes he'd made, but also loads of pictures of the fun he'd had with his friends – especially China, Kiera and Ellie. After going through everything I wanted to see and copying some photos to my phone, I gave Anthony's laptop to Paul. He was pleased about that – not just to have a better laptop, but also because now he could now have something of Anthony's to keep.

Our Kate popped in one day around this time and we sat reminiscing, keeping Anthony's memory alive, as we so often did. It was a strange thing – even though the trial had proved that we parents had tried everything we could to make the police investigate, I still felt guilty that I felt happy with the verdict. It exhausted me . . . I suppose because I didn't know what to feel, what it was OK to feel.

More meetings with the others at the solicitors in Leeds progressed our case, but very slowly. Our joint action would now become a key part of the inquests on all four boys, which were to be held with a judge and jury. So there was a lot to be organised and the months passed by, until finally an approximate date was set for these inquests to take place in late 2019, which was later postponed to sometime in 2020, then again until January 2021, nearly seven years after Anthony's death. Yet again, gathering sufficient evidence was one of the major problems, but things began to look more promising as time wore on. Our solicitors were meticulously thorough in their preparation and our barrister was increasingly optimistic that the police would in all likelihood offer an out-of-court settlement before the inquests began.

Throughout this period since Anthony's death, everyone at work has been very understanding and I've had time off whenever I've needed it. My work colleagues were great too. I led a team of eighteen staff for a national company, so I travelled all over the place. Everyone worked together well and we achieved a lot. However, I'd done my job as a project manager for fifteen years and I was getting jaded with it.

'Your brain needs to be kept busy,' said my boss. 'So I was thinking about asking you to do this.' She handed me a leaflet about HR training. That was good because it took my mind off everything else, especially the legal case building up again. I do HR for nineteen stores now and I find it very interesting. It keeps my brain well occupied, working with our legal team, and it does take my mind off everything else during working hours, which is great.

Roll on the day when I don't have to take my mind off anything.

Two years after the trial, I had another unexpected phone call, this time from our press agent, via our solicitors. She told me she had had been approached by a BBC drama producer to see if all the families might be willing to collaborate with a proposed new BBC dramatisation of our story.

'It will be about the murders,' she explained, 'but in a different way.'

'What do you mean?'

'Well, the angle the production team want to take is threefold: the boys themselves and their lives and their potential; the impact on you and the other murdered lads' families and, in particular, how hard you had to fight to win justice and get to the truth.' She paused. 'What do you think?' I talked to the other families and we all agreed for the BBC to go ahead.

Neil McKay, the scriptwriter, came a few times to interview me and then I didn't hear any more. Until, finally, the first script arrived in the post. I started reading it straight away and was thrilled to see it had a lot in it about the lads' lives, suggesting how much promise and talent died with them and what a great deal we, their families, had lost. It wasn't long before I found out who was going to play my part and I was thrilled: Sheridan Smith is one of my favourite actors. She starred as Cilla in a previous TV drama series and was in *Gavin and Stacey* too. Sheridan was brought up in north Lincolnshire, only a few miles from Hull, so she was perfect as she was a local girl and already used to my accent.

The first time I met Sheridan, after ten minutes with her, I felt I'd known her forever. She came over to see me, to chat with me and pick up how I talked, my facial expressions and my mannerisms, like the way I move my hands. She's a lovely lady and we became good friends during those weeks before the filming started. She texted me quite a lot as well, trying to make sure she did her best to take on the way I am, the way I speak and the way I move. She'd text me about the smallest details, saying: 'I really, really want to get this right.'

The next thing I knew, I was invited to bring any family or friends to go and watch a scene being filmed in Manchester. Sami and Kiera came up on a train from London to meet me and Kate and her husband Phil came to join us as well. When we arrived, Sheridan spotted us and came straight over to say hello.

When it was time to start, we walked through to an area where the filming was going to take place. Suddenly I saw it: what a shock, but in a wonderful way. They'd built a catwalk down the middle of the long room, with rows of chairs along each side and across one end. But the thing that took my breath away was the far end, where the models would come through the curtains, under a sign with lights all round it, and there, in big letters across the sign, was Anthony's name, lit up in a hundred lightbulbs. A shiver ran through me as I struggled to contain my emotions. Anthony had always said: 'You mark my words, Sezzer, I'll be famous one day. I'll have my name up in lights.' He was right. He'd made it. But how tragic that it wasn't real, and he wasn't here to see it.

But still, I went to bed that night with a warm heart. 'This would have been your heaven,' I whispered to Anthony in the darkness and the faint echo of his voice and his laughter lulled me to sleep.

CHAPTER 24

Anthony's Legacy

My focus continues to be on keeping Anthony's memory alive and doing what I can to ensure that his death was not in vain. A lot of learning should come from what happened to Anthony, to prevent this situation ever happening again, but it seems that such learning may be slow in being embedded into everyday police work.

In the long letter of apology I received at the end of the trial from Stuart Cundy, Commander of Specialist Crime Investigations in the Metropolitan Police Service, his penultimate paragraph stated:

> *Whilst it may be of little comfort, the MPS [Metropolitan Police Service] has already made important changes to how we respond and the guidance we give our front-line officers dealing with similar cases. If we need to make further changes following the IPCC investigation, then you have my commitment we will.*

It sounded positive but, in the event, it will have been more than four years from that letter by the time the IPCC report is published, so I hope they will have made many of the required changes a lot sooner than that. There does seem to be some evidence that police guidelines now exist regarding 'chemsex' crimes and liaising with the LBGT community, but I hope that their other failings are also fully addressed, especially what the newspapers have called the police's homophobia.

The picture regarding dating app crimes is an even greater concern. While the latest statistics suggest that 40 per cent of all couples, and 60 per cent of same-sex couples, now meet on dating apps and that for most of them it is a positive and relatively safe experience, meeting strangers for the first time in unfamiliar places, with no certainty of their backgrounds or criminal records, is of course far from risk-free. In fact, most people have heard stories of times when dating app meetings went wrong, or worse, when crimes were committed, as in Anthony's case.

On 11 April 2019, the *Independent* ran a headline which read: 'Dark Side of Online Dating: Crimes Rise Dramatically in Last Five Years'. It's hard to see what regulatory arrangements could be made to safeguard users of dating apps so the only other option is to do a lot more to raise awareness of the dangers.

Since June 2014, almost everything I've felt has been grief for Anthony and anger at the police. Although the commander of the Met police apologised, what I really want is an apology from the Barking and Dagenham police. Port getting life imprisonment wasn't the only thing I needed to help me move on. The other is an apology from Slaymaker and O'Donnell, or the head of their team. They and their colleagues made everything 150 times worse than it already was.

However, there have been some positives. Despite the fact that Anthony was killed before he was able to complete his degree studies, his tutors at Middlesex University were so upset by the tragic death of one of their most promising students that they posthumously granted him an honorary degree. At the same time, they instituted the annual Anthony Walgate Award for the most promising fashion student of the year. This news brought tears to my eyes.

We still have Anthony's first sewing machine. After the funeral it went back to Tom's house – to his bedroom there. That's where we all used to live until Tom and I split up, so we both agree that's the right place for it to stay.

I often sit and wonder, what if he hadn't gone to London? What if he'd gone to university in Hull instead and carried on earning his spending money stacking shelves at the supermarket? Would he still be here? Probably yes. But would he have been happy? At least the time he had studying fashion in London gained him some wonderful friends and a lot of happiness. There is no right answer to any of these 'what if' questions. Fashion and friendships were his two great loves and he was very successful at both. His friend Kiera's words will always stay with me: 'Anthony was a friend like no other. I doubt in this life I will ever meet anyone even a fraction like him.'

We still talk about Anthony at family gatherings and keep his memory alive that way. Not long after Anthony died, my nephew Dillon had another baby. 'Can we call him after Anthony?' he asked me.

'Yes,' I said. 'As long as it's his middle name. I don't want anyone to have his first name.'

I've spoken to all the rest of the family too: 'From now on, whoever has a boy in this family, his middle name is going be Anthony, and we'll pass it along.'

They all made a face! I suppose it has to be their decision but I don't want him to be forgotten. I've got no grandchildren. I have one son but he's not married. I don't know whether he'll ever marry, but if he does, I wish he'd hurry up.

I've always been a doer: a logical, level-headed sort of person; somebody who takes no nonsense and always works to find a solution. Tell the truth and damn the devil – that's always been me. Even at work, if I do something wrong, I laugh and exclaim 'Shit!' because I wouldn't do anything wrong intentionally, so I'll always own up to my mistakes. We did an analogy test at work a few years ago: 'How good a people person are you?' I came up about 90 per cent task-driven and 10 per cent people. We all laughed.

I said: 'No, it's about fifty-fifty.' I have eighteen staff and most of them have worked with me for years, so I can't be that bad.

But losing Anthony has changed me forever. I have less tolerance now for other people's problems. One of my staff came into my office a couple of years ago, weeping and wailing that her husband was going to leave her because she'd got into debt and she'd done this and she'd done that, so I just looked at her and said 'Has anybody died?'

'No,' she replied.

'You know what?' I continued. 'There is nothing in this world that you cannot change or put right other than death, so go and sort yourself out. At the end of the day, it's money. So what?' I know that must have sounded harsh, but she went back home and confessed and they're still together now.

I say that to everyone these days because it's true. Nothing is so big that it can't be sorted, whether money, love, jobs . . . The only thing that can't is death. In fact, my staff laugh and say, 'We come to you because we know you'll tell us straight.'

I rang a member of my team last night who I've known for donkey's years. She recently found out she's got breast cancer. I was the only person she had told. I went to the hospital with her for the diagnosis. She was advised that a mastectomy was her best option but she was worried. I told her, 'At the end of the day, Penny, it's a lump of fat. Get it taken off, so what? If it's saving your life, you need to have it done.'

In my own life, I've always gone straight at things and dealt with them. That's why it hit me so hard when Anthony died. Because I couldn't do that and it made me feel helpless. No matter what I did or how hard I tried, I couldn't get anywhere. I felt as if I'd been standing on what I'd always believed to be firm ground and suddenly it was pulled away by a sinkhole, so that I had fallen and was clinging onto the edges with my fingertips without the strength to pull myself up again. I've been struggling like that for nearly six years now – with the legal case, suing the police, still to come in a few months' time, along with the inquests. I feel as if I can't breathe fully until that's all over and done with.

I know it sounds strange but I can't remember who I was before. It's been so long. I can't remember what I used to do before, or what I was like, or who I was, because this has totally and utterly consumed everything since June 2014. So maybe, when it's all over and done with, I might get back a little of who I was. But I don't know. I am myself but it's very much more about my mindset. What is the point of stressing about something when you can fix it? It's only when you can't fix it that things are at their worst.

However, my emotions are all over the place. The anti-depressants help. They make it so that everything passes straight over my head. It has to, because otherwise, after all these years, I'll never be able to finish this off.

I don't even have any sense of direction for the future right now. If people ask me what I am going to do after the final legal case is over, I don't have an answer any more. I used to think I'd want to be active in campaigning for better policing and against homophobia and unregulated dating apps. But I feel too exhausted by everything to be heard: all the fighting, the coping with people saying I wasn't a victim, the court cases and everything else. I need to have a calmer, quieter life, for a while at least. Then maybe, one day, I'll change to a job that's more for pleasure than a wage – something that will make a difference to someone or something. Or do a job that will make the world a better, safer place, so nothing like this nightmare happens to any other lad and his mother ever again. Not now or yet, but perhaps one day . . .

I still think about Anthony at all sorts of odd moments of the day and I'm sure I always will. I talk to him too, in my head, all the time. I don't suppose that will change either. I hope it doesn't because these thoughts and memories brighten my moments and make me smile.

Only the other day, I turned the radio on in my car just as the presenter announced the next song: 'It's "All About You" by McFly.' I felt as if my heart missed a beat. This was the song that I chose for his funeral because, for Anthony, everything was 'all about me'.

Other painful memories come to mind at unexpected moments. When it's my birthday or Christmas, I feel his loss so much as he always made a fuss of me and chose very thoughtful gifts. For my last birthday before he died, he gave me a bottle of perfume called 'Je t'adore', that he'd paid extra to have beautifully gift-wrapped.

'Why did you do that?' I asked.

'Well, next year, I'll buy you some Botox,' he joked. 'I won't be able to gift-wrap that!'

The last gift he gave me was for no reason, other than that he saw it and thought I'd like it – a coloured lantern. I have it in front of me now.

'I bought it in Shepherd's Bush Market,' he said. 'Next time you come down, we could go there together.'

I'd have loved that . . . but it was not to be.

I now cherish my memory of the last ever time we spent together. It was 3 March 2014. Sami and I had spent our second wedding anniversary in London with Anthony. We'd had a wonderful time exploring and having meals out. When it was time to leave, Sami took a Tube back to his restaurant in Essex and I was going to take a train back to Hull. We had time to spare, so Anthony and I sat together, just the two of us, on a wall outside King's Cross Station, chatting for thirty minutes about nothing special.

Finally it was time for my train, so we stood up. We hugged and I kissed Anthony's cheek, saying 'Missing you already, Baby.'

He laughed. 'Sezzer, you're such a geek!'

I watched him walk away and smiled to myself. He was happy in himself, doing everything he wanted to do and loving every minute of it.

Now, as I write this, I've come to the realisation that the anguish and pain is not over yet. First it was the murder trial I had to contend with and now it's the parents' joint action, suing the police, the inquests . . . and I have to make sure once again that I can run out of the reports about Anthony's injuries. I know the basic facts but I still couldn't bear to hear all the awful details. We have only one chance of getting all this right, so it's a challenge, an obsession with me. I *have* to do it.

Since his death, I have always referred to my younger son as Anthony, when in fact I never called him his full name before. He was always Ant to me. But I still can't bring myself to call him that. It's far too personal and I'm even filling with tears as I think of it. When everything is over and finished with, I will be able to call my son Ant again. But then I will have to deal with the fact that Ant has gone forever . . . and forever is a long, long time.

I began to write notes for this book from the very start, in June 2014, when we'd only been back in England for a few days and I've been writing them ever since. But when I was ready to write the book itself, I arranged for a writer friend to come over to my house and help me get going.

As I've often said to my friends, I can't dream about Anthony. I don't know why. I try to force myself but it just doesn't happen. He's always the last thing I think about before I go to sleep. But that very morning, when my writer friend was due to come, the strangest thing happened. Very early, just when I was about to wake up, Anthony's face was there, right in front of mine. He gave me a big smile and, within the blink of a second, I woke up, feeling very calm and warm. It was just a smile, like a grin, then he was gone.

I felt as if he was saying 'We're nearly there, keep going,' as if he knew this was the day she would be coming and we'd start on the book – his book. He was giving his approval. I'm sure of that. He'd have been so taken that we were doing this book. He'd have been telling everybody: 'Told you! Told you! I told you I'd be famous.'

I've written this book so the truth can be known, but also for Anthony himself. This is a way to carry on his memory. I really can't bear the thought of him having died for nothing. If reading it helps to save someone else's son by realising the dangers of dating apps like Grindr, then it will have been worth doing. My boy was far from stupid but he died as a result of meeting the devil on Grindr. Don't let your son or anyone else you know make the same mistake.

I want this book to have a picture of Anthony on the cover and I want it dedicated to him, so that everywhere in the world where it's sold he will be seen. I want him to travel the world. And even in twenty years' time, in second-hand book shops around the country, there will be Anthony's picture, smiling at anyone who picks up this book.

It had always been my intention to retire one day to a caravan by the sea. Well, I'm not retirement age for a long while yet but I have changed my life-plan. I now see that life really is too short not to follow your dreams, however big or small they may be, so I've moved out of the city to live a calmer life in my new caravan in a beautiful spot on the east coast of Yorkshire, right by the sea. I still commute to work each day but it's a joy to come back home to the birdsong and the sounds of the waves lapping the shore.

I love living here. I love the peace of it. I don't even switch my telly on. I just put my feet up and read a book. I enjoy the solitude but I've made plenty of friends here too. The kids come over now and then, which is great, but I'm perfectly happy on my own, or with Sami when he comes up here, but it's usually easier for me to go down there for occasional weekends, so that he can keep the restaurant going at full strength. Our marriage has weathered the terrible storms of the past few years and Sami's gold watch (his plane ticket back to Turkey) still lies untouched in its drawer!

When the joint action, the inquests, the IOPC Report, the BBC drama and this book are all finished, I will find a big stick, go down to the beach and draw a long line in the wet sand. I shall stand on one side for a few seconds . . . then, like a ceremony, I'll step over the line to the other side, where Anthony becomes Ant again and that will be my new start.

Epilogue

The Inquests

I feel sick. It's Sunday afternoon on 3 October 2021 and my stomach is churning. After all these years and many cancellations, the inquests are finally going to happen . . . or at least I hope they are. Surely nothing will stop them now? I've waited so long for this, but I'm dreading it too.

Tomorrow I'll take the train to London, but not just London, this time to Barking – the one place I never wanted to go, the last place Anthony was alive, where he took his last, rasping breath.

I can't just sit here and think about it. I'm too restless. I must do something, so I go out for a brisk walk in the fresh sea air. A couple of friends poke their heads out of their windows as I pass by. They know my story, Anthony's story.

'Good luck!' says one.

'You'll be strong,' calls another. 'I'll be thinking of you.'

Thank God for my friends and my family, shoring me up when I feel at my worst. I'd be a wreck without them.

Back home again, I do feel a bit fitter and stronger now, so I get down my rucksack and start to pack. As I try to decide what clothes to take, I can almost hear Anthony talking to me:

'No, you can't wear that Sezzer. You're doing this for me, so you'd better look smart!'

I put the jumper back in the wardrobe.

'Wear your black and white top.'

I smile. He was always very particular about what I wore, so I pack the black and white for the first day in court.

The rest of the afternoon and evening drags by very slowly until my phone rings and it's Kate. She's great. She always knows when I need a bit of TLC.

'How are you feeling?' she asks.

'Rubbish,' I reply. 'I can't stop thinking. Suppose the police twist everything round and the jury believe them?'

'They don't have a leg to stand on,' she says. 'And they don't have a brain between them!'

I laugh out loud – the first time I've laughed properly for days.

After a restless night, I'm up early. Today's the day I leave for London. While the kettle boils, I check that my ticket is secure in my purse. I have a mug of tea but nothing to eat – I don't trust my stomach today.

What am I going to do all morning? I google the inquests update, which tells me that the jurors have been empanelled and they will go through everything with the coroner today. She is the judge as well in these inquests, so it's an unusual situation with a full jury and loads of barristers and witnesses involved. I look through the timetable I've been sent that sets out everything very precisely – who will be interviewed, when and for how long. Each witness will also be questioned by each of the barristers, including one for the police, and even the jurors can submit questions to the coroner to ask on their behalf.

I wash up my mug and look at the time. My train isn't till after lunch and it's still only 8 o'clock, so the empty hours between seem daunting. I need to fill them, so I get in the car and go to work.

'What are you doing here?' asks my boss. 'Aren't you going to London?'

'Yes, but not till later. I don't want to sit at home worrying all morning, so I've come to work to keep my mind busy.'

I'm soon glad I made that decision. There is plenty to do. But as the morning wears on, I develop a stress headache and start snapping at people, so now it's time to leave.

The London train is on time and I find a seat by the window. There are very few people on the train today, so I just sit back and start thinking ahead again. I can't help it.

My head starts pounding and I'm all over the place, my thoughts in a tumble and my nerves jangling. I need something to calm me down, so I pick up the newspaper I bought at the station and that fills some time. I usually love reading – books, newspapers or anything. But today I can't concentrate and have to keep rereading the same passages, so that's no good.

I get my phone out and play games on that for most of the journey, until I have a sudden panic. Have I brought the commemoration piece I wrote about Anthony to read out in court on the first morning? I've worked so hard at that, writing and rewriting what I wanted to say. But now I can't remember packing it. I unzip my bag and go through that, praying it will be there . . . and it is, right at the bottom. Phew!

I unfold and reread it for the umpteenth time. The funny bit makes me smile and I feel more relaxed now . . . until we're nearly there.

From King's Cross I have to go on to Barking, but first I walk outside to sit on the wall where I sat with Anthony the last time I saw him. I wonder whether he can see me. Well, it makes me feel good anyway, this last link with him, remembering his confident, happy wave as he left to go back to his university friends.

As I get out at Barking station at 6 p.m., I try to take a deep breath. I am now walking in Anthony's last footsteps, leaving the station on that fateful night in June, seven and half years before.

There's no Wi-Fi, so I ask a security man how to get to my hotel. He points to the exit and gives me a map, adding a cross where the hotel is. I follow the map to where it shows a green area labelled 'park'. That looks like a handy shortcut, so I go through the gate and into a quiet grassy oasis away from the traffic noise and fumes.

As I walk across, I notice a church with some gravestones and, up to the left, a sign that says 'St Margaret's Church'.

I freeze. The sudden realisation hits me. Horrified, I stop breathing for several seconds. This is where the other three boys' bodies were left – Gabriel and Daniel in the church-yard and Jack just the other side of the wall.

It's such a shock. I take several steps back, away from where the bodies had been, right back to the edge and follow that round to the exit.

★

I arrive at the hotel to find Vicky and Lyndsey, two of my legal team waiting for me.

'Have you eaten?' asks Vicky.

'Not since . . .'

'Good. Let's go out for a meal,' suggests Lyndsey.

So I leave my rucksack with reception and off we go.

Once we've ordered, I ask them questions about the next day, wondering how different it will be from the murder trial. Mostly we chat while we eat, which gives me a chance to chill out after the long train journey. They explain what is going to happen in the morning.

'Neil's coming to meet us first thing,' says Lyndsey, 'and we'll all walk to the town hall together.' Neil Hudgell is our senior lawyer.

'There are quite a few changes to the usual arrangements because of Covid-19,' explains Vicky.

'Yes, the court room is all long tables with dividers between them and video screens for each person to see what's going on at the witness stand.'

I'm pleased I know what to expect and we go back to chatting about other things, so it's a friendly, relaxed evening – just what I need.

Later on, lying in bed, my mind is in a spin again. I can't stop going through what might happen the next day. Will the press be there? Will I make a mess of reading out my favourite memories of Anthony? I'm up and down, walking around the room, then back into bed. I think back to that terrible day in Turkey when I first found out, then through all the awful ways the police treated us, the cruel things they said, their contempt for Anthony and for us and, worst of all, their refusal to investigate the evidence in front of their noses.

I have to stop going over it all, so I keep telling myself: 'For God's sake, get some sleep or you're going to be useless tomorrow.'

I try to breathe slower . . . the next thing I know is it's the morning and time to get up. I reckon I only had about two hours of proper sleep but I have a shower and I do feel better than yesterday.

I'm here now, so bring it on!

Arriving outside Barking Town Hall is quite an experience. The press have their cameras pointed at us and shout questions, which we ignore as we walk past. Neil takes us through security and upstairs to the room that has been set aside as a family room.

'You can come up here any time for a break,' he says. 'You can watch the proceedings by video-link on these screens if you like, or just chill out with a cuppa.'

'That's great,' I say. 'Just like at the Old Bailey.' Being with the other families always breaks the tension so I'm relieved that we can have some chill-out time together. We support each other.

Just then, the door opens and in come Daniel's father and stepmother, followed by Mandy and Jack's two sisters, Donna and Jenny.

'Gabriel's brother Adam couldn't come,' explains Neil. 'Because of the Covid travel restrictions, so his memories of Gabriel will be read out for him.'

Just then, our solicitors' lovely press agent, Kerry, arrives to join us.

'The press are all still waiting outside,' she says, 'wanting to take photos of you all together.'

'Let them wait,' I think, trying to keep calm for the court. But they're only doing their jobs, so we all agree to go and pose for them.

Finally, it's time to go into the coroner's court. As Neil leads the way, I feel a great sense of satisfaction that at last we are here and it's actually happening.

He opens the door into a large room, much more spacious and set out very differently from the cramped Court 16 at the Old Bailey, where Port's murder trial took place. This will be the home of the inquests over the next couple of months and it's fully compliant with Covid-19 regulations. The whole room is like a huge open-plan office area, with dividers between people for social distancing and video-screens everywhere.

An usher shows us to our seats, all of us in a long row, with a wall behind us and our screens on the tables in front of us.

Just as we are settled, we all stand up again as the coroner and her officials come in. She looks round with a smile for everybody, then takes her place, followed by the jury and then the legal teams all file in. This is our only opportunity to look at the members of the jury as they pass by and I'm relieved to see that they look quite a mixed bag, so hopefully representative and unbiased, but we'll have to wait till the end to find out for sure.

Finally, some senior police officers walk in and I'm pleased to catch sight of Ian Atkinson, my lovely second family liaison officer. He gives me a smile as he passes. I'm glad he's going to be in court for my speech.

The coroner begins by telling the jury who we all are. She then makes her opening statement, directing the jury: 'Putting the matter in its starkest terms, we will have to consider whether, had the investigations in the earlier deaths been conducted differently, the lives of those who died later might have been saved.'

There's a slight pause as we all take that in.

I'm relieved to hear her words, that this is the main focus of the whole proceedings as it has also been the focus of my sense of guilt over the years, the guilt that I couldn't make them do more. How can the answer be otherwise?

Knowing I'll be the first to speak, I feel apprehensive, but somebody has to do it. I get out my pen-portrait of Anthony from my bag and, as I flatten the creases, I suddenly feel a great sense of calm flooding me. I have practised reading it enough times and I'm always happy to talk about Anthony. Now I've got a captive audience. So let's go!

The coroner calls my name and I get up with a sense of relief – *at last*.

But as I enter the witness stand, with the cameras on me, the nerves hit me again. I'm worried about talking too fast. I must remember to speak slowly.

The voice in my head says, '*Go for it, Sezzer.*'

I take a deep breath, put my head down and I'm off. I don't look up once. My whole focus is on reading out those words in memoriam for my murdered son.

'Thank you for allowing me to tell you about my boy. Anthony was quite a quiet, shy child. I've always said that when he first tried to stand up, he grabbed my leg and never really let go. Anthony was never naughty as such. He just did what he thought were the right things to do, like dialling 999 while I was upstairs and asking the police to arrest his older brother for going out to play and leaving him behind!'

I go on to tell the court my favourite stories of his childhood, like the time he lost his first tooth and pushed it right into his ear for safe-keeping, which required a full operation the next day, and the time he dug up his recently buried pet hamster to show his friends. What a caution Anthony was. Then on to his teenage years.

'I genuinely cannot remember Anthony ever being in trouble at school. He was like that all the way through, just sitting quietly and doing his work. He only changed when he went to college. I could see and feel his confidence growing daily. He developed a very dry wit and really made me laugh, usually at the most inappropriate times.

'Just before he turned eighteen, he told his dad and me that he had an interview at a university in London. I begged him not to go, to stay in Yorkshire. But he replied that he would be famous one day, with his name in lights. He loved fashion and London was the only place to achieve his dream.

'The longer Anthony was in London, the more I could see the cygnet becoming the swan. He seemed to blossom and find who he really was, and could dress and act how he wanted. He loved London, his friends and his life there.

'When he came back to Hull, he used to say we were all asleep, as we walked around so slowly. He just couldn't slow down and said he would never live up north again, as London was his life. He even had to change the way he spoke, as nobody in London could understand his Hull accent . . .

'We would speak at least three times a week, with Anthony telling me what he'd been up to. He'd also ask me what was going on at home. He was a terrible gossip and couldn't keep a secret. This is one of the things I miss most about my boy – the phone calls. He either had me laughing or threatening to throttle him!

'Even now, after all this time, whenever I hear some gossip or read something in the local paper, I think, "I'll ring Anthony to tell him." Then I remember that I can't.

'For the past seven and a half years, every time I talk about my son, I call him Anthony. I never actually called him that. It was always Ant. But I still cannot bring myself to use that familiar name. It is so personal. To me it would mean my boy has really gone forever, and I realise now that forever is a very long time.'

It has all gone well, until I've got to the bit where I say 'Ant' – the name I haven't uttered since he died. It chokes me, but I knew that would be the most difficult thing to say . . . and now I've said it. Fortunately, it's at the end, so I can keep my head down and return to my seat.

As I travel back to Hull that afternoon, I feel quite relaxed, for the first time in days. I think the thing that helps most is having seen how varied in ages and types these jury members are. That's a big plus. I relax as the miles speed by along the tracks. The rest of this week and some of the next will be mostly about Anthony's autopsy and I can't bear to hear all of that again, so I decide to go back to work until the coast is clear.

★

Once the witness statements and interviews start, I watch a couple of them at home on my video-link, then travel back down to Barking to hear what some of the police have to say for themselves.

I suppose I should be gunning for particular individuals among the Barking and Dagenham police, for all the pain they caused me in so many ways. But what I really want is for it to be fair, to hear some sort of apology and for the outcome to make a difference in the future.

My train arrives a little late on 13 October, so I run all the way from Barking station, arriving just in time as Detective Constable David Parish steps up to the witness stand. He was on the bottom rung – one of the most junior policemen working on Anthony's case. He just had to do what he was told.

As I settle down to watch him on my screen, he looks worried. He answers questions with a nervous smile to begin with, but he soon starts apologising that there were so many key things he didn't do. As a trainee, some of them were due to lack of direction from his line manager, DS O'Donnell – a familiar name. Others were his own omissions.

Now I'm angry. I do believe Parish is sorry, but why didn't he at least do everything he was told? And why wasn't he supervised?

A couple of days later it's one of the big ones for me – Detective Sergeant O'Donnell's turn to give evidence. This is the day I've waited seven and a half years for. He was the first policeman to know Anthony's name, when China reported him missing, and the first one I spoke to on my return from Turkey.

The man I watch entering the witness stand looks so different from the man I remember. He has lost a lot of weight and most of his hair. His confidence has been replaced by a nervous, haunted expression. I wouldn't recognise him in the street.

He answers clearly to start with, but as the questioning becomes more probing, he starts to mop his brow. If I wasn't watching this live in an English court, I would think he was a spy being interrogated under the spotlight.

He keeps apologising when he answers questions and explains he can't pass the blame up the line. He accepts that he didn't do many of the things his superiors told him to do and he acknowledges his failures.

'In hindsight,' he says, 'I'm so sorry.' He repeats these words throughout. I do think his apologies are genuine. He clearly feels out of his depth. Being only a sergeant, he is close to the bottom and, as the saying goes, s**t rolls downhill. But it shouldn't be like that. Where was the supervision, the challenge from his superiors?

I almost feel sorry for him now, but it doesn't last when we leave the court. I'm relieved that after all this time he has apologised and acknowledged his faults, but I'm fuming inside.

All these years I've been tormented by guilt – could I have done more to make them investigate Anthony's death and prevent the other three deaths? But no, whatever I did was no use. I tried the local press and our MP, but now I know that I could have gone to 10 Downing Street and it wouldn't have made any difference.

After a week at home and work, while various other police officers are being questioned at length, making apologies and shifting blame by turns, I travel down to Barking again, to take my turn to give evidence on the witness stand. My nerves are building up already. Last time I spoke, it was to read out my memories of Anthony, so I was in control. But this time I'm facing the unknown.

My two barristers are at the hotel to meet me. I hope for encouragement, to dispel my fears, which they do give me, so that helps, but that's not all. They give me lots of reminders about everything I need to say. I'm tired from the journey and full of trepidation. My head fills up with noise and my stress levels are soaring. If I don't get some fresh air and open space, I'll explode. So I go to the middle of the car park and have a shouting meltdown . . . witnessed by some bemused passers-by. That feels better.

By the time I get to my room, my heart is pounding, so I ring my sister Kate.

'They just kept telling me how important it is to remember everything. So I'm worried I'll forget what to say. I was nervous coming down on the train, but now I'm dreading the whole thing. What if I don't give the right answers or I say the words all wrong? I might give the jury the wrong impression and let Anthony down.'

'Stop right there,' says Kate, finally getting a word in. 'Just calm down. You've been wanting to tell your side of things ever since Anthony died. Now it's your time.'

'Yes, but I have to do it right.'

'Just remember you are not an actress. You're a mother. Just tell the truth and you will be fine.'

As I reach the town hall the next morning and go into the inquests, I feel strangely calm. My legs are a little shaky as I walk to the witness stand but I've done nothing wrong and here is my chance to gain justice for Anthony. He would have said '*Go for it, Sezzer*.' So that's what I do.

I'm on the stand for fifty minutes and tell the truth, answering every question just as it all happened. Then, finally, it's time for me to stand down. I feel a stone lighter!

Flooded with a great sense of relief, I go straight to King's Cross, where I meet up with Anthony's father, Tom, and his brother, Graham. Tom also gave his evidence today. He called the Barking and Dagenham police 'Keystone Cops'! I bet that will go into the newspapers.

'The train's not due for ages,' I tell him. 'I just want to get home.'

'Me too. Let's see if there's an earlier train,' he suggests.

There is, so we both agree to pay the extra and go to the platform. As we board the train, who should we bump into? Karl Turner, my lovely local MP, with another Hull MP, Emma Harding, both going home for the weekend.

'When's the BBC drama going to be shown?' asks Karl.

Emma looks at me. 'What's that about?'

'It's called *Four Lives*. Sheridan Smith plays me,' I explain. 'I wanted a gobby northern bird to play me and she's perfect.' We all laugh. 'She's even got the accent. She came to see me a couple of times and we get on brilliantly.'

'I'm in it, too,' adds Karl.

Emma looks bemused.

'Well, not me exactly – an actor playing me.' We explain how it all came about and how strange it feels to see someone else being you.

A few days later, I take the day off work to watch the video-link. This is the other big one for me. I know it will be difficult to listen to Slaymaker and I'm right. It's the hardest day of all the evidence.

He looks calm, even brazen to start with, but as the questions challenge him harder, he goes red in the face and takes sips of his water. I always knew he would argue black is white in the court, as he so often did to me. But not to this extent. He clearly has no intention of apologising and instead implies I'm a liar, again and again.

I'm livid now, shouting at the screen.

Finally, he goes too far. Our barrister challenges him with what all of us, the boys' families and friends have separately and consistently said in evidence about him. Now he's on the hook. Surely there's no way the jury will be convinced by his wriggling.

At this point our barrister corners him with a memo he'd written, telling his superiors that Anthony had been to drug and sex parties and he can't wriggle out of that.. At last he has to admit he's wrong.

'GOTCHA!' I yell at him.

If only he could hear me.

Only two more weeks of evidence to go. Most days, after work, I follow what's happening via the WhatsApp group that our lawyers set up for us all. They update us and we can chat to each other. This is great. Some days I also check out the newspapers online, so I don't feel I'm missing anything.

Finally, it's the turn of one of the country's top police officers – Detective Assistant Commissioner Stuart Cundy.

To release the tension, the other families and I put bets on how many times we think he will say 'lessons have been learned'. I reckon eight times, but in the event we all lose count – he keeps repeating the phrase throughout his evidence. I'm in shock. He admits what a cock-up the police had made, due to bad management and inexperience. He talks of police failings and the lack of leadership.

'Opportunities and lines of enquiry were missed,' he admits, and 'improvements were needed'. All this is in the first few minutes.

He goes on to speak directly to us, the boys' families and friends.

'The murders of Anthony, Gabriel, Daniel and Jack I know have left all your family members, friends and others absolutely devastated, and every single one of you absolutely had the right to expect a professional investigation to the standards that all of us would have expected . . . I don't think those standards were met.' He pauses. 'I can't imagine putting myself in any of your shoes . . . and I know there is nothing I can possibly say that can take away or undo what has occurred in the past, but I am deeply sorry, personally and on behalf of the Metropolitan Police Service, that we didn't conduct the initial investigation to the standard you rightly expected and rightly deserved.'

I'm astonished. He does seem genuine.

'It's a matter of personal disappointment to me that many things were not done that should have been done . . . Please accept my sincerest apologies.'

After a short adjournment, DAC Cundy is then questioned by our barrister, who asks him about changes that have been made 'to reduce the risk that the trauma these families have suffered' and their experiences of 'being given false narratives about what happened to their loved ones and being ignored and dismissed, will not be suffered by other families'.

He agrees that these were unacceptable failings. 'Some changes have already been made,' he explains, 'as a direct result of lessons learned from these investigations.'

I am both amazed and relieved to have such comprehensive apologies and promises for the future of policing. We will have to wait and see. Cundy cannot admit there was any prejudice, especially homophobia, against our boys, which is disappointing. However, he outlines many changes that have already taken place since 2014 as a result of lessons learned, which is good to hear.

The next day, I receive my divorce papers. It's not a surprise. It's sad, but I suppose inevitable. I know how tough I was on Sami during the police's refusal to investigate Anthony's death; how rough it was throughout the murder trial, then the long delays to the inquests.

We've seen less and less of each other and we agreed it was time to go our separate ways. So I've lost my son and now I've lost my marriage too. But at least now the inquests are coming to an end and I hope against hope that I will soon be able to look forward again.

★

Four weeks later I'm running the Christmas party at work, but I'm expecting to get the call that I've been waiting for so long: the call to come back down to Barking to hear the jury's verdicts. I'm on tenterhooks.

I keep looking at my phone. Eventually, I hear the beep and the text says it's happening at midday tomorrow. I dash into an empty office to book my train ticket. Once that's done, I'm almost shaking. I'm a bag of nerves.

It's midnight when I get to bed, but I can't get to sleep. I'm in absolute turmoil. My stomach is in knots. Eventually I drop off but I only have about two hours of sleep before I need to get up at four.

This is IT.

I arrive at the train station about forty minutes early, desperate not to miss the train. Tom is on the platform too, with his brother, Graham, so I join them. We chat most of the way down to Barking, talking, a bit about how we think the outcomes will be on this final day, but also about other things, to help us relax a bit. Our main lawyer, Neil, is there on the platform, waiting to meet us. As soon as I catch sight of him, I feel all the tension wash away. He's such a calming influence.

'Come on,' he says. 'I'll take you to the coffee shop.'

As we enter Barking Town Hall for the last time, I remain calm, thinking, '*Que sera.*' I can't change it now. It will be what it will be.

We go upstairs to our room. All the other families arrive just after us and Kiera, one of Anthony's best friends, comes in too. (The other two, China and Ellie, are both working abroad so sadly they can't join us.)

We chat for a while till it's time to go down to the court room.

'Look at the jurors' faces,' I say to myself. If they smile, it's good. If they don't, it's not.

'I'm all tingly and nervy,' I say to Henrietta, our barrister. 'Please could you give me the thumbs up to let me know how it's going? That will help.'

The coroner is already in the court and the jurors file in. I'm watching their faces, but nobody looks at us. Maybe they've had instructions not to, but I think the worst. Oh God! I hardly dare to listen.

'*Go on, Sezzer*,' says Anthony's voice in my head. '*You'll be all right.*'

The coroner reads out the first questions to the jury.

I grit my teeth and hold my breath . . .

The foreman starts reading out the jury's answers to her questions, unanimously agreeing that if the police had properly investigated Anthony's death, they could have prevented the other three murders.

All these years I have carried a lump in my chest – a lump of guilt that I couldn't get the police to do anything to avoid more deaths. Now that guilt evaporates. Anthony is right. Every answer is what I want to hear. Fantastic! I'm buzzing now.

In her closing speech, the coroner confirms that there were a number of police omissions and failures and I'm glad to hear that she 'will be producing a report with a view to preventing further deaths'.

'Finally,' she says. 'I would like to address the families.' She thanks us for 'your composure and your dignity throughout'. That's the first time anyone has used those words to describe me! She continues: 'May I also express the hope that you finally feel you have been listened to, and that you have answers to some if not all of your questions.'

Wow. This is it – the confirmation that if only the police had done what I said, the other three boys wouldn't have died. I feel vindicated at last. Triumphant too, especially after Slaymaker implied we were all liars. He was the only one who never said sorry to us.

The jury members come to talk with us and I thank the foreman. They are genuinely happy for us.

We all troop back upstairs in jubilation, to prepare for our final duty. The press conference. Some of us go outside for a smoke and a chorus of 'We Are the Champions'. Kiera bursts into tears at this release of tension. I comfort her briefly, but we soon have our last call.

'The press are waiting for you.'

Here is our chance at last to raise the one big issue that had not been permitted for discussion in the inquests 'for legal reasons'. The barristers were strongly for it, but the police were dead against, and they won the argument.

Neil has prepared a speech on behalf of all the families and reads it out:

'We feel fully vindicated by the jury's findings . . . The inadequate investigation by the Metropolitan police in respect of Anthony, Gabriel, Daniel and Jack should be on public record as one of the most widespread institutional failings in modern history.

'The jury have been unanimous in finding fundamental failings and basic errors in the investigations . . . We are incensed by the police's successful attempts to prevent the jury from examining whether prejudice played any part in the police's actions . . . Based on the treatment we received, I firmly believe that the police's actions were, in part, driven by homophobia . . . The approach of the Met on the issue of homophobia demonstrates to us that, even today, seven years on, they have learned very little . . . The killer has rightly been held accountable, but the police have not. It distresses us hugely that many of the officers who failed us so badly continue to serve as police officers, without any significant sanctions, and we cannot be confident that their performance has improved. In fact, we understand that at least ten of the officers involved in the investigation have been promoted.'

There are a few questions to us and then it's finally time to end, so we all go up one final time to the family room.

'You should all be so proud of yourselves,' says Henrietta, our barrister. 'You are completely vindicated. This is recognition that everything you said is true.'

We say our jubilant goodbyes, knowing we will all keep in touch.

'Come on,' I say to Kiera. 'I'm taking you to McDonald's for a late lunch and a good chat.'

As we walk there are still tears in her eyes.

'You can stop crying! We've done it. It's all over now. This is a fantastic day, so no more crying.'

She tries to smile. 'OK.'

'What would Anthony say now?' I ask.

Kiera does his accent perfectly: 'There, you're all still talking about me!'

Now we can't stop laughing.

'You know,' I reassure her, 'you've really done well. You've been here all this time. You've been a true friend.'

As arranged, I meet up later with Neil, Tom and Graham at the station for the journey back up to Hull. I think we're all a mixture of tired but happy, discussing how it all went at the end of this momentous day. Neil looks shattered but somehow he keeps going as we chat about our one disappointment.

'It's a disgrace that the jury were not allowed to make judgement about the police's institutional homophobia,' says Neil.

We all agree.

'Oh well,' I say. 'It will be all over the internet and the papers tomorrow.'

As the train pulls in at Hull, I check my phone and find a message from Dame Cressida Dick, the Commissioner of the Metropolitan police. I tell the others.

'What does she want?' asks Neil.

'She says she wants to have a constructive meeting with me, at Scotland Yard.'

'Will you go?' asks Tom.

'Of course I will. It will be a chance to tell her exactly what I think about the police failings and their institutional homophobia.'

'In a constructive way?' asks Neil, with a half-smile.

'Yes of course. I also want to tell her how I think things could be improved.'

'Good luck!' says Tom. 'I hope she takes it on board.'

That evening, some friends take me out for a few drinks and we have a brilliant time. I'm so elated that I don't even feel tired until I get home. It's the first time I've truly relaxed since Anthony died.

I'm still on a high, finally winning our case. I hope this never happens to anyone else. But whatever happens, I want to tell everybody: 'Just stand up for yourself. You can be heard. Do what is right and it will turn out right.'

I've always known what I want to do when the inquests are over. Now I call six close friends – Mary and Keith, Gary and Tracey, Nick and Pat – and they come over the next day. We all go down to the beach, just after the tide has turned.

I find a big, sturdy stick and draw a line in the wet sand. They stand by and watch me as I take a single stride across the line and cheer as loudly as I can: 'HOORAY! JUSTICE AT LAST! JUSTICE FOR ANT!'

They all cheer with me.

'JUSTICE FOR ANT!' I shout the name I used to call him, the name I can now say again.

I'm ecstatic I've done all I can do. Now is my time to let go. The fight is over, so at last I can grieve for Ant.

Acknowledgements

Thanks to all of the following people:

My sister Kate for suggesting the book and finding my writer.

Sami for being so patient.

My work friends: Angie, Nikki, Katie, Denise and Tracy for all their support.

Ian Atkinson, the one policeman who was truly born to be a family liaison officer.

Amanda Harris and Vicky Eribo, my publishers at Orion.

Clare Hulton, my literary agent.

Jacquie Buttriss, my ghostwriter.

Help us make the next generation of readers

We – both author and publisher – hope you enjoyed this book. We believe that you can become a reader at any time in your life, but we'd love your help to give the next generation a head start.

Did you know that 9 per cent of children don't have a book of their own in their home, rising to 13 per cent in disadvantaged families*? We'd like to try to change that by asking you to consider the role you could play in helping to build readers of the future.

We'd love you to think of sharing, borrowing, reading, buying or talking about a book with a child in your life and spreading the love of reading. We want to make sure the next generation continue to have access to books, wherever they come from.

And if you would like to consider donating to charities that help fund literacy projects, find out more at **www.literacytrust.org.uk** and **www.booktrust.org.uk**.

THANK YOU

*As reported by the National Literacy Trust